Contemporary Issues in Education:
an introduction

Contemporary issues in

Education

···

an introduction

Edited by Keith Crawford

Peter Francis Publishers

Peter Francis Publishers
The Old School House
Little Fransham
Dereham
Norfolk NR19 2JP UK

A CIP catalogue record for this
book is available from the British Library

ISBN 1-870167-40-6

Printed and bound in Great Britain
by Biddles Ltd, King's Lynn.

Contents

Introduction   1
Keith Crawford

1 The Historical Development of Educational Provision   7
Mike Davis

2 Ideology and Curriculum Theory: whole-school approaches   25
to education for sustainable development
Dean Garratt and Tony Shallcross

3 Critical Perspectives in Early Childhood Studies   52
Philip Prescott

4 Towards Firmer Foundations? An Exploration of   72
Developments in Early Years Education and Care
Ian Barron

5 The Politics of Identity and Schooling   88
Cedric Cullingford

6 Children's Rights   101
Dominic Wyse

7 The School Curriculum   120
Keith Crawford

8 The Politics of Effective Schooling   135
    Graham Boyes and Adrian Smith

9 Inclusive Education: principles and practices   155
    Brenda Judge

10 Citizenship Education: origins, challenges and possibilities   171
    Ian Davies

    Notes on Contributors   185

    Bibliography   188

    Index   199

Introduction

Keith Crawford

E DUCATION is the foundation of a democratic society and is undeniably the basis of our personal, social, and economic well being. The core of education is teaching – a demanding, complex dynamic process that involves a myriad of decisions made on behalf of the students and our societal needs. Drawing upon a range of intellectual resources, theoretical perspectives and academic disciplines education studies promises to illuminate our understanding and provide opportunities for those with a commitment to education to engage with fundamental questions concerning the aims and values of education, its relationship to society and the problematic relationship between educational theory, policy and practice.

The field of educational studies experienced considerable growth during the last decade of the twentieth century and continues to do so, since all those who are concerned with the education and welfare of children, including teachers, parents and those working in allied agencies, have engaged in a national and international debate exploring a range of issues, themes and problems facing the education system. Each of these stakeholders has a role to play in developing an education system which furnishes individuals with the opportunities to grow, learn and develop their potential – as educators we owe them no less. Yet this task is not without its problems in a contemporary political context within which the education system is the site of intense public scrutiny, speculation, and change, particularly during the 1980s and 1990s. One of the problems faced by educators is that everybody knows what the problems of education are; in some sense we are all experts whether we are professional educators or simply because we have all been to school. In some quarters this perspective might be seen as being at best problematic and, at worst, downright confusing and has led to ideological conflict, competition and contradictions as battle lines are drawn. Yet it can also be refreshing, stimulating and exciting as educators and parents share views and opinions regarding what education should be about. If we begin from the viewpoint that education involves the development of constructive partnerships between all those with an interest in educating children, then the potential for change and development which offers lasting and tangible improvements in the quality of educational experience is there for all to see.

This book is a contribution to that debate and the chapters that follow are designed to provide a range of thought-provoking arguments, perspectives and narratives to develop further our knowledge and understanding of education. The book focuses upon a number of core issues which lie at the heart of contemporary educational debate.

Understanding the historical development of the education system is crucial to the development of a deeper, richer and more grounded analysis of the condition of contemporary education. 'Knowing' about education, what it is for, who controls and manages it, requires this sense of history. In Chapter 1 Davis examines policies and practice in the provision of compulsory education in the years since the end of the Second World War. One indisputable fact regarding education since 1945 is that the period has been one of intense social, economic and cultural change. Davis explores the manner in which the education system has also had to change to provide a system which responds to wider social and economic needs. Politically and ideologically this has resulted in considerably tensions and competition impacting upon school organization and management, curriculum change and the inevitable conflict that exists between providing a system of education that educates the individual while striving towards meeting both economic and cultural expectations.

There are numerous ways of viewing the processes of education and all are predicated upon sets of values, beliefs and assumptions regarding the aims and objectives of education. These ideologies are used as the basis for action and behaviour by a range of interest groups who seek a voice in controlling the education system, in influencing curriculum construction, teaching and learning styles. Each interest group 'imagines education' sometimes from a complimentary, but more often, from an alternative and competing position. These perspectives often have socio-economic and cultural roots and are locked into issues to do with socio-historical precedence characterized by debates over aims, territory, status and resources. This is the site for Chapter 2 by Garratt and Shallcross which, building upon the narrative in the previous chapter, focuses upon educational ideologies by exploring how ideas about education are presented, through a case study analysis of the relationship between educational ideology and practice within the context of sustainable development. It explores a number of political and ideological motives and intentions in the public presentation of education. The chapter moves beyond describing the manner in which education is organized and managed to exploring the underlying political and ideological principles that condition education provision. It sees education as being socially constructed, the result of debate and tensions between competing interest groups.

Chapter 3 written by Prescott takes us into the realm of early childhood studies. He critically explores the current knowledge-base that underpins early childhood studies within educational and 'care' contexts, and within a framework of adult-child relationships. In analysing discourses of childhood politically and ideologically, Prescott explores areas similar to those in Chapter 6. He places childhood and children within contexts where their relationships with society, and with adults, are dominated by the differential nature of power and responsibility, and seeks to broaden our understanding of the nature of early childhood studies by putting meanings into context within broader social and cultural discourses. In doing so he asks fundamental questions about the nature and experience of childhood and posits the need to 'challenge the construction of childhood as separate from adulthood and to problematize adult power in the context of structural relations and social arrangements of childhood' (see page 69).

In Chapter 4 this theme is continued and broadened by Barron within the context of early years education which he points out is not well understood and has often been under-valued by politicians, who have tended to see it as not part of formal education but more the responsibility of parents and agencies other than the education service. In exploring issues to do with who should have responsibility for early years education and the nature of provision within contexts characterized by poverty, abuse, difficult family circumstances or disability, Barron critically explores the potential difference early experiences can make to the development and learning of young children.

The context of the two previous chapters places children within a sociopolitical and cultural context and explores the theoretical definitions of childhood and debates surrounding provision. Writing in a wide-ranging and discursive style, Cullingford takes us in Chapter 5 into the social world of the child and their school experiences, and from their perspectives offers insights into what it is actually like to be a child seeking to construct a sense of both identity and belonging within an increasingly demanding and complex world. Cullingford analyses questions which are fundamental to our understanding of childhood: how and what do children learn; and, fundamentally, where do children learn? In exploring the relationship between the formal school curriculum and what children learn from their peers and from the environment in which they live and work, Cullingford asks us to question the fundamental role of the school in educating children. Do children learn more about their world, their identity and sense of belonging from experiences which are outside the formal curriculum? Indeed, does the formal school curriculum pay enough attention to the social education of children, or are schools now merely sites for the acquisition of testable bodies of subject knowledge driven by agenda which focus too much attention upon national debates regarding standards, rather than the social growth and maturity of young people? These are vital questions.

In Chapter 6 Wyse explores an area which had become increasingly important during the 1980s and 1990s, a time when it became recognized that children have 'rights'. While the United Nations' convention focused upon child protection, including abuse, neglect and exploitation, and children's needs such as education and healthcare and participation, acknowledging a child's capacity to make decisions and play a part in society, was adopted in 1989, the area is still under-explored and under-represented in the experiences of many young people. Focusing upon the role of schools councils in increasing pupil participation in their schooling, Wyse's position is that childhood can be viewed as a social construct. He explores ways in which schools can give greater prominence to re-configurating the way in which children and childhood are viewed and ways in which they can be given greater voice in their legitimate participation in their education.

The second half of the book broadens debates over educational provision by exploring a range of issues which are of contemporary concern to educators and parents. Crawford in Chapter 7 analyses the major issues, themes and problems associated with the development of the school curriculum from 1976 to 2000, a period during which, against a background of profound socio-economic change, the curriculum experienced radical and permanent changes which have exerted a profound effect on what pupils are taught, how they are taught and how their knowledge and understanding is assessed. Crawford charts the changing nature of the school curriculum and explores in detail the manner in which centralized and bureaucratic control of what is taught and how it is to be taught and assessed dominated the politics of curriculum.

Intimately linked to issues of curriculum is the debate over effective schooling in the United Kingdom. This in turn is closely linked to the manner in which government during the last twenty years of the twentieth century took a central role in controlling the education system. Lying at the heart of this strategy was the belief that effective schooling was only provided via strong managerialism characterized by a targeted commitment to raising standards of teaching and learning coupled with the desire to give 'value for money'. Arising out of 1980s neo-liberal and neo-conservative Thatcherism, this discourse dominated key educational agenda. So much so that, allied with the Office for Standards in Education (OFSTED) inspection service, schools found themselves very much in the market place with issues of consumer accountability a powerful driving force. Here issues to do with the way in which resources were allocated and, crucially, the way in which schools were managed offered a key framework within which schools were expected not only to be effective but seen to be effective. In Chapter 8 Boyes and Smith explore this theme by analysing questions such as the following. Is the effective schools movement driven by internal or external pressures? Does the drive for effectiveness stop with professionals or are other stake-holders involved in the process? This chapter examines some of the questions raised above and puts forward ideas for discussion.

The final two chapters in the book are linked in the sense that the issues that they explore focus upon the nature of schooling in its relationship to wider socio-economic, political and cultural issues. In Chapter 9 Judge explores the debates over inclusive education which lie at the heart of much contemporary educational practice. Given the managerialist context driven by the externally motivated drive towards ever higher educational standards, value for money and public accountability, many schools are faced with severe problems. A fundamental concern is how they manage and reach externally set targets within a climate in which they are expected to deliver high quality provision for pupils who come from a variety of socio-economic contexts; and how they cope with the practical realities of pupil alienation from schooling, truancy, disruptive behaviour, gender and multi-cultural issues, sometimes in deprived inner-city environments which present their own acute challenges. Inclusive education focuses upon education for all and equality of educational opportunity for all, but how are such slogans experienced in practice and what can schools do to achieve this aim given the multi-faceted contexts within which they are expected to perform?

In May 1998, the Labour government ordered a comprehensive review of the school curriculum to allow more time for classes in citizenship and parenting. The Qualifications and Curriculum Authority (QCA) were asked to consider what schools should be doing to prepare young people for the opportunities, responsibilities and experiences of adult life, including training in citizenship. In September 1999 the QCA (HMSO, 1999) recommended that citizenship should be taught as a statutory entitlement for all pupils aged 5 to 16 from the year 2002. In the book's final chapter Davies describes how citizenship education came to prominence. He discusses the problems and challenges associated with securing a place for it in schools and other educational institutions and offers suggestions on how teachers and others might work towards the effective implementation of citizenship education. Given the complex nature of contemporary society and the centrality of issues in popular discourse focusing upon political illiteracy and youth alienation, debates regarding community involvement, or the lack of it, and social and moral responsibility, Davies' chapter offers a timely reminder of the absolute necessity of schools becoming sites of active citizenship aimed at the development of participatory approaches to teaching and learning.

The pages of this book vividly illustrate that at the heart of education studies is the task of understanding how young people develop and learn and the contexts within which such activities take place. Methodologically, having a critical engagement with a variety of perspectives, it must encompass studying the nature of knowledge and ways of knowing and understanding, drawn from a range of appropriate disciplines. What each chapter in this book also illustrates is the highly complex and politically inherent nature of what it means to be educated. Education studies must also involve the intellectually rigorous study of educational processes, systems and approaches, and the cultural, societal, political and historical contexts within which they are embedded. This is an important task and the pages of this work are a contribution to this vital debate.

Chapter 1

The Historical Development
of Educational Provision

Mike Davis

T HE purpose of this chapter is to examine policies and practice in the provision of compulsory education in the years since the end of the Second
World War in 1945, a period of intense social and economic change. The
years leading up to the war were characterized by powerful social divisions,
crushing unemployment and associated poverty and poor health. Opportunities for social mobility were extremely limited and accordingly, class divisions
were insurmountable. The chapter explores the development of educational
provision following that war through:

- 1944 Education Act (The Butler Act)
- The post-war educational consensus
- Circular 10/65: towards the end of consensus
- Human capital: social and economic growth
- The 'secret garden' of education
- The Great Debate on education, 1976
- The 1988 Education Act

The 1944 Education Act

Among the consequences of warfare in much of the twentieth century was an
attention to social, medical and educational conditions of the fighting forces
as low self-esteem, poor health and limited education became vividly obvious

when men were put under conditions of severe emotional, medical and intellectual stress. Accordingly, wars tended to be followed by attempts at social engineering to alleviate social and educational inequalities. Legislation often follows changes in thinking and levels of acceptance by the populace at large, and thus there was increasing reluctance to countenance the desperate socio-economic conditions that much of the population was enduring. Consider this short extract from George Orwell (1937: 36):

> I have before me five pay-checks belonging to a Yorkshire miner, for five weeks (not consecutive) at the beginning of 1936. Averaging them up the gross weekly wages they represent is £2 15s 2d. But these pay checks are for the winter, when nearly all mines are running full time. As spring advances the coal trade slacks off and more and more men are temporarily stopped. It is obvious, therefore, that £150 or even £142 is an immense over-estimate for the mine-worker's yearly income.

Social reformers recognized that this condition could not continue. However, among the consequences of the war was a re-invigoration of the economy and despite the horrors of the Blitz and the fighting on the various fronts around Europe, Africa and the Far East, there appeared the germ of social change that seemed to be characterized by social reform across three major planks:

- the abolition of poverty through the introduction of a more generous welfare state;
- the provision of a national health service to offer medical and related care, free at the point of delivery;
- the introduction of compulsory and universal secondary education.

These aims attracted general all-party support, none more so than the education reforms. Planning for this began as early as 1941 when civil servants and ministers began to think about a (hopefully victorious) post-war period. In 1943, as victory became more likely, plans were set in motion to make the necessary legislative changes. The 1944 Education Act created a tripartite system of secondary education. This reflected current thinking both in psychology and psychology of education and divided pupils at the age of 11 on the basis of what came to be known as the eleven-plus examination, comprising an IQ (intelligence quotient) test and tests in English and mathematics. The Act assumed that children could be divided into categories with three different types of ability and aptitude. It was thought that ability was fixed by the age of 11, could be reliably measured through IQ tests and was unlikely to change. The intelligence quotient was said to represent a person's intellectual capacity in relation to peers. The average score was 100 and 85 per cent of the population fell between 85 and 115. A child would need a score above 115 to win a place in a grammar school, depending on where in the United Kingdom a person lived and the number of grammar school places that existed. The Act created three types of school:

- the grammar school, based on existing grammar schools; (up until this point these had been fee-paying, although in the main they were day, rather than boarding schools;)
- secondary technical schools, designed to educate potential engineers and those with technological, rather than academic potential; (very few of these schools were created, so in essence, the provision was more bipartite rather than tripartite;)
- secondary modern schools, designed to educate all of the rest. (Their curriculum was more general, with an emphasis on vocational and domestic education.)

The top 15-20 per cent of children who passed the eleven-plus went to grammar schools where they followed an academic curriculum preparing them for GCE 'O' and 'A' levels. The less 'academic' children who showed more practical ability were sent to technical schools aimed at occupations such as engineers and skilled manual workers. The large majority of children who failed the eleven-plus (60-70 per cent) were sent to secondary modern schools thought more suited to lower attaining pupils. The tripartite system was based upon the principle that it was possible to predict at the age of 11 the type of occupation which would suite children when they were adults.

Teachers were also segregated. The former grammar school teachers stayed in their schools and apart from a slightly higher number of working class children, the schools continued much as before. Teachers were mainly graduates and the schools saw their priority as an academic education for the small élite that would attend university; and a general education in the arts, sciences and humanities for the remainder, who would aspire to clerical and other jobs in the civil service, banking, insurance and the more highly sort after apprenticeships. The curriculum would include Latin – a requirement for university – and sometimes Greek, and one or more modern languages as well as the more conventional diet of English, mathematics, sciences, geography and history. Sport was important. The majority of grammar schools continued their tradition of being single sex.

Secondary technical schools did not make a significant impact for a variety of reasons, among them being a need for new and potentially expensive buildings. By the time the economy was beginning to improve in the 1950s, the impetus for secondary technical schools, with other provisions of the 1944 Education Act, had dissipated. Many secondary modern schools stayed in, or took over the old elementary school buildings. Classes were large, teachers were often poorly trained – products of post-war emergency training colleges which offered one-year courses to returning servicemen.

While the 1944 Act was the product of a Conservative Minister of Education, it was a member of the Labour government of 1945-50 who had to implement it. As reported by Beckett (2002: 28):

> [Ellen Wilkinson], according to the historian Peter Hennessy in his study of the 1945-1950 government, was 'appalled at the prospect of boys and girls doing practical things in their secondary modern schools which they would, perforce, spend the rest of their lives doing. She didn't want children of different IQS going to physically separate schools'. She hated the idea, she told her civil servants, of giving 'the real stuff to a selected 25 per cent while steering 75 per cent away from the humanities, pure science, even history'.

As a consequence of the bartering Wilkinson had to do to fund the new programme of development, particularly school building, she lost the eleven-plus battle, and that did not resume with any seriousness until the mid 1960s.

The other major consequence of the 1944 Act was the triangular division of responsibility between:

- central government, which set national policies and allocated resources;
- local education authorities (LEAs) which set local policies and allocated resources to schools;
- headteachers and governing bodies, which set school policies and allocated resources within the schools. (Gillard, 2001)

While this gave new powers to central government, previously somewhat indifferent to the nature of the provision apart from indirect expressions of control through, for example, Her Majesty's Inspectors of Schools (HMIs), this control was limited to prescriptions about the need for religious education. Local education authorities exercised some influence on the curriculum, particularly through advisory/inspection services but the real power lay in the headteacher's study. Theoretically, the curriculum could be comprised of religious education and Portuguese grammar and nobody would have any redress. Needless to say, this never happened. The system as a whole would be a 'national system, locally administered' (Bartlett *et al.*, 2001: 93).

The post-war educational consensus

In the years following the Second World War, there were a number of shared assumptions about the quality of life people could reasonably aspire to and education was seen as being central to this. As Dalin (1978: 3) wrote:

> education was looked upon as the main instrument for individual and economic development as well as the major social force for equality of opportunity.

However, the impact of post-war reform was slow to take effect, mainly as a product of the shift from a wartime to a peacetime economy, shortages of food and clothing – rationing of some items continued into the early 1950s – and the costly implementation of the nationalization programmes of coal, steel and the railways. However, once into the 1950s, there were the beginnings of prosperity: the economy started to grow and it was during this time that there were the beginnings of the implementation of educational reform. Initially, this was for organizational, rather than educational reasons: Anglesey, a rural local authority with a relatively small population, was the first in England and Wales to adopt the comprehensive model of education. This, somewhat piecemeal development, continued through the 1950s and by 1967 the distribution of schools types was quite varied (see Table 1.1). These figures demonstrate the slowness of the transition: Anglesey re-organized in 1954 and thirteen years later there were still only 500 comprehensive schools as against almost 6,000 organized along selective lines. Not only was there a degree of organizational separation, but the grammar schools continued to se- lect more pupils from middle class backgrounds, as Table 1.2 illustrates. This data is drawn from a survey conducted in Huddersfield in 1954. The national situation was remarkably similar in 1964 (see Table 1.3). This discrepancy be- tween opportunities offered by the grammar schools to working class pupils was a pre-occupation among educational researchers and subsequently some Labour politicians at that time. As Morrison and McIntyre (1971: 21-2) wrote:

> ... children of non-manual workers were several times more likely than those of manual workers to gain a grammar school place. Especially in

Table 1.1:   Types of secondary schools

Type of school	Number of schools	Number of pupils	Average school size	Number of teachers	Pupil teacher ratio
Modern	3,494	1,459,377	418	71,105	21:1
Grammar	1,236	694,898	562	39,004	18:1
Technical	141	69,704	484	3,948	18:1
Comprehensive	507	407,475	804	21,307	19:1
Other	351	201,397	574	10,132	20:1
Total	5,729	2,832,851	424	145,496	20:1

Source: Adapted from Jackson and Marsden, 1962

Table 1.2:   Social class origins (by paternal occupation) of entrants to grammar schools

Social class	Girls (%)	Boys (%)	Girls and boys (%)
Higher professional	17	10	12
Lower professional	32	35	35
Clerical	20	14	17
Skilled manual	22	34	29
Semi-skilled	5	5	5
Unskilled	4	2	2

Source: Adapted from Jackson and Marsden, 1962

Table 1.3:   Children in each social class entering grammar schools

Social class	Children in LEAs where over 1/5th go to grammar schools	Children in LEAs where 1/5th or under go to grammar schools
Non-manual upper	100	100
Non-manual lower	99	72
Manual upper	85	60
Manual lower	72	52

Source: Adapted from Douglas, 1964

those areas where a relatively small number of grammar school places were available, upper middle class children obtained, relative to others, many more places than their scores warranted.

For almost all of the 1950s and the first third of the 1960s, there was a Conservative government, which at least aspired towards one nation conservatism. The consequence of this, and of a degree of fatalism among Labour opposition MPs, led to a situation where there was not a systematic opposition to the educational *status quo*; rather quiet expressions of delight at the progress being made towards educational reform and increased spending (approximately 15 per cent per year in OECD countries). As Dalin (1978: 3) wrote:

> Most educational systems were quite successful in 'expanding', that is, in making the same opportunities available for more individuals 'doing more of the same'. But the reasons for expansion were mainly based on the belief that somehow education could cure societal ills, helping us to overcome some of the social and economic inequalities by providing everyone with the same opportunities.

It took some radical thinkers to begin the process of unravelling the consensus with the aim of re-writing the educational agenda for the last third of the twentieth century.

Circular 10/65: towards the end of consensus

In 1964 a Labour government was elected with a majority of six. Another election in 1966 gave Labour a substantial victory and laid the foundations for Prime Minister Harold Wilson's technological revolution. Tony Crosland, who became Secretary of State for Education in 1964, was one of the Labour Party's theorists and dedicated to notions of equality of opportunity which he believed was a key to social transformation. Price (1998: 19) concluded:

> No Labour minister since the war has a better record of opening up opportunities to those who would otherwise have been denied them and acting as an advocate for an inclusive education system.

By the mid-1960s the tripartite system of education was under sustained attack, questioning the fairness of selective education, leading to doubts about its suitability in providing equality of educational opportunity. It was argued:

- The eleven-plus was unfair, unreliable and inaccurate. Some bright pupils failed the eleven-plus; the examination did not allow for late developers. It became clear that intelligence was not fixed at the age of 11 as many children began to be sent to the wrong school. There was no such thing as parity of esteem. Grammar schools had higher status than technical and secondary moderns schools. They were seen by parents, pupils and employers as being better schools. They had better teachers and better facilities and better employment opportunities for the children attending them.
- Selective education reinforced social class divisions. More middle class children passed the eleven-plus than working class children. The education system, therefore, divided people along social class lines as it had done pre-1944.
- The self-fulfilling prophecy meant that many children were almost guaranteed to fail. Children and others began to label children as failures, expectations and self-esteem were low because of the school they attended.

Crosland was also widely known for his opposition to grammar school (although tolerant of public schools) and is quoted as threatening to destroy 'every *fucking* grammar school in England'. He set out to achieve this, not by legislation, but by persuasion, albeit backed up by some strong guidance in Circular 10/65 which 'required' local education authorities to submit plans for comprehensive re-organization. This was followed up in 1966 by suggestions that local authorities who did not comply with Circular 10/65 would suffer financial penalties. On the one hand, this could be seen as a Secretary of State interfering in the prerogative of local education authorities to run their own affairs – and indeed some chief education officers who supported comprehensive re-organization resented his intervention – and on the other, it could be regarded as an inevitable product of the equality agenda.

Comprehensive re-organization in the late 1950s and early 1960s was an attempt to achieve equality of educational opportunity and to overcome the in-built inequality of the tripartite system. Comprehensive education abolished selection at 11 and the three types of secondary school and entrance examinations. The advantages of comprehensive schools were said to be that:

- the possibility of educational success and of obtaining qualifications remained open throughout a child's school career;
- late developers whose intelligence and ability improve later in life could be catered for;

- talent was less likely to be wasted, particularly among working class children, and so there was greater opportunity for all children to fulfil their potential;
- the large size of comprehensive schools meant that there would be more teachers, teaching a wider range of subjects, with a wider variety of equipment and facilities;
- if all children attended a comprehensive school then children of differing social classes would mix avoiding social segregation.

Bartlett *et al.* (2001: 216) described the comprehensive movement as:

> born from an alliance of three groups. Leading sections of the Labour Party were keen to promote social reform through education, the organized sectors of the teaching profession who favoured a more egalitarian system and some key intellectuals in the new education-related disciplines were able to exert some influence on government thinking.

There were mixed reviews of Circular 10/65. Some commentators considered it to be an inadequate response to the issue of social and educational equal opportunity and that legislation to deal with reluctant local authorities was essential. Tony Benn, wrangling at that time with Harold Wilson about his cabinet appointment was asked if he were serious about wanting education. 'Yes, providing I could have an Education Act and make the comprehensive schools thing a really living issue' (Benn, 1988: 54). Other analyses were more favourable as Whitbread (1995) testified:

> Imperfect though it was, that Circular proved immensely popular. Nearly half the LEAs met the initial early deadline with plans for comprehensive re-organization of their whole area and most others gradually developed a variety of schemes for local circumstances. 10/65 accelerated and smoothed the way in all LEAs for a process already under way in many to eliminate the hated eleven-plus selection in favour of planned comprehensive systems.

> Support for comprehensives derived from hatred of the flawed and discredited eleven-plus selection. Released from that straitjacket, primary schools could abandon streaming and forge ahead educating all their pupils. Comprehensive secondary schools had to develop curriculum, teaching methods and internal organisation for a new educational context. Circumstances were so diverse that dull uniformity was always a myth.

This retrospective politicization of the debate reflects some of the thinking in the 1960s, although there is ample evidence that among the Labour leadership, particularly Harold Wilson himself, there was support for the continuation of grammar schools, alongside new comprehensives (Benn, 1988).

Human capital: social and economic growth

While these reports had independent membership, they were reflecting some of the prevailing concerns in society, particularly in respect of the insidious nature of the selection process, which, among other things, also impacted on the children of the increasingly larger middle class as well as the aspirant working classes. There had been little expansion in higher education which was seen as a potential block to social mobility and Robbins (1963) addressed this directly through the recommendation for the creation of new universities throughout the United Kingdom, allowing for an additional percentage of 18-year-olds to aspire to graduation. This was supplemented by Crosland's other great achievement: the creation of the polytechnic system, which awarded degrees accredited by the Council for National Academic Awards (CNNA) and offered a more vocational type of undergraduate opportunity. These institutions came under the control of local education authorities and were expected to be responsive to local industrial and commercial needs. They finally achieved their independence in 1992.

By the end of the 1960s, the majority of local education authorities had produced plans to introduce comprehensive schooling and the decision was made to raise the school leaving age to 16, with effect from 1972. Both of these contributed towards record spending on education as new schools and new accommodation for the additional pupils were built. Education had become a major investment, with the expectation of high rates of return both for individuals and for society. This was generally known as 'human capital theory'. Its core thesis is that peoples' learning capacities are comparable to other natural resources involved in the production process; when the resource is effectively exploited the results are profitable both for the enterprise and for society as a whole. From its inception in the United States of America after World War Two, human capital theory tended to equate workers' knowledge levels with their levels of formal schooling, to rely on quantitative indices of the amount of schooling in estimating individual economic returns to learning and to infer that more schooling would lead to higher productivity and macro economic growth. Throughout the post-1945 expansionary era, the simultaneous increase of school participation rates and earned incomes in advanced industrial market economies lent support to this perspective and encouraged the popular view that more schooling would inevitably lead to economic success.

Expectations that society would benefit from quick returns on investment in human capital were soon to be disappointed. It would indeed be naïve to expect it, but the nature of politics and the inability to protect national economies from international economic phenomena combined to create, in the early 1970s, the beginnings of resentment towards the apparent failure of schools to transform the national economy.

The change of government in 1970 and the arrival of Margaret Thatcher as Secretary of State for Education finally buried the hatchet in the corpse of the post-war consensus. She rescinded Circular 10/65 but paradoxically, was responsible for the closure of more grammar schools than any other Secretary because of the advanced state of development towards comprehensive education arising from Circular 10/65: to turn the clock back on those developments was by this time impossible. As Beckett (2002: 28) wrote:

> Although the Tory Education Secretary, Margaret Thatcher (1970-74), withdrew [Crosland's] request, the momentum behind comprehensive education was such that many local authorities continued to submit schemes to introduce it.

This coincided with further movements in the liberalization of the school system (Table 1.4). There were experiments in school organization, curriculum, school governance, and an increasing professional empowerment of teachers, their professional standing and their salaries rising dramatically.

The 'secret garden' of education

This phrase was used by Prime Minister Callaghan to indicate the closed nature of the debate about education. It was, in fact, the creation of one of the civil servants at the Department of Education and Science (DES) (now the Department for Education and Skills, DfES), who was frustrated at teachers' unwillingness to open up to ideas from civil servants and politicians. Up until this point, the curriculum was thought of as solely the responsibility of teachers and to a lesser extent, through the university-based examination boards, academics mindful of their duty to identify able students through their matriculation examinations. Both the GCE 'O' and 'A' levels (the precursors to the existing system of GCSE and AS/A levels) were examined via

Table 1.4:   A summary of educational developments

Policy	Year	Measure
Curriculum development	1964	Creation of the Schools Council for curriculum development
MACOS (Man: a course of study) (Bruner, 1977)	1968	Classic examples of 'centre-periphery' curriculum development projects, emerging fully formed from university departments of education and the Schools Council
Integrated humanities programme (Stenhouse, 1975)	1970	
Black Papers 1 to 5 (so called in contrast to government policy statements (White Papers)	1969 to 1974	Beginning of backlash against progressive education
Election of Conservative government	1970	
Raising of the school leaving age	1972	100,000 more pupils in schools
World oil crisis	1972	Massive 400 per cent rise in price of oil by OPEC countries
The Houghton Report	1974	A review of teachers' pay which gave substantial rises
Miners strike and three day week	1974	Insufficient coal at power stations to maintain electricity supply; TV closed at 10.30; no street/shop lighting
Election of Labour government	1976	Following Ted Heath's attempt to gain a mandate for taking on the National Union of Mineworkers.
Ruskin College speech and the Great Debate	1976	An attack on the 'secret garden' of control over the school. Signalled the beginning of the end for teacher control of state schooling.

these boards and teachers were represented on them. The Certificate of Secondary Education was wholly in the control of teachers, through subject representatives, many themselves ex-teachers. This situation, it could be argued, created an arrogant assumption about the right of teachers to maintain control of the curriculum. Teachers were almost certainly hostile to the notion that politicians and others could make a contribution to the debate. This had serious consequences for the way in which the educational establishment reacted to the planned intervention by Prime Minister Callaghan in his well signposted Ruskin College speech.

The Great Debate on education, 1976

James Callaghan, one of the few senior labour politicians not to have attended public school and university, took the opportunity in his Ruskin speech, to encourage teachers to listen and debate with parents, employers, civil servants and politicians about their expectations and ambitions for the education service. It was largely the product of years of frustration with a service that seemed to be a constant and expensive drain on national resources, refusing to allow open discussion, particularly in respect to discussions about value for money, that is, a return on the investment in human capital. The substance of the speech had three main themes:

- relationships between schools and industry, particularly teachers' attitudes on employment in industry, and standards of numeracy;
- concerns about innovation, particularly informal teaching methods;
- the need to return to a basic curriculum.

This speech, introducing the Great Debate was no surprise: news of it had been released to the press; in the *Times Educational Supplement* of the previous week Callaghan had been warned off – he was not welcomed in the garden. Callaghan (1976) referred specifically to this when he wrote:

> I must thank all those who have inundated me with advice: some helpful and others telling me less politely to keep off the grass, to watch my language … It is almost as though some people would wish that the subject matter and purpose of education should not have public attention focused on it: nor that profane hands should be allowed to touch it.

Schools and industry

Almost since the inception of compulsory schooling, there had been an uneasy relationship with industry and the work place. Among the intentions of the early framers of education legislation in the late nineteenth century, was a desire to have a more skilled and more flexible work force who could carry out increasingly complex work in manufacturing and other industries. In curriculum terms, however, there was a lack of clarity about what was required, beyond the '3Rs' (reading, writing and arithmetic) with obedience, punctuality and respect for superiors thrown in. Accordingly, vocational education had assorted manifestations as schools, particularly elementary and then secondary modern schools struggled with the desire to provide an appropriate, but totally de-contextualized vocational curriculum intended to lay the foundations for apprenticeships and other less formal models of work-based learning. The reality was that in times of low unemployment, young people found it easy to enter the job market and have low level training on the job. Expectations of 15/16-year-olds' competences were not high and in any event, much of the work was undemanding and repetitive.

Callaghan was concerned about the way in which he believed that teachers undermined industry. He argued that teachers did not understand industry, that they had no experience of it and that they subverted its attractiveness to young people. This was particularly thought to be the case in relation to science and he recounted evidence that there were 30,000 vacancies in science and engineering courses in universities while humanities courses were full.

While comprehensive education may have succeeded in improving overall educational standards in comparison with the tripartite system, the education system came under increasing pressure in the 1980s for failing to meet the needs of industrialists and employers. The consequence of this was an attempt to raise educational standards further and to link all parts of the education system to the needs of the economy. In a complex industrial society, the education system plays an important role in preparation for working life in producing a skilled labour force. A literate and numerate work force is essential in an industrial society and there is a need for specific skills related to particular jobs such as engineering and computing etc. What is learnt at school generally influences the kind of job and training people undertake when they leave school. The examination system helps to select people for different occupational pathways used by employers and educators to dictate patterns of training and employment. Attempts included:

- sending teachers into industry to develop their understanding which they could then apply to their teaching;
- work experience programmes for pupils between 14 and 16 to ease the school to work transition;
- new courses more closely related to the adult world of work, including vocational courses such as CPVE (certificate in pre-vocational education), and the TVEI (technical and vocational educational initiative) aimed at increasing understanding of technology, industry, wealth creation and enterprise.

Educational innovation: a return to basics

The five Black Papers of 1969 to 1974 (see Chapter 7) were opportunities taken by right wing commentators to reclaim some of the field from progressives who had dominated the educational system since the early 1960s. In some ways the problem was difficult to visualize: on the one hand, there had been reforms, predominantly in structure but also in curriculum and through the introduction of versions of mixed ability teaching, but schools in the 1970s were not wildly dissimilar from schools in the 1930s. Despite this, as early as 1957, Lester Smith, a historian of education could claim:

> in the bad old days of canings, birchings, sarcasm, impositions, and other customary forms of torture many [people] acquired in their school days a permanent dislike of their teachers, and this led them to hold a poor opinion of teachers in general. Although schools are no longer like that, centuries of iron rule have, it is suggested, left their mark on the popular attitude to teachers. And it must be admitted that even in this century – the age of the child as it has been called – people sometimes speak of their teachers as if they are echoing some unhappy memories of their schooldays. (150-51)

Many children educated in the 1960s and 1970s would not have recognized the 'age of the child'. Nevertheless, there were some innovations threatening conventional notions of what should be learned and how, and it was this that led the Black Papers to begin their campaign. Significant curriculum development projects like the integrated humanities programme worked to democratize the curriculum and give control of aspects of learning to pupils through the use of, for example, neutral chairmanship of discussions. MACOS never had many adherents in the United Kingdom; where it was employed, it was often for pragmatic reasons. The school I worked in during the early 1970s adopted it for use with 1st year pupils when building delays and overcrowding forced the use of an additional site across town.

The 1988 Education Act

In 1988 the Conservative government of the day introduced the Education Reform Act. It was described at the time as one of the most radical and far-reaching changes in education for a hundred years. At the heart of the Act was the Conservative government's intention to exercise central control over the work of local education authorities, schools and teachers. Key words of Conservative thinking at the time were 'choice', 'competition' and 'standards'.

Ideologically and politically one aim was to take control of education away from teachers and local authorities and put it more closely into the hands of government and parents (as consumers). In an interview with the *Times Educational Supplement* (31st May, 1996: 3) Kenneth Baker, who was Secretary of State for Education, acknowledged the importance of education as an electoral focal point:

> I knew perfectly well, because here was an election coming up, that I had to get this on the road ... If you look at our manifesto in 1979, I think we had about three inches on education and in 1983 we had about nine inches. In 1987 we had about ten pages.

The outcome of the Education Reform Act was that it provided the Secretary of State for Education with over 100 new powers to control education. There were three elements in the Act:

The National Curriculum A range of ten subjects was be studied by all pupils aged 5-16. The core subjects of mathematics, science and English dominated over the non-core subjects of history, geography, art, music, PE, technology, foreign languages and religious education. Since 1988 the National Curriculum has been reviewed three times and a new model introduced in September 2000, continued to emphasis the core subjects reducing the amount of time being spent on non-core subjects. In addition, in September 2002 citizenship education was introduced as a cross-curricular theme in the primary school and as a subject in the secondary curriculum. This curriculum is supported by national tests at the age of 7 and 11 in the core subjects. The results of these tests are publicly announced in the media in the form of 'league tables', the objective being to provide parents with one source of information from which they could make choices regarding the school they wish their child to go to.

Local Management of Schools (LMS) The 1988 Education Act gave powers to schools to mange their own budgets and increased the power of parents and local business people on governing bodies. This portion of the Act meant that headteachers were now responsible for how they spent the money allocated to them. In their financial planning they had to consider the total resourcing of the school in terms of salaries, equipment for the children, maintenance of the buildings etc. etc. In some large schools this budget could run into millions of pounds.

Grant Maintained Schools Schools could choose to 'opt out' by gaining grant maintained status (GMS). These schools ran their own budgets and made their own decisions on staffing, resource allocation and could make them more responsive to the educational market (parents and employers). These schools were free to select their pupils at the age of 11. Since the introduction of the 1988 Act, while hundreds of schools have become grant maintained, they have remained, however, in the minority and the overwhelming number of schools have stayed in local authority control.

After their election in May 1997 the Labour Party did not attempt to make fundamental changes to the structure of the 1988 Education Reform Act. The basic provisions were left in place. The Labour Party successfully re-invented itself. Despite their election in May 1997 educational politics in the United Kingdom were characterized not by change but by continuity. New Labour and Conservative politics showed a strong degree of congruence. The Labour government colonized the discourse of conservatism and attempted to create an uneasy alliance with policies originating from an ideology of the right.

Conclusion

The historical development of contemporary education since 1945 has been marked by significant and far-reaching changes. It is crucial in developing an understanding of these changes to appreciate that they are very often the product of wider socio-economic imperatives. The education system does not grow and modify in a vacuum, rather it is changed by powerful political and ideological groups in direct responses to issues, problems and themes which are considered to be of contemporary concern. Often, educational change, in terms of curriculum, accountability, organization and management, have economic conditions of existence. When the economy is secure and growing then it is assumed that schools and teachers must be doing their job; in times of economic crisis the opposite is often the case. Given the contemporary state of society it is easy to conclude that nothing in the world of education is secure or certain. However, one thing is sure, the education system will continue to be modified as society and its core values are forced to respond to global and national issues.

Task

Everybody has alternative and, perhaps, competing educational experiences which have shaped their values and attitudes towards what constitutes appropriate and relevant state schooling in the late twentieth century. Consider the following questions:

(1) What should be the aims and objectives of state schooling?
(2) Who should decide what those aims and objectives ought to be?
(3) Should education be about educating the individual or about preparing individuals for their role in society?

Indicative reading

A selective reading of particular chapters in each of these books will provide you with evidence to help frame answers to the questions above.

Bash, L. and Coulby, D. (1989) *The Education Reform Act: competition and control*. London: Cassell.

Flude, M. and Hammer, M. (1990) *The Education Reform Act*. London: Falmer Press.

Lawton, D. (1989) *The Education Reform Act: choice and control*. London: Hodder and Stoughton.

Chapter 2

Ideology and Curriculum Theory: whole-school approaches to education for sustainable development

Dean Garratt and Tony Shallcross

THE task of addressing the linked concepts of ideology and curriculum theory is one that is closely tied to the question: what are the aims and purposes of education? Prospective answers to this question provide the underlying rationale to the concept of education, where educational ideologies create the foundations upon which expressions of formal curricula are based. However, the question of how a curriculum should be constituted and hence what should count as knowledge has long been contested (see for example, Peters, 1973, 1966; White, 1990, 1982; Laura and Cotton, 1999). Of the numerous presentations made, we identify five possible purposes of education:

- vocational;
- social replication of labour;
- cultural socialization;
- liberal;
- transformatory.

Although there are contradictions within current educational policy, we suggest that modern education in the United Kingdom is largely concerned with the first two instrumental purposes and with the products or outcomes of education. In contrast, more radical forms of education for sustainable development (ESD) takes a fundamentally liberal humanist, intrinsic perspective on educational purpose that includes the last three examples, and so remains fundamentally concerned with the nature of education in a way that emphasizes process. In this chapter we propose to explore what this means in practice through the example of ESD, by providing an analysis of the concept of 'ideology' in relation to a range of different curriculum models. Before developing our case study, however, we shall explore the meaning of ideology within and through a selection of historical and educational contexts.

The complexity of ideology

Throughout the history of ideas the concept of 'ideology' has come to mean different things to different people at different times. It is a promiscuous word the meaning of which has been notoriously difficult to pin down, with the appearance of almost as many different definitions as there have been attempts to understand the term. Yet where many commentators, sociologists and writers of political science seem to reach agreement is on the view that the concept can find no position from which its meaning can be universally determined. This is because there can be no single or correct interpretation of ideology, nor any closure to the countless disputes regarding its numerous definitions. As various commentators have attested:

> What ideology means is problematic usually. (Apple, 1990: 20)

> [It is] an essentially contested concept. (McLellan, 1986:12)

> Every concept in education has varying and various interpretations but perhaps none more so than ideology. (Matheson and Limond, 1999: 15)

> Such a variety of available definitions can be bewildering. The links between beliefs, a society's self-image, the production of meaning and the creation of individual identity may not be immediately apparent. (Cormack, 1992: 9)

For scholars of education and students of social science these perspectives and others raise critical questions concerning the way in which one should attempt to make sense of the term. Equally they pose the dilemma of how it is possible to proceed from this apparently relativistic position. One useful strategy may be to consider that in spite of its plurality of meanings 'ideology' is a term that has travelled along a distinctive historical path, where key philosophical milestones may be used to reveal the various ways in which the concept has evolved over time. The following analysis seeks to identify such moments in the history of its evolution, portraying both its positive and negative conceptions, while acknowledging at the same time the complexity that different theoretical perspectives bring to bear upon our understanding of its meaning(s) and usage.

The genesis of ideology

The concept of ideology (Cormack, 1992) was first used in post-revolutionary France by a group of intellectuals known as 'ideologues' (the principle architects of the French Enlightenment), who conceived the term as an expression for the 'science of ideas'[1]. This move was closely matched to the prevailing mood of the time, where a previous reliance upon religious dogma and all things metaphysical was exchanged for the project of establishing a true and universal knowledge of the social world. 'Ideology' was, therefore, conceived as the device through which all enlightened thinking was expressed and all pernicious falsehoods rebuked. However, as circumstances changed in France at the beginning of the nineteenth century, Napoleon, following the defeat of his army in Russia in 1812, denounced the ideologues for propagating spurious ideas – blaming their practical naïveté and political ignorance for his own misfortune in battle. From this point on, ideology was bequeathed a negative meaning, where it was often invoked as a representation of 'undesirable and misguided sets of ideas' (Matheson and Limond, 1999: 16). Ironically, then, there was a significant inversion from the view of ideology as the essence of all that is good and true to its negative conception as a mystification or deception of ideas and beliefs.

The negative conception

For Marx and Engels (see Cosin *et al.*, 1971), this pejorative meaning was used to express the distortions that ideology had inflicted upon the social and economic world. In *German Ideology*, for example, Marx and Engels described the relationship between subordinate and dominant classes within society, where only the latter were seen to possess a consciousness that enabled them

---

[1]   It should be noted that ideology was linked with earlier concepts developed in the work of Machiavelli, Bacon and Hobbes (see Cormack, 1992).

to think and which allowed them to produce meaningful political ideas. These ideas informed the dominant ideology that operated a self-justifying and persuasive rhetoric. In Marxist terms, this effect was achieved through the illusion of class, where a line of cleavage was formed between the rulers and the ruled. The ideology worked because its illusion appeared real, and because subordinate classes were denied the luxury of contemplation. They had 'less time to make up illusions and ideas about themselves' (in Cosin *et al*, 1971: 179), and, therefore, scant opportunity to recognize the conditions and extent of their oppression. In this way the dominant class was assured that all interests, power and social and economic resources remained, to their advantage, unevenly distributed. Accordingly, as the passive recipients of the dominant ideology the working classes were said to experience 'false-consciousness', where the concept of ideology worked perniciously to distort their true material existence and perpetuated their absolute subordination.

Building upon the work of Marx and Engels, but in marked contrast with their notion of ideology as a set of ideas or beliefs, Althusser (1981) in his essay "Marx's new science", developed a theory of ideology as structure:

> Ideology is indeed a system of representations, but in the majority of cases these representations have nothing to do with 'consciousness': they are usually images and occasionally concepts, but it is above all as structures that they impose on the vast majority of men, not via their 'consciousness'.

By referring to 'structures' Althusser (1984) meant both the overt and covert operations of what he called the 'ideological state apparatus'. In the case of covert operations, he described the way in which ideology was perpetuated at a structural level through the existence of various institutions, including religious, educational, media and governmental. These institutions, which formed part of the state apparatus, represented the interests of the dominant class, because they operated in ways that preserved the dominant class's political interests and ideological supremacy.

While Marx and Engels' account of 'ideology as false-consciousness' and Althusser's theory of 'ideology as structure' are important analytical tools, both share conceptual difficulties. For example, with respect to the problem of ideology as false-consciousness, Foucault (1980: 118) explained that

> the notion of ideology appears to me to be difficult to make use of ... [because] like it or not, it always stands in virtual opposition to something else which is supposed to count as truth.

Of course, this not only raises the ontological (to do with the nature of being) dilemma of what truth is, but generates an epistemological (to do with the nature of knowledge) one that asks how Marxists may presume to know what is best for others. This apparent display of arrogance by Marxists, in suggesting how is it possible to demystify ideology so that the subordinate classes may better understand the conditions of their oppression, has been criticized elsewhere (Smith, 1993). The second point in connection with the structural theory of ideology is that its monolithic tendencies invoke a negative imagery in which the concept is seen as a totalizing and repressive force. However, as Foucault (1980: 122) elaborated:

> I don't want to say that the State isn't important; what I want to say is that relations of power, and hence the analysis that must be made of them, necessarily extend beyond the limits of the State ... because the State for all the omnipotence of its apparatuses, is far from being able to occupy the whole field of actual power relations, and further because the State can only operate on the basis of other, already existing power relations.

What Althusser's notion of the ideological state apparatus denied, then, was the possibility of subjectivity and autonomous decision-making, concealing as it did important variations in the values and ideas of ideological subjects. This produced a tension where the subordinate class was apparently subject to the totalizing control of the dominant ideology, yet consumed by the particularities of its own economic situation, with its corresponding demands that might be at odds with the dominant ideology (Cormack, 1992).

The resulting incongruence, that lay at the core of Althusser's negative articulation, was rectified in the work of Gramsci (1971), who revealed how structures and individuals may be reconciled. Unlike the previous theorists, who in their different ways presented a negative conception of ideology, he mapped out a looser conceptual model that acknowledged the more positive role of ideology as a political, social and economic device. Gramsci argued:

> The term 'ideology' assumed in Marxist philosophy implicitly contains a negative value judgement ... 'Ideology' itself must be analysed historically, in the terms of the philosophy of praxis, as a superstructure ... ideology is given both to the necessary superstructure of a particular structure and to the arbitrary elucubrations of particular individuals. The bad sense of the word has become widespread, with the effect that the theoretical analysis of the concept of ideology has been modified and denatured.

This suggests that there is an important symbiosis between the conception of ideology as a set of ideas and beliefs and its more deterministic structural relation. For Gramsci, this implied that subordinate ideologies might be accommodated by the dominant one as a way of preserving the latter's supremacy. This means that the dominant ideology may sometimes tactically concede power in order to retain its own hegemony (dominance). In educational terms this can be illustrated, for example, through the introduction of vocational courses to the secondary curriculum. These may be introduced to accommodate the needs of lower academic achievers who might otherwise be disadvantaged by an over narrow academic curriculum. 'Empowerment', then, is the root metaphor of this Gramscian notion of articulation, since the language of improved 'choice' and 'range' of curriculum subjects can be seen to produce a chimera of enhanced participation. It does so because the cultural dominance of academic subjects is preserved, while the curriculum is expanded in order to extend provision to the wider school population, to satisfy the needs and aspirations of lower academic achievers and the demands of the economy[2].

What this brief and somewhat crude account of the Gramscian model highlights, then, is that ideology is a more subtle and complex concept than originally conceived. In contrast with the earlier perspectives of both Marx and Engels, and Althusser, ideology is not always monolithic or omnipotent, but may sometimes be shown to reveal contradictions that present opportunities for the circulation of power within relationships of dominance and subordination. In breaking the stereotype of ideology as a repressive force, Gramsci suggested that it could be a structure of variable strength (see Cormack, 1992), which through interaction with its subjects could be seen to display a variety of overlapping and conflicting positions. Through this more sophisticated conception of ideology positive features may be illuminated.

---

[2]   There are numerous examples of this 'smuggling-in' of vocational-type subjects under the auspices of improved choice and empowerment of the individual. An obvious example concerns the former Secretary of State for Education, Sir Keith Joseph's idea of introducing the Technical and Vocational Educational Initiative (TVEI) for the bottom 40 per cent of achievers, whilst seeking to maintain the 'high-culture' and dominance of academic subjects in the school curriculum during the early 1980s. Similar moves have been made in conjunction with General National Vocational Qualifications (GNVQ), which have entered the curriculum through a rhetoric of 'widening participation' but have yet to challenge seriously the dominance of either the National Curriculum, GCSEs and/ or 'A' level qualifications, particularly in terms of student access into higher education.

Positive conception

In 1936 Mannheim advanced the idea that in order to understand ideology more fully the concept should be analysed historically, since its meaning is not associated with any one single group, process or intellectual position. In subjecting the concept to a sociological analysis, Mannheim believed that ideology took on a relational meaning so that different theoretical conceptions might be bound up with different ways of seeing the world, each of which had played a part in the evolution of the term. For Mannheim, then, Marxism merely discovered a clue to understanding the workings of society, a view that was shaped and influenced by 'the gradual rounding out of which the whole nineteenth century participated' (see Cosin *et al.*, 1971: 174). In contrast to the classical position of Marx and Engels, Mannheim suggested a shift from the negative articulation of ideology as a narrow theoretical statement 'showing that the adversary suffers from illusions or distortions on a psychological or experiential plane' (see Cosin *et al.*, 1971: 174), to one in which the analysis could be seen to acknowledge the co-existence of different competing views. This positive transformation revealed a complex inter-play between differing perspectives, where the 'narrowness and limitations which restrict one point of view tend to be corrected by clashing with the opposite points of view' such that 'all elements of meaning are qualitatively changed and the word ideology acquires a totally new meaning' (174-6). It is this qualitative change in the meaning of ideology that potentially has the most powerful contribution to make towards our understanding of curriculum issues.

Ideology and the curriculum

To the extent that any curriculum programme is an amalgamation of ideas, values and beliefs, which are the products of a cultural heritage shaped by prevailing social structures, it may be viewed as inherently ideological. This, of course, assumes that ideology refers 'to some sort of "system" of ideas, beliefs, fundamental commitments, or values about social reality' (Apple, 1990: 20) and that these in turn are enabled to find expression through the product (knowledge), process (pedagogy) and praxis (mediated experience) of the intended curriculum. Apple suggested that this expression requires ideology to play a dual role that recognizes the scope of the rules governing the curriculum and the rhetorical function of the concept in arguments over power and resources. This becomes critical when the positive articulation of ideology is paramount, for it implies a conceptual framework of overlapping theories and justifications that in turn give rise to potential conflicts of power. Yet in spite of this possibility, resulting from the clash of divergent curriculum orientations, ideology has in common certain defining features:

> *Legitimation* ... ideology is concerned with legitimation – the justification of group action and its social acceptance ...
>
> *Power conflict* – all of the sociological literature links ideology to conflicts between people seeking or holding power ... power conflict is always at stake in ideological disputes, whether or not those involved expressly acknowledge that dimension ...
>
> *Style of argument* – many writers note that quite a special rhetoric, and heightened affect, mark the argumentation that takes place in the realm of ideology ... The rhetoric is seen to be highly explicit and relatively systematic. (McClure and Fischer, 1969; cited also in Apple, 1990: 21; our italics)

For ideology to function in its role as a purveyor of meaning in complex situations, especially those found within bodies of socially organized curricula (Young, 1971), it is imperative that its features are managed within an interpretive framework which recognizes the construction of curriculum theory as a plural enterprise.

The question of what should count as knowledge, however, has historically proved difficult to answer. Meaningful analyses of differing educational ideologies that have conflicting curriculum aims and purposes, rely upon the negotiation of variable and often contrasting visions of educational quality, since, as Mannheim suggested, 'thought' itself is a 'particularly sensitive index of social and cultural change' (Cosin *et al.*, 1971: 176). Rarely is it true, then, that curriculum programmes are based upon one-dimensional thinking. It is more common to find that educational interests are diffuse and that curriculum programmes comprise competing definitions of aims and purposes, with contrasting pedagogical styles and strategies of mediation. Yet what educational ideologies have the power to do is to render the complex more intelligible. They work heuristically by constructing ideal-type versions of educational quality that present a simplification of the reality they are purporting to describe. While this is undoubtedly their strength, a weakness lies in their tendency to be taken too literally. Accordingly, while advancing a framework of several versions of educational quality in the following section, these educational ideologies do not represent 'reality' in any concrete sense, but are only indicative of general tendencies in the development of curriculum theory.

Three educational ideologies

In a sociological analysis of the nature of curriculum theory, Grundy (1987) explored a framework in which the foundations of organized curricula were subjected to detailed critical scrutiny. Curriculum was not a concept, she argued, but rather a cultural phenomenon. It was a construction that could be elucidated through a framework of 'knowledge-constitutive interests' which was developed by the German philosopher Habermas (1972). He elaborated a three-fold theory of fundamental human interests that could be seen to bear directly upon the construction of curriculum knowledge. As Grundy (1987: 10) elaborated 'these knowledge-constitutive interests do not merely represent an orientation towards knowledge or rationality on the part of the human species, but rather constitute human knowledge itself'. These can be expressed according to three basic cognitive factors, namely, technical, practical and emancipatory interests:

> The technical interest, like each of the fundamental human interests, is grounded in the need of the species to survive and reproduce both those aspects of human society which are deemed to be of most worth. To achieve this purpose, persons have a basic orientation towards controlling and managing the environment ... this is a form of knowledge known as positivism ... [that] consists of certain theories about the world which are grounded in our 'positive' observation and experience of that world. (11)

The preoccupation here with control and the presentation of propositional forms of knowledge has strong resonance with Marxist theories of dominance and subordination. On this view, the ruling élite is at liberty to determine what counts as knowledge through the 'technical exploitation' and control of learning and teaching.

Transmissional model (technical)

The technical version of educational quality implies a transmissional model of teaching and learning that makes the following assumptions about the acquisition and mediation of knowledge, namely that:

- knowledge is certain, indubitable and unproblematic;
- teachers are universal bearers of knowledge that is conveyed through an expert-novice relationship;

- learning is a linear, uniform and unproblematic process;
- knowledge is contained within and exclusive, to the cognitive domain.

In many respects this model is divisive since it serves to maintain the stratification of knowledge along the lines of the prevailing social order (Young, 1971). This order is determined through the interests of the élite, which in turn are legitimated through an apparently neutral curriculum, which at the same time generates a framework of knowledge serving particular social, cultural and economic interests. This is a perspective that has much in common with the classical humanism of Plato, where the prevailing rationality was to secure the submission of the learner to an externally-driven and pre-determined body of knowledge. In this scenario, the hegemonic function of ideology works through the differentiation of individuals to whom Plato referred as men of gold, bronze and iron (Skilbeck, 1976). This hierarchy, in descending order of status and importance, determines the social ranking of individuals and thereby establishes the process by which their entitlement to different forms of knowledge is granted. In modern programmes of education this model can be recognized through a curriculum that places significant emphasis on the acquisition of academic knowledge. This ideological stance is preoccupied with the division of pupils according to their performance against academic targets. The system of ranking operates through a series of technical procedures and systems of measurement, including examination league tables, assessment targets and the ability to master cognitive aspects of knowledge. Although presenting itself as a neutral and fair curriculum it can be seen as culturally biased, since the privileging of academic knowledge over other forms may disadvantage groups of children through class, gender and/or ethnicity (Edwards and Whitty, 1992; Ball, 1993b; Arnot, 1997).

Transactional model (practical)

The transactional version of educational quality is one that shares much in common with the second of Habermas' knowledge-constitutive interests, where curriculum emphasis is more practical than technically oriented:

> The practical interest is grounded in the fundamental need of the human species to live in and as part of the world, not to be, as it were, in competition with the environment for survival ... the production of knowledge through the making of meaning is the task associated with the historical-hermeneutic sciences ... [where] access to facts is provided by understanding of meaning, not observation. (Grundy, 1987: 13)

The emphasis here on interpretation signals a departure from the previous model of control to one in which actions and behaviour are dealt with in a more holistic fashion. In curriculum terms, practical interests are realized through experience, where knowledge is rooted in participation so that understanding the 'environment' (that is, different forms of curricula) becomes a process of interaction that acknowledges the centrality of judgement (Grundy, 1987). This model makes the following assumptions about the nature of knowledge and process of teaching and learning, that:

- knowledge is less certain and more problematic;
- knowledge is to be acquired and constructed through experience;
- teachers and learners form part of a reciprocal relationship;
- learning is messy and individualized;
- knowledge is as much concerned with feelings and emotions as it is cognition.

In curriculum terms these interests have found expression through the implementation of forms of experiential learning, where the relationship between teacher and pupil is partially subverted by a model that is less transmissional and more participatory – this will be illustrated later in the section on educational ideologies. Sharing common ground with this view in contemporary curriculum practice is the philosophy of naturalism advocated by Rousseau (Skilbeck, 1976). Ideologically speaking, Rousseau was the pioneer of progressive thinking – a version of educational quality in which 'growth' is recognized as the root metaphor in a process that addresses the individual requirements of children. In contrast with notions of division and classification which are characteristic of humanist beliefs, progressivism seeks to address education in more equitable terms, focusing instead on the impulses of the developing child. This transactional and more progressive ideology was popularized through The Plowden Report (DES, 1967a) and pedagogy of child-centred education during the 1960s and 1970s. Even today, aspects of this educational ideology feature in the espoused ethos and curriculum approach of Summerhill School (Neill, 1969).

Transformatory model (emancipatory)

Within the triad of knowledge-constitutive-interests, it is emancipatory interests that display the strongest resonance with the transformatory version of educational quality. For Grundy (1987: 16), emancipatory interests conveyed the following meaning:

Emancipation for Habermas means 'independence from all that is outside the individual and is a state of autonomy … it is only in the act of self-reflection … that emancipation is possible … Although emancipation must ultimately be an individual experience if it is to have any reality, it is not simply an individual matter.

Whereas the central premises of technical and practical interests were control and participation respectively, the central feature of emancipatory interests is social change and transformation. This transformatory aspiration sometimes finds expression in the desire to free persons 'from the coercion of the technical and possible deceit of the practical', where for the latter 'consensus can be false when powerful interests are participating in the meaning-making and agreement process' (17). Interestingly, the transformatory ideal has been articulated elsewhere in Skilbeck's (1976) notion of reconstructionism. This perspective works from the premise that in order to function more effectively society requires stability and coherence, of which the essential preconditions, especially in times of social and political upheaval, are critical and reflective change. In the history of curriculum reform, aspects of reconstructionism have entered into ideological debates concerning the purpose and aims of education. However, these have tended to be economically driven (see for example Moore, 1984; Patten, 1993) rather than egalitarian or socially transformatory. The transformatory model makes the following assumptions about the nature of knowledge and process of teaching and learning:

- that all knowledge attempts to conceal the assumptions and interests that are contained within;
- that teachers and learners should be critical of and reflective upon knowledge;
- that teachers and learners while participating in a reciprocal relationship of mutual dependency are entitled to a degree of autonomy and independence;
- that learning should involve continuous reflection;
- that knowledge is contestable and always open to revision.

It is our purpose in the following section to illuminate this model through a discussion of whole-school approaches to education for sustainable development, discussing the implications of this version of educational quality in practice.

Ideologies and education

In this section we view ideologies as cultural phenomena, as systems of conflicting ideas that co-exist and intertwine, that justify group action and its social acceptance. Ideology will be viewed as positive but open to conflict.

We must acknowledge that educational ideologies exist in a subordinate, nested relationship to other more dominant socio-political and economic ideologies and within educational ideologies such as transmissional, transactional and transformatory there lie nested concepts of childhood and the nature of knowledge. In terms of power, education is a following rather than a leading discipline in the expression and generation of ideological ideas (Bernstein, 1970; Begg, 2000). Besides the conflictual nature of ideology there is frequently a gap between ideology as a system of ideas and values and the manifestation of these ideas in educational practices in classrooms. The notion of ideology in educational thinking and practice is further complicated by the fact that we live in a technically pragmatic, purportedly non-ideological age which claims that education is based on policies that work. Is this rejection of ideology in itself an ideological stance?

Sustainability and education for sustainable development

Definitions of sustainability (Table 2.1) tend to share the idea of maintaining systems. One conception of sustainability is to see it occupying the space at the intersection of three domains: the economic, social and scientific (see Figure 2.1). Sustainability requires that all three types of system operate in

Table 2.1:   Definitions of sustainability and sustainable development (SD)

Term	Definition
Sustainability	'A characteristic of a process or state that can be maintained indefinitely' (Webster's Dictionary).
Sustainable development	'Improving the quality of human life while living within the carrying capacity of supporting ecosystems' (The World Conservative Union, United Nations Environment Programme, World Wildlife Fund).
Sustainable development	'Sustainable development is development that meets the needs of the present without compromising the ability of future generations to meet their own needs' (WCED, 1987).

ways in which they can be sustained indefinitely. Sustainable development means meeting the needs of human beings now and in the future while living within the ability of natural systems to support us.

Sustainability, like ideology, is a complex and problematic concept, yet also the most important idea facing humankind (Dimbleby, 2001). Sustainability is equated with an economic, quantitative concept of yield rather than a qualitative regard for richness and variety implicit in sustaining biodiversity. A sustainable forest becomes a crop grown to sustain an economic yield indefinitely, not necessarily a forest that is promoting biodiversity. The ethics supporting such a view of sustainability are based on the idea that humanity is either the only thing that matters or it has greater value than anything else, ethics so deeply embedded in the Western psyche, so conditioned by cultural and economic systems, that they are learned and re-enacted as second nature for most people in Western societies (Orr, 1994; Bowers, 1997).

Sustainability is not about saving the planet; it is about saving ourselves. Whether our concern is with socio-economic or with ecological concepts of sustainability, it has many human overtones. We have to sustain ecosystems to sustain ourselves. The Earth is not fragile; it has recovered from numerous catastrophes such as asteroid strikes, colossal volcanic eruptions and ice ages which have caused major extinctions. Our current ecological pathology is producing a similar catastrophic extinction, from which humanity will probably

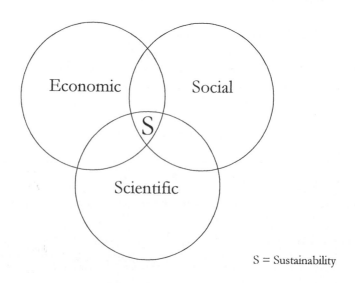

S = Sustainability

Figure 2.1:   The three domains of sustainability

be one of the casualties, not the Earth itself. On the other hand there are those who have a more radical understanding of sustainability which is built on reducing the impact of our lifestyles, respecting the Earth and avoiding damage to natural systems. Ethical sustainability is about considering nature of equal value to humanity. So does the language of sustainability attempt to convey a unified conception that does not exist?

While definitions of ESD also differ, they usually contain relatively consistent commitments to changing values, attitudes and actions (Orr, 1992; Uzzell, 1999; Shallcross and Wilkinson, 1998). These three strands can be clearly identified in the UNESCO (1997: 4) description of the purposes of ESD.

> The effectiveness of awareness raising and education for sustainable development must ultimately be measured by the extent to which they change the attitudes and behaviours of people as both consumers and citizens. Changes in lifestyles as reflected in individual behaviour, households and at a community level must take place.

Before we look at the ideologies associated with ESD clearly the purpose of it is to change values and actions in ways which will result in more sustainable lifestyles. Thus, ESD is concerned with changing how we act. Sustainability requires both global and individual changes in the way we live our lives. Can education alone ever initiate changes in actions on such a scale?

ESD and educational ideologies

Again we should recognize that we are using categories here that are designed to enable understanding, categories that in the real world overlap and conflict. No teacher, policy maker or headteacher is locked exclusively into one of the ideologies we shall examine in this section. The three ideologies we shall discuss are very closely related to Grundy's (1987) division of educational ideologies into the technical, practical and emancipatory. As earlier, we shall use three different but equivalent terms here (see Table 2.2), transmissional (technical), transactional (practical) and transformatory (emancipatory).

Transmissional ideology underpins some approaches to ESD. Transmissional ESD has been based on a top-down, centre-periphery model of curriculum development, which because it is based on an individualistic model, emphasising behaviour modification, and has not produced significant changes in the way people act sustainably. Despite recognizing environmental complexity, the transmissional approach to ESD has applied a simplistic, psychological model of human behaviour based on the belief that if people are aware of a problem they will act for its resolution (Roszak, 1995). Yet, an education committed to changing people's actions through cognitive routes alone will not produce large enough changes in action to make societies sustainable. 'Over these years, I came to see that the early assumption, shared by most people in environmental education, was a simplistic and deterministic one: that if people learnt about environmental issues, their behaviour would change' (Sterling, 2001: 19).

Transactional approaches to ESD are more concerned with critical pedagogy which takes the view that knowledge is both socially constructed and problematic. Identifying the issues surrounding social and ecological sustainability requires critical pedagogy which is at least transactional in approach: 'In this perspective, teachers would be involved in the invention of critical discourses and democratic social relations. Critical pedagogy would represent itself as the active construction rather than the transmission of particular ways of life' (Giroux, 1996: 695). However, it is also an ideology that recognizes that knowledge and rationality are not the keys to human motivation but values and emotion (Kagan, 1984). Thus transactional approaches to ESD would be based on the thesis that in order to change actions one first needs to change values and attitudes. The problem with such an ideology is that it often fails to distinguish between the values we claim to hold and the values implicit in our actions (Posch, 1993).

No matter what values individuals or groups of people espouse, there will often be inconsistencies between these stances and their environmental actions. People may adopt different value systems for different circumstances (Clayton and Radcliffe, 1996); for example there may be dissociation between private economic decisions and public social decisions. This dissociation

Table 2.2:   The curriculum and educational ideologies

Ideology	Some typical features
Transmissional or technical	Pupils are seen as passive recipients of traditional, disciplinary knowledge in a uni-directional system of education that is downward.
Transactional or practical	Pupils are seen as active participants and constructors of their own learning in a system of education based on dialogue between pupils and the curriculum using e.g. discursive and problem-solving approaches.
Transformatory or emancipatory	Children are seen as whole people in a system in which education is viewed as a holistic cognitive, affective and active process of personal, social and ecological development.

applies to young people as well, as Rickinson (2001: 258) observed in his review of research into their environmental attitudes:

> These report generally positive environmental attitudes, i.e. greater agreement with pro- rather than anti-environmental sentiments. However, several studies find students to be less environmentally conscious in relation to certain issues – in particular, those linked to their own lives and material aspirations.

Brennan (1991) used Aristotle's concept of incontinence to describe this failure of people to act in ways that they believe to be right (see Table 2.3). The plight of the weak-willed is at the heart of the environmental crisis. Too many people who are aware that there is an environmental crisis and feel that something should be done about it do not act for its resolution. Sustainability is much more likely to be achieved if such incontinent behaviour can be transformed into virtuous behaviour. Some people are sufficiently affected by a transmissional or transactional education or their own personal experiences to act more sustainably, otherwise we would not have eco-warriors (Scarce, 1990) and other committed environmental activists. While such people exist, the United Kingdom is far from becoming a more sustainable society. Some would argue that our record on traffic congestion, waste disposal and energy use is worsening. The World Economic Forum's 2002 Environmental Sustainability Index ranked the United Kingdom 98th out of 142 countries.

Transmissional educational ideologies are based on a functional model of social influence, that is, how education affects changes in actions. Transactional and especially transformatory ideologies are much more firmly rooted in a genetic approach to social influence. Moscovici's (1976) genetic model of social influence in Table 2.4 shows that the pertinent level of social influence is the interpersonal, between social actors, including between children. In this

Table 2.3:   Aristotle's account of the relationship between knowledge, values and actions

Relationship	Cognition	Emotion	Action
Virtue	Y	Y	Y
Incontinence	Y	Y	N
Control	Y	N	Y
Vice	N	N	N

Source: Adapted from Brennan, 1991

context the non-formal curriculum becomes a more important arena for values education than the formal curriculum.

> The child is a witness; the child is an ever attentive witness of grown-up morality – or lack thereof; the child looks and looks for cues as to how one ought to behave, and finds them galore as we parents and teachers go about our lives, making choices, addressing people, showing in action our rock-bottom assumptions, desires and values, and thereby telling those young observers much more than we may realize. (Coles, 1997: 5)

How can education promote competent and sustainable actions that will turn incontinence into virtuous sustainable actions on a societal scale? One answer is to develop whole-school or whole-institution approaches (see Table 2.5) rooted in a transformatory educational ideology and a genetic model of social influence. A transformatory educational ideology espouses, amongst

Table 2.4:   Functional and genetic models of social influence

Feature	Functional model	Genetic model
Source/target relationships	Hierarchical asymmetrical	Horizontal symmetrical
Source of influence	Parent, teachers, only adults	Parents, teachers, support staff, children
Target of influence	Children	Parents, teachers, support staff, children
Function of behaviour or action	Reaction and adjustment	Interaction
Direction of influence	One way	Reciprocal
Purpose of influence	Social and environmental control	Social and environmental change
Personal and social role of children	Passive	Active
State of social system, environment and participants	Predetermined and static	Dynamic
Reality	Objective	Subjective
Socio-environmental context	Consensus	Conflict

Source: Adapted from Uzzell *et al.*, 1994 and Moscovici, 1976

other things, process-focused whole-school approaches based on inclusive collaborative cultures of caring, participation and democratic education. ESD in the English National Curriculum, however, is largely the property of citizenship, geography and science.

The Crick Report (QCA, 1998) on citizenship mentions whole-school approaches, but these are not included in the citizenship guidelines (DfEE, 1999) that have their origins in a transactional educational ideology with strong transmissional overtones.

In simple terms whole-school approaches mean practising what we teach through the integration of formal and non-formal curricula. It is education as a way of life that must be immediately and fully satisfying. Whole-school approaches integrate pedagogy, with the social/organizational and technical/economic aspects of school practice (Posch, 1999). Orr (1994) argued that an ecological education has to transform educational buildings, the substance and processes of the formal curriculum, the purposes of learning and how education institutions work. However, all these prescriptions omit evaluation and research which are integral to whole-school formulations and when added (see Figure 2.2), complete a plan, do, review cycle (Rauch, 2000). Whole-school approaches are not simply a reaction to the limited success of environmental awareness and values education in promoting action through ESD, they encapsulate positive motives through their foundation in transformatory ideology.

Table 2.5:   Ladder of participation

	Levels of participation	Degrees of participation
(1)	Child initiated, shared decisions with adults	
(2)	Child initiated and directed	
(3)	Adult initiated shared decisions with children	
(4)	Consulted and informed	
(5)	Assigned but informed	
(6)	Tokenism	
(7)	Decoration	
(8)	Manipulation	Non-participation

Source: Hart, 1997

Many relevant attitudes and values will be expressed in the ethos and daily practices of the school, in the literature that it directs people to, in the versions of life that it holds up as being successful and the status it accords to different activities and relationships. These will need to be carefully evaluated from the perspective of sustainability if damaging inconsistency of message and pupil cynicism are to be avoided. (Bonnet, 1999: 323)

Whole-school approaches have much greater potential to realize the transformation to sustainable lifestyles because they give priority to the socialization and transformatory purposes of education. The focus on action in whole-school approaches to ESD has psychological benefits because teachers are able to identify values in action much better than the beliefs from which these values stem (Stenhouse, 1983). The professional culture of primary teachers prefers the practically active to the theoretical (Alexander, 1984). Being active members of a community based on whole-school approaches is also more likely to reduce defection and increase attachment.

Attachment theory suggests that cycles of abuse can be broken when children establish one good relationship with an adult. Separating environmental awareness from action socializes hypocrisy with the result that armchair

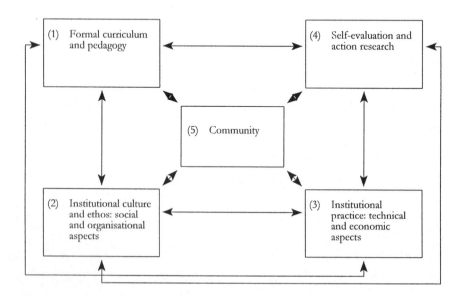

Figure 2.2:   The five strands of a whole-school approach to ESD

environmentalism that espouses concern for the environment without doing anything significant for it becomes normal behaviour. Whole-school approaches imply a behavioural role for teachers in minimizing incontinent actions by closing the gap between espoused values and values in actions. By experiencing democratic continuity in social relationships children may find the social support that persuades them that co-operation is better than defection (Posch, 1999). 'It is by belonging to a social group that children will be agents of change' (Uzzell *et al.*, 1994: 37).

> For example, if parks are litter free, it is often easier to persuade people who would otherwise litter not to do so. It is also usual to tolerate a low level of defection within such a hypothetical community. However, as soon as the numbers defecting increase significantly, and the park starts to fill with litter, the social pressure diminishes and a widespread outbreak of defection and littering tends to follow. (Clayton and Radcliffe, 1996)

> This kind of democratic planning, at both the school and classroom levels, is not the 'engineering of consent' towards predetermined decisions that has too often created the illusion of democracy, but a genuine attempt to honour the right of people to participate in making decisions that affect their lives. (Beane and Apple, 1999: 10)

We shall now move on to look at the implications of a transmissional ideology on our ideologies of childhood and teaching.

Children

> Would it deflate our vanity too much to face the strong likelihood that the highest source of creative power in our schools is the students themselves and the teachers who are there to serve as mature guides illuminating the path toward sorely needed wisdom? (Harrington, 1996: 1)

A transformatory educational ideology argues for authenticity in ESD that includes high levels of child participation (Table 2.5 above) and links with real issues. This view is shared by children: 'What you learn in school needs to be put in perspective in the real world' (Connell *et al.*, 1999: 103). Children also identify action and participation as key features of an authentic ESD project. Environmental education and ESD have been the major influences, along with the children's rights movement, in promoting the children's participation in education (Freeman, 1999). Such authenticity can only be the consequence of transformatory rather than transmissional or transactional educational ideologies. Better understandings of the role children play as present and active citizens are vital in ESD.

Children want more challenge in classrooms, more space to make their own decisions, tasks that allow them to identify and use their own ideas, tasks that allow them to discuss things and work together. At the school level they want to be trusted, to have more responsibility and to be treated in a more adult way. Children work well in schools that communicate the message that they matter. The danger is that national concern about targets, testing and measurable performance, a technical educational ideology, may be so dominant that we neglect how different groups of pupils experience learning in the widest sense.

A democratically-based ESD requires that children have the voice to let them develop a critical awareness of their own ends, means and capacities in enactive learning. It also has to operate with a conception of pupils with plural abilities rather than general ability, and multiple intelligences rather than just IQ, where intelligence features: a clear cut developmental path, localization in the brain and observation in isolated forms, for example, prodigies.

> By minimizing the importance of other intelligences within and outside of schools, we consign many students who fail to exhibit the 'proper' blend to the belief that they are stupid, and we do not take advantage of ways in which multiple intelligences can be exploited to further the goals of the school and the broader culture. (Gardner, 1993: 80)

Mature intelligence involves the integration of rational (IQ), emotional (EQ) and spiritual intelligences (SQ). This mature intelligence can appear in the sophisticated thinking of primary school pupils. EQ consists of knowing and managing one's own emotions, recognizing emotions in others, motivating oneself and handling both social and ecological relationships. SQ additionally allows us to change the rules, it leads to unitive thinking (Zohar and Marshall, 2000). SQ and EQ are then crucial to the transformatory ideology of education associated with the societal changes that sustainable lifestyles require (Zohar and Marshall, 2000) as they lead to collective capacity; to social intelligence.

Integrating these three intelligences is crucial to the sustainability project, for IQ is a measure of cleverness, rather than intelligence (Orr, 1994). Cleverness is short-term and fragmentary, associated with transmissional ideology, it separates cause from effect, and distinguishes know-how from know-why. Authentic intelligence is long-term, emotive, transformatory and integrative.

Cleverness on the other hand gives us the capacity to do many more things than intelligence would have us do. Intelligent action does not violate the principles of morality.

> The classroom, of course, is as much a social situation as an academic one; the socially awkward child is as likely to misread and misrespond to a teacher as to another child. The resulting anxiety and bewilderment can themselves interfere with their ability to learn effectively. Indeed, as tests of children's nonverbal sensitivity have shown, those who misread emotional cues tend to do poorly in school compared to their academic potential as reflected in IQ tests. (Goleman, 1996: 122)

Teachers

> It is the beliefs and practices of environmentally motivated teachers which are the most significant elements [in school] in prompting young people to undertake environmental action. (Morris and Schagen, 1996: 20)

At the heart of ESD is the teacher as role model, not in the sense that teachers are stewards of the right values and attitudes, but that they strive to act in a virtuous way by seeking consistency between the values they and their institutions espouse and their values in action. Role models, who are consistent in how they judge moral predicaments, generally have greater impact on children's moral reasoning than those who disagree with each other (Bandura, 1986). While the indoctrination of pupils by teachers into their own values is clearly unethical, to avoid discussion of teachers' values is equally unethical.

Fullan and Hargreaves' (1992) concept of total teachers is highly consistent with transformatory ideologies. They have four important characteristics: purpose, person, the real world context in which teachers work, and the culture of teaching. According to Rauch (2002) total teachers also provide a counter-balance to the declining role of traditional networks. Fullan and Hargreaves (1992: 28) maintained that the total teacher addresses the moral role that teachers have in society.

> With the decline of the Church, the break-up of traditional communities and the diminishing contact that many children have with parents who can 'be there' for their children on a regular basis, the moral role and importance of today's teacher is probably greater than it has been for a long time.

Total teachers locate and articulate their inner voice, reflect in, on and about action, develop a risk-taking mentality, trust processes and people, appreciate others as total people, work with colleagues, seek variety and avoid balkanization. They re-define their role so that it extends beyond their classroom, balance work and life, push and support headteachers and managers to develop interactive professionalism, commit to continuous improvement and perpetual learning and monitor and strengthen the link between their professional improvement and student development. Total teachers focus on positive images, professional reading, professional dialogue, teacher support groups and research, through diaries, autobiographies and life narratives.

Thus, the professional, institutional and personal become integrated in total teachers. ESD requires teachers who can demonstrate that people can choose to transform to a higher order of understanding and to act convergently with this understanding. Their role shows that the acquisition of skills and understanding can be enhanced by interaction with a more knowledgeable other (Holden and Clough, 1998). To increase participation we need teachers with educationally-focused democratic values who will embrace children's involvement in decision-making within and outside classrooms. In order to develop pupil participation teachers should identify the qualities and characteristics they wish to encourage in children, develop action competence, and decide the levels at which participation should be promoted (see Table 2.6). Participation may need to be differentiated in terms of provision and resources, and on the basis of age and gender, in order to recognize the different ways in which girls are treated in different cultures (Holden and Clough, 1998). This participative agenda also places responsibilities on other adults associated with schools.

> Thus, alongside a wish to help with the process of observation and inward looking I saw an obligation upon adults to participate equally. I also saw that rules must apply to all and be seen to be applied fairly for children to realize that their own struggles and efforts are supported by the adults around them. (Farrer, 2000: 4)

There are a number of themes central to teaching ESD. Catering for multiple intelligences requires skilled teachers who can open different windows on the same concept (Oelschlaeger, 1995). Identifying the issues surrounding social and ecological issues requires critical pedagogy. It requires teachers who in themselves, their classrooms, their schools and communities are able to integrate the cognitive, affective and active domains within a holistic educational agenda the aim of which is transformation through such approaches as

Table 2.6:   Teachers' roles in relation to social and ecological change

Relationship with change	Characteristics
(1) Instrumental	The social and physical environment is only of value as the location in which education occurs or the context about which education is implemented.
(2) Osmotic	Environmental concern emerges naturally from outdoor experiences. Social concern results from social interaction in schools. Specific educational strategies to address social and environmental justice are not required.
(3) Cognitive	Teaching and learning strategies are used to develop environmental and social awareness. No concern with social or environmental action, as action is assumed to develop naturally from awareness.
(4) Affective	Specific strategies to develop social and environmental attitudes and values. Where there is a concern for appropriate social or ecological action, such action is seen to result from values or attitudinal change.
(5) Active	Specific strategies are used to develop social or environmental intervention. Education is directly concerned with environmental change in the school and its grounds.
(6) Integrated	Institutional actions, the curriculum and evaluation are integrated in whole-institution approaches to social and environmental change. High-level pupil participation is encouraged within the school and/or its local community.

the emotional and ecological literacy movements (Orr, 1992; Goleman, 1996). As Greig *et al.* (1989: 20) discussed:

> Holistic education does not necessarily depend upon a rearrangement of the curriculum, a shift to inter-disciplinary timetable slots, although that might well help; it calls, rather, for an attitude of mind on the part of teacher and student alike which prioritizes and searches out relatedness to the whole.

It is possible to identify a number of different roles that teachers adopt in relation to their treatment of social and ecological change. While teachers will move between these roles according to professional circumstances, a transformatory ideology requires relationships five and six.

Teaching is at heart a cognitively and emotionally relational activity between human beings. Where good relationships are established these can open the door to high self-esteem and the determination of pupils to please not only teachers but themselves. ESD also requires teachers and other adults who recognize that children can teach adults as much as adults can teach children (Farrer, 2000). Such relationships are not built solely through the teachers' professional knowledge; they are deeply rooted in their body language. 'In kindergartens the body language of the respected people taking care of small people is decisive. The care and respect manifest in every interaction with every living thing has immediate and strong effect' (Naess, 1993).

Conclusion

What emerges from this discussion, then, is that there is a symbiotic relationship between our ideologies of teachers' and children, their roles and the success of whole-school approaches. For transformatory ideology and whole-school approaches to succeed, the teacher's role has to extend beyond that of classroom practitioner to include the teacher as individual and member of a school and local community. This educational ideology cannot treat the child as citizen-in-waiting, it has to consider children as presently active citizens. Yet in the day-to-day practice of schools committed to transformatory ideology there will be examples of transmissional and transactional teaching. This may be because of time constraints or because of the imposition of teaching strategies, such as those contained in the national literacy and numeracy strategies for primary schools in England.

The example of ESD illustrates both the importance of ideology and its elusiveness when analysing its impact on practice. When discussing ideology we often have to distinguish between ideology as a set of values and the ideology implicit in the practices of schools. These never match totally. For example, does a school that espouses a transformational ideology have a school council. If it does, we need to ask who makes decisions and how are they made. If the school council is in effect controlled by the headteacher, we have transmission disguised as transformation. How many other wolves in sheep's clothing have you seen in schools? Be aware of these and seek out good practice and the ideology that underpins it.

Task

(1) Using the matrix on educational ideology above, take each of the educational ideologies below and explore the *practical* advantages and disadvantages of each in terms of their role in providing an ideological basis for the construction of an education system which meets both

the needs of the individual and wider social needs.
(2) What conflicts and tensions exist within each of these models?
- transmissional or technical;
- transactional or practical;
- transformatory or emancipatory.

Indicative reading

The Institute of Education at MMU (Manchester Metropolitan University) has, for six years, been involved in a professional development project for practising teachers called the SEEPS Project (Sustainability Education in European Primary Schools) based on the transformatory educational ideology discussed above. There is also a website for those in initial teacher education called "Educating for a sustainable future" (http://www.education.ed.ac.uk).

Chapter 3

Critical Perspectives in Early Childhood Studies

Philip Prescott

THE relatively new academic arena of early childhood studies has been influenced by some key concepts and perspectives presented here, which are predicated on a belief that all those concerned with young children should, as Moyles (2001: 81) argued for researchers and early years practitioners,

> engage in high level, critical (and passionate!) reflection on their own practices, [to] link associated theory and [to] challenge political prescription.

To present a general familiarity with some of the underpinning knowledge in this subject area and to foster an interest in developing a deeper and wider enquiry into the study of young children, identification of key areas of analysis is the main aim of the chapter. I shall take a critical view of some of the underpinning knowledge that informs early childhood studies to encourage an analytical and 'suitably sceptical' approach to this subject. Early childhood studies has many varied origins, absorbing large swathes of ideas, concepts and theories from a variety of disciplines and sources. The key source areas will be considered in a broad but critical overview of their central ideas, concepts and debates in the context of the early years.

The early years debate spins largely around the education/care axis which relies upon understandings of child development and the very nature of the adult-child relationship. At the time of writing children and families can be seen to be a political priority, looming relatively large in United Kingdom national policy. One question to be addressed is whether a true child-centredness pervades the early years curriculum and whether, in fact, it should.

Research into early years has led to the promotion of a holistic view of the young child (Hazareesingh *et al.*, 1989), contending that all aspects of health, development, and emotional and social need have to be addressed in order to provide for young children's well-being. The efficacy of 'educare' was promulgated in the recent past as an underpinning philosophy for work with the youngest children. The debates about the meanings ascribed to 'education' and 'care' appear to have led to a mainstreaming of how to meet children's needs via a combined model addressing both their cognitive and care needs. The early years curriculum contained in the National Curriculum foundation stage sees the 'educare' model developed and stresses the need to merge care and education in all environments for young children.

In an academic frame, the study of early years concerns the issues that affect the real lives of children in their first life-stage in the contexts of family, society and culture. A social constructionist position underpins this chapter's analysis of early years studies. Essentially childhood is a social construct that is historically and culturally specific. As such it is a contested and contestable concept. The cultural relativism of the concept of childhood must be acknowledged. The concepts of children and the way children are cared for must be seen from a perspective of challenge and change.

To achieve the contemporary holistic vision some measure of interdisciplinary working must be reached, and a multi-professional approach to early years work has been strongly promoted and supported by legislation. This can be exemplified, for instance, by the importance given to 'working together' under the Children Act 1989, but the difficulties that appear in any attempt to work multi-professionally must also be acknowledged. An underlying problem is one of producing coherent assessments and plans for children with the involvement of ever-increasing specialisms in the field of early years. This problem of 'coherence from diversity' is as true for the study of children and their needs as it is for professional practice with them. The difficulty is grappling with a range of disciplines underpinning its knowledge-base, and their concomitant theories and concepts. Four perspectives on young children are addressed in this chapter, with some weight being given to the area of child abuse.

The 'socialized' child

Sociological perspectives on early childhood address the accepted common assumptions and beliefs about children. They attempt to situate children in a social world that has considerable influence upon them and they upon it. The child could be said to exist in a relational and contextualized setting. Decentring the child in this post-modernist way questions any notion of the child as an essentialized or universalized subject (Dahlberg *et al.*, 1999). Sociology's role is to problematize a child's position in society and deconstruct the very meanings of child and childhood.

A contemporary sociological analysis of childhood requires engagement with social constructionism as a framework for the exploration of social problems, addressing the tensions and contested boundaries concerning adult-child relationships. The significance of contested discourses is ably demonstrated by the dilemma in trying to define a child. Critical theory attempts to deconstruct the symbolism of the term 'child' by adopting a critical stance towards knowledge that is taken for granted. The traditions of positivism and empiricism are challenged for their objectification of the world (Burr, 1995). Perceptions of childhood and other social constructions are contextualized in terms of history, society and culture.

The different meanings ascribed to childhood have traditionally been presented from an adult perspective as part of an over-arching position that consolidates ideological and cultural commitment to the family and the universalism of the state of childhood. In this same context imagery has played a major role in the representation and construction of the 'universal child' (Gittins, 1998). Representations of children in the twentieth century were powerful weapons to legitimize or challenge many ideas held in society.

> Arguably, the sheer number – the deluge – of images of children has helped to create a myth of a universal child and a universal childhood. Images of children are invariably constructed by adults to convey messages and meanings to adults. The meanings that are used to convey childhood change and vary, although there are certain recurring and central themes: dependency, victimization/helplessness, loss, nostalgia, innocence, danger and nature. (Medforth *et al.*, 2000: 3)

Imagery attempts to corral children into particular and boundaried fields of meaning. Images of childhood can be seen to label, categorize and limit (Holland, 1992). Sociology has provided the means to challenge a dominant construction of the young child as an undifferentiated entity and to embrace the lived realities of different children's lives. The importance of this lies in the ability to deconstruct a model of childhood focused on children's innocence and vulnerability, which has largely determined the experience of children because of its reference point for adults responsible for meeting children's needs.

Sociological perspectives have enabled a critique of the way childhood is conceptualized and distinguished. They have delivered childhood as a contested and contestable construct of historic and cultural specificity. Social constructionism as a particular framework for analysis clearly argues against any natural distinction that identifies the separateness of children and adults. One historical perspective pursued by Aries (1962) demonstrated an emerging construction of difference between adult and child from the fifteenth century onwards. The needs of children were categorized separately, beginning with early educational provision.

Contesting Aries' time-frame and methodology, Shahar (1990) argued this construction of difference was evident in much earlier times through Judao-Christian beliefs about innocence and evil exemplified in the new born: essentially the construction of 'original sin'. Enlightenment romanticism moved the construction towards a view of children as being 'cute' and 'innocent'. Such a childhood discourse could be seen to pervade nineteenth century sentimentalism, the early twentieth century development of a 'Peter Pan syndrome' and the more recent 'Disneyization' of movie children as 'sweet' and 'cutely inventive'. The construction of children as 'evil' entities is also well documented and the symbolic and institutional demonization of children has been carefully examined (see: Hendrick, 1990; Goldson, 1997; Stainton Rogers, 2001a). The dominant discourses of welfare and control continue to contest the meaning of childhood. The protectionist perspective pervading the welfare approach to children and their needs is exemplified by social policy in the United Kingdom. Education policy can be seen to be informed by a discourse of control. It demands regulation and promotes standardization, and is exemplified by the introduction of 'early learning goals.'

From an early history of children seen as property whose needs were objectified, there has emerged a number of perspectives on the status and role of children in society. A particular construct which sees children as smaller adults for example has implications in terms of status and citizenship and therefore for social and political relations. If, as Reynolds (2000) argued, citizenship is constructed within the public arena of law, politics and social welfare services as a basis for excluding those without the means of access or participation, then young children can clearly be seen within this public sphere and are again constructed as 'becoming' or 'citizens-in the-making'.

Children exist within a range of social systems; seeing them as people first moves beyond a protectionist attitude towards them and challenges the discriminatory way in which most societies perceive and treat children. This then allows for a more rights-based position to be taken where children's entitlements are clearer and more specific. Traditional constructions of the child focus largely on individual incompetence and dependency. The 'new paradigm of the sociology of childhood' (Prout and James, 1990) established childhood as a structural component of society. From an anti-foundational perspective childhood is distinguished as being important in its own right but also as part of a life-course. From a post-modern perspective children as social agents are co-constructors of knowledge contributing to social resources. Children have to be seen as being embedded in relationships of power with adults.

Summary box

- The complexity in providing a definition of childhood must be acknowledged. Sociology has attempted to provide the means for analysing childhood as a social construct and for exploring the position of young children in contemporary society.
- As a social construct childhood has to be seen as historically and culturally specific and different constructions of childhood will determine different types of intervention in children's lives.
- Young children's position in society must be seen in the context of key discourses of welfare and control and within relationships of power with adults.

The 'developed' child

The value of promoting actively the development of young children is widely acknowledged amongst professionals, academics and politicians. Parents, carers and particularly early years practitioners emphasize the massive benefit to children of quality experience in their early years and therefore quality resource. There has been much historical interest in early childhood as a particular life stage (for an analysis of the history of childhood see Aries, 1982), as can be seen from the work of Plato, Froebel's *kindergarten*, and the analysis of the socially constructed curriculum of Reggio Emilia.

An understanding of psychological theory is very significant for all early years practitioners in their attempts to predict, describe, explain and indeed control young children's behaviour.

These processes of describing, explaining, predicting and controlling are the very essence of theory, and professionals in child education, health and welfare need to do all these things on a daily basis. In many cases, far reaching decisions about a child's future will have to be made on the basis of such theorising. (Greig and Taylor, 1999: 17)

For students a sound understanding of developmental psychology is required and remains a cornerstone of training and practice. Theory and research in this area constitute perhaps the largest body of knowledge on children. There are many different theoretical perspectives in child development; those adopted by individual professions can have enormous impact on types of intervention in children's lives and the futures they will experience. Assessments on the problems faced by an individual child, for example, can range from a focus on poverty and its impact on parenting skills to the labelling of a child as having a learning disability. Inter- and intra-professional concerns and debates about children's development must be carefully examined not least to avoid children being left in the limbo of professional divergence and disagreement, and therefore at potential risk. Generally, child development theories have had a major impact upon society's perceptions of children and childhood.

The key theories relating to child development require acknowledgement. Early 'common-sense' approaches to observed behaviour can be found in the work of Locke (cited in Crain, 1992). Children's individual characteristics are formed by their experience and as a *tabula rasa* each child is seen to be moulded in to a particular individual. Rousseau (1762, see reprint, 1993) moved the developmental debate towards what was described as a naturalistic view where children had their own distinct processes of thinking and learning which developed independently.

The nature versus nurture debate underpins much of psychological theory. Ethological approaches focus on the survival or adaptive nature of behaviour and this area of study provides important concepts for students of early years such as the meanings given to 'critical periods' or 'imprinting'. Attachment theory raises important questions for the professionals in the context of parent-child relationships, and the early work of Bowlby (1982) and Rutter's (1981) re-visitation of that work provide a foundation for exploring this perspective that centres on adaptation to the environment.

Psychoanalytical ideas are still to be found well embedded in early years psychological literature. With a focus on the individual overcoming a series of challenges, this perspective may be seen to have developed from the early and profoundly influential work of Freud centering on internal forces and biological maturation that govern development, to the later, eight-stage, life-span approach adopted by Erikson which emphasizes the social and cultural impact on an individual's development (Stainton Rogers, 2001b).

Learning theory addresses observable behaviour rather than experience or the relevance of internal processes. Reward and punishment are key elements in a behaviourist approach. The theoretical concepts here move from Pavlov's (1927) classical conditioning where learning is seen in terms of a reflex action conditioned by particular stimuli; through Skinner's (1974) operant approach to how the environment may control behaviour and the importance of reinforcement; to a social learning perspective that recognizes the importance of imitation in learning (Bandura, 1973).

Piaget's (1950) stage theory of cognitive development has had a major impact upon relatively recent thinking and practice in early years. As a genetic epistemologist concerned with the growth and development of knowledge, he stressed the importance of biology in understanding the development of the child's mental apparatus. Here, cognition is a process of adaptation where stages of development follow a sequence of differentiated steps. The theory is transformative in the sense that children undergo major changes in *how* they think. These stages are invariant sequentially, each one being an integration and consolidation of its predecessor. Learning takes place through the complete reconstruction of knowledge from one stage to the next.

Socio-cultural perspectives on child development have had increasing influence in academic literature and professional practice. The understanding of human behaviour is developed by a cross-cultural approach that acknowledges diversity and does not succumb to a universal standpoint on human behaviour. Vygotsky (1978) introduced an understanding of cognitive development moulded through interaction with the social environment. The pedagogic and modelling roles of adults were emphasized where they 'scaffolded' the context of learning for children. In what might be seen as a process of synergy, complex cognitive functioning is more possible in the interaction between adult and child than is possible by the autonomous individual child, or indeed adult (Leather *et al.*, 2000). Interactionist positions have been further developed for instance through Sameroff's (1991) transactional model of development as a continuous, dynamic process between child and environment that traverses time.

The theoretical perspectives briefly outlined provide evidence for a solid rationale for the inclusion of child development in early years studies. The understanding of how children grow and the factors that influence growth are of crucial importance. Nevertheless, a critical analysis of child development has to be undertaken. Child development theories are largely the product of North American and European academia and science. In a largely Western and Northern context child development theories may be seen to be ethnocentric. Sanders (1999) considered this point, arguing that there were great dangers in applying Western norms of child development to other cultures, not least in the context of child abuse for example. Underpinning much of this still dominant child developmentalism is a modernist, positivist tradition that strives for discovery and understanding of the 'universal' child. Further, much developmental theory emphasizes children's 'incompetence' and does not consider their political position of powerlessness.

A developmental problem?

The twentieth century's increasing domination of the field of child affairs by psychology and medicine saw many child-orientated services develop as psycho-medical provision. By establishing standardized norms the majority are likely to reach, children can be measured against those norms. Ostensibly, the measurement of child development is done to support and promote the potential of the individual child. The definition of appropriate care and education, according to individual social, emotional and cognitive development, is constructed in this way. Theories of child development search for universal 'stages', 'patterns' or 'milestones' that all children move through.

The critique of universal child development perspectives is now well embedded in academic discourse. Bronfenbrenner (1979) began to stress the importance of social context in terms of research with and about children. In considering the way meaning is constructed through written, spoken and enacted practices discourse analysis has enabled an examination of the way a developmental perspective can contribute to a view of children and childhood. Such a perspective tends to stress the position of children as 'adults-in-the-making' and to endorse a construction of children as 'other' in the sense of being perceived in contrast to an explicit or implicit image of the 'adult norm'.

The implicit standard model of the child in the traditional developmental approach at best marginalizes the impact of class, culture, gender, disability and indeed history. Diversity and potential may be seen to be negatives in the pursuit of 'normal progression' (Morss, 1996). Developmentalism can also be criticized for 'objectifying' children; individualizing them to the point of being research targets, isolated from 'the social' but containing the answers to the meaning of 'natural development' which are waiting to be discovered.

Developmental discourse can also be seen in the context of social control by considering its role in structuring the personnel and the process of caring for children. It has been argued that developmental psychology has responded to particular moral and political agenda where particular individuals or groups are singled out as the cause of society's ills. A normalizing taxonomy of development allows for comparison with the 'norm' and thus for the construction of problematized groups of children.

Woodhead (2000) argued that child development is 'an idealized construction', that actually under-emphasized the diversity of Western childhoods and diminished any consideration of childhood in a global context. He advocated a socio-cultural model of development where young children are attuned to engage with the social and cultural environment of activity and meaning. The environment in this context is a cultural construction, (see Cole, 1992; Rogoff et *al.*, 1993; Trevarthen, 1998 and Woodhead, 1999).

Developmental psychology has been utilized in the study of families, mothers and fathers as a tool for classification and evaluation of sections of the population that then determines welfare intervention and its supporting legislation. Again the social control of particular groups can be seen to be embedded in the developmental discourse. Students in seeking a reflective approach to their study need to consider the influences apparent within the curriculum and its delivery. Penn (1998) argued that, despite the criticism of traditional child development theories, the move to a recognition within cultural psychology that cognition has to be seen within institutional and cultural practices and a postmodernist discourse that acknowledges the importance of 'multiple voices', a 'universal' child developmentalism, the precepts of which have been derived from research with Anglo-American middle class children, still pervades professional practice with young children.

Psychological developmentalism remains a contested area. It still has to be acknowledged that monitoring the development of children is a major part of early years professional work. However, sensitivity and flexibility in applying developmental norms may demonstrate a move towards a different construction of children's needs. If the ideas of 'developing' and 'specified progression' are abandoned, can a more creative model of understanding how children 'grow' be found? The answer to this may be in the making but whatever is done with young children they must be prepared for the unknowable world. Young children require confidence in dealing with the different and the challenging. In pursuing the 'right', 'universal', 'developmental' way of caring for and educating them there is the danger of not seeing *their* energetic, creative, eager and non-standardized ways of encountering the unknown and making sense of it (Kress, 1999). Developmentalism then can be seen to determine outcomes for children rather than children co-constructing meaning with adults and determining mutual outcomes with them.

Summary box

Ideas about growth and development are critical areas for academic debate especially in the context of early years. Developmental theories can be placed in four broad groupings or models (Oates, 1994) that stress particular positions:

- an emphasis on innate abilities (nativism);
- an emphasis on the role of the environment (behaviourism);
- an emphasis on the interaction of biological and environmental factors (constructivism);
- an emphasis on the history and culture of the social group where development occurs (social construction).

Theories of child development must be critiqued for the contribution they make to, rather than their reflection upon, particular views of children and childhood.

For a critical discussion of psychological developmental theories see Burman (1994) and Messer and Millar (1999).

The 'educated' child

Spontaneity, exploration and creativity are the cornerstones of early childhood experience. As they remain the key points of concern for the practitioners and academics, ideas and debates about children's learning and pedagogy must receive critical analysis. Their learning and development must be contextualized and individualized. Discipline, knowledge and practice experience alone no longer suffice as curriculum content; teaching and learning processes have to be considered (David, 2001). Curriculum may be seen as the imposition on children, both formally and informally, of knowledge, attitudes, skills and understandings deemed to be of most importance to the child's culture and society. A curriculum for the youngest of children will have long-term consequences for society as research in brain development recognizes the optimum plasticity of the young brain and the reality of life-long learning.

A dominant academic perspective on early childhood education is one that tends to refer to an instructivist approach to education where children are dependent on the instruction of adults for academic knowledge (Katz, 1996). In contrast, a constructivist, interactive perspective posits children as constructors of knowledge. Katz (1999) presented a 'third way' that highlighted curricula and teaching methods which went beyond the instructivist/ constructivist dichotomy. Her 'intellectual developmental' approach differentiated itself from instructivist academic learning and the constructivist emphasis on play and self-direction by focusing on an almost mediating role for adults. The balance to be achieved lies somewhere between the poles of an educational continuum with the 'heavy' and potentially undermining influence of academic instruction at one end and the dangerous, 'progressive' waste of children's capacities and dispositions for knowledge, at the other.

It is important to emphasize that anti-universalist, multiple-voiced curricula have been developed. New Zealand's *Te Whariki* 'woven' curriculum identifies learning and growing as part of a developmental continuum. Embracing something of a post-modern account of diversity and subjective experience in young children's lives, this curriculum focuses on children's well being, communication, contribution and exploration. In also acknowledging the importance of belonging and a children's rights perspective in the early years curriculum, it centralizes the critical importance for children of 'responsive and reciprocal relationships with people, places and things' (Carr and May, 2000: 60).

The Reggio Emilia curriculum model is a pedagogical approach to early years learning that focuses on children's social, cultural, historical and environmental lives. The 'rolling narrative' of what is described not as a curriculum but a project with shared aims centering on the promotion of independent decision-making, celebrates the richness and power of young children's learning. 'Curriculum' is developed from children's interests through, 'creative learning processes with various tools, the arts, visual communication and pedagogical documentation' (Lind, 1998: 151).

Concern with early years education identifies a variety of discourses. The alleged decline in educational standards from the 1970s onwards has been linked with a particular focus on child-centred perspectives and the marginalization of what has been called the 'structured curriculum' (Wagg, 1996). Despite the New Zealand and Italian examples of non-traditional curricula and the broad acceptance of early learning goals and the centrality of play in early learning, the current dominant discourse in the United Kingdom increasingly emphasizes standards, accountability and outcomes exemplified by numeracy and literacy strategies and the language of 'performance', 'targets', 'special measures' and 'league tables'. This position may be seen to be countered by claims about the decline in children's creative and social development. Adultist perspectives also abound which advocate higher work rates and continued testing of children despite evidence of considerable mental distress in children's lives (The Mental Health Foundation, 1999). Early educational problems must be critiqued in terms of an anti-oppressive approach to children and their situation. For instance, educational issues must be put into context in terms of ethnicity and gender while school exclusions focus disproportionately on children from ethnic minorities and differential rates of achievement are seen between boys and girls (Robb, 2001).

Schooling and 'educare' in the United Kingdom are developed on the premise of meeting the needs for individual development, socialization and the future needs of society via the market economy. A particular construction of childhood is at work here: one that views children as adults-in-the-making. Children are separated from adults in this discourse and difference is constructed around age, vulnerability and economic power. The separation of childhood from adulthood involves time, space and action and maintains an adult perspective that dominates children's lives and can be seen as having an oppressive function (Nasman, 1994). All aspects of social justice should be addressed as they impact upon young children.

It is of critical importance to raise issues in early childhood education in a powerful and sustained way in order to 'hook' an international community into the debate. Research into early years demands an analysis of the tensions, issues and outcomes for children in these situations and settings. A double focus is needed, providing a structural critique and a particularized, subjective analysis. A post-modern perspective, as referred to earlier, can be seen to celebrate co-construction of knowledge, diversity and context. A clear example of the need for such research is the importance of examining the differences in outcomes for minority and majority world nations' children.

'Curriculum as policy' requires a persistent critique not least because of the impact of curriculum on practice. The opportunity for oppressive and anti-oppressive practice stands clear, so the potentially socially divisive context of curriculum policy must be examined. International, national and local curricula require examination as complex, dynamic phenomena. A deeper exploration of the impact of national and international politics and economics on young children is required. Early childhood discourses function within other normalizing discourses that utilize particular constructions of nation, community, family and child.

The potential for providing a critique of the use of the construct of childhood within national and international politics and economics has been clearly identified (Woodhead, 2000). One obvious example that highlights the need for continued research in this context is the area of child labour. Contradictory political positions can be seen where the advocacy of children's rights, 'at home', is evident in many Western countries. At the same time the toleration, maintenance or development of insidious child labour, abroad, abandons any children's rights perspective.

Summary box

- All curricula are underpinned by values, principles and ideologies concerning children.
- Learning and development need to be contextualized and individualized.
- The dominant discourses that underpin curricula must be unearthed and problematized.

The 'protected' child

Within the early years curriculum child abuse and 'child protection' are recognized as important areas for serious consideration. However, child abuse appears still to be dealt with as a specialist 'subject' shrouded in mystery and dominated by professional discourse. If, as Johnston and Rahilly (2001: 4) identified, even some inspectors of early years childcare provision show, 'a lack of knowledge about child protection issues' then the full integration of a child abuse and child protection curriculum in the early years curriculum must be developed and sustained. The argument here is for a position that sees the safeguarding of children as the backbone of an early years philosophy until the nature of adult-child relationships no longer require such a position. The curriculum needs to address fully child protection literature and research, and give deep consideration to a general ecological approach to child abuse.

A social constructionist analysis of child abuse addresses the tensions and contested boundaries between the public and the private in the context of adult-child relations. The history of violence to children demonstrates considerable evidence to show that children have suffered at the hands of adults throughout history (May, 1978; Thane, 1981). By the end of the nineteenth century, a problem of 'family violence' had been identified, defined mainly in terms of cruelty to children. Primarily this was understood in the context of wider concerns about working class families and social order (Hall, 1998; Mooney, 1998). However, apart from the last quarter of the nineteenth century, the problem was rarely seen as a major social issue (Behlemer, 1982).

The post-World-War Two American emphasis on tackling the physical abuse of children demonstrates the strength of a medical model of abuse which steered the social construction of the problem towards physical harm (Nelson, 1984). Since the 1970s new discourses of child abuse and child protection have developed. Professional responses have also varied, oscillating between measures to rescue children and attempts to prevent abuse, and support for families. The changing constructions of child abuse demonstrate the historical and cultural specificity of the problem and, at another level, the shifting and contested boundary between public and private.

Centering on physical injuries Kempe *et al.* (1962) launched the issue into a public arena and began to bring about the pathologization, medicalization and professionalization of the problem. 'Diseased' individuals were seen to need to be treated by medical professionals for the harm they inflicted on their children. Parton (1985) examined the development of child abuse as a problem in the United Kingdom, recognizing the same early emergence of physical abuse as the focal point. The dominant discourse here was an individualist 'disease' model that defined child abuse in terms of a deviation from 'normal' functioning. The pathology resided primarily in the parents but manifested itself in the relationship with the child. Essentially, psychological or interpersonal family factors were seen as the causative model where character 'defects', or 'abnormalities' were addressed by individualized identification, prediction and treatment. In a processual analysis Parton identified the stages of discovery, diffusion, consolidation and reification of the problem constructed through social forces.

In its diffusion stage professional, political and media interests had begun to exert influence over the meanings attached to child abuse. Through a developing public awareness the Maria Colwell inquiry (DHSS, 1974) played a significant part in the consolidation of child abuse as a social problem. Framed within a political economy of welfare that concerned itself with the 'failure' of the family, moral decline and social work impotence, the problem of child abuse was embedded as a social problem and was to become reified through the emphasis placed upon it within social policy.

Through the 1980s and into the 1990s a 'social model' of child abuse emerged, emphasizing the importance of taking economic, social and psychological pressures on families into account. The social context, particularly in terms of class and poverty, was seen as critical in understanding the nature and social distribution of child abuse. Rooted in social inequality and values the problem could be seen to involve frustration, repression and aggression in response to social problems and as such is a potential problem for many children. The use of social work's individualizing problem-solving techniques becomes, at best palliative, at worst futile. For an overview of the social policy issues concerning children's needs and child abuse see Saraga (1998).

Through the 1980s and 1990s there was evidence of a shift in emphasis from care and support for families who fell within the child abuse system towards discipline and surveillance. This was represented as a shift from a medico-social construction of child abuse to a socio-legal model of child protection (Langan, 1998). Legal, rather than medical experts, predominated. Clearly the different approaches to the problem had particular consequences for definition, intervention and the reality of the lived experience for the relevant children and families. As the constructions of the social problem changed their transition, fragility and contingent properties became evident.

Gil (1975) considered a 'global dimension' to the problem arguing that the early and dominant construction of the problem in terms of individual disease served to hide the abusive practices of industrial, corporate and state agencies. He criticized the location of the primary genesis of abuse within families by maintaining that any act of commission or omission, by individuals or the whole society, together with their resultant conditions, which 'deprive children of equal rights and liberties and/or interfere with their optimal development, constitute, by definition, abusive or neglectful acts or conditions' (347). Child abuse can be manifested at both the institutional and societal level but this is rarely seen as legitimate for discussion within debates about its nature, extent and causes. Here lies a further demonstration of how a constructionist framework helps provide a critical appraisal of social problems. Constructions such as child abuse are legitimated and organized in the context of power relations. The influences of early years settings, schools, institutions, unemployment, welfare systems, racial discrimination and class and gender differentiation may have far more deleterious effects upon the life chances and development of children than the traditional concerns of child abuse literature and policy.

Sexual abuse entered the public arena largely in the 1980s and this awareness was attributed to the disclosures of adult survivors. A feminist perspective that challenged the medical model of abuse asserted that a discourse of power enabled a more critical analysis of child abuse. Essentially structural, patriarchal oppression and male socialization resulted in the sexual abuse of girls by men (Driver and Droisen, 1989). A challenge to such a feminist analysis had a significant effect on social work training in the late 1980s. The family systems model, propounded perhaps most forcefully through the work of Dale (1986), identified child sexual abuse as a dysfunctional issue. This model can be seen to marginalize power inequalities in family relationships, stress the role of women as stabilizing influences in the family and therefore, dangerously, identify women as collaborators or colluders with abuse.

Through the 1990s a variety of issues arose in the child abuse context. A focus on 'stranger-danger' and the 'placing' of paedophiles within the community exercised public interest and moral panic. Major inquiries occurred in the residential children's sector and the Church. Importantly, the professional and academic communities began to stress the criticality of 'listening to children', and the children's rights 'movement' to move the debate along.

Within the British child protection system there is no coherent or precise definition of child abuse. The safeguarding of children remains its clearly stated aim and children have a right to early protection from physical, sexual, emotional and neglectful harm. The difficulty of definition lies partly in the variation of experience and impact of that harm and therefore generalizations about abuse, particularly concerning its consequences, are always problematic. Heterogeneity is applicable in the context of causation as well as definition and impact.

The battle for causation is well documented (Gelles, 1979; Irvine, 1988; Corby, 1993). Child abuse has been variously constructed as a crime and, as identified earlier, an illness. Tensions abound in the camps of the 'syndromites' and the 'labellers' where identification is clearly set in either pathology or in categorized behaviours. No models of causation are singularly satisfactory. However, particular theoretical positions can be presented, including psychiatric, sociological and interactive models as suggested by Belsky (1978) or psychodynamic, social learning theory, social/psychological and sociological models proposed by Sweet and Resick in 1979 and cited in Kingston and Penhale (1995). Tensions between the models reside in the arenas of individual pathology and social context.

The critique of child development theories, as outlined earlier, informed the debate about the way child abuse is constructed at macro- and micro-levels. The child-centred pedagogy that stems from developmental psychology constructs the child as an object to be normalized. For instance the technologization of developmental assessments can be seen to determine the assignation and measurement of children according to normalizing standards of skill and competence. According to Popkewitz hierarchical positions are achieved by children through achievement or otherwise of developmental tasks and personal and social identity becomes determined (Dahlberg, 1999).

The Foucauldian view of 'dividing practices' elucidates the position of children in terms of normalizing systems of classification. Children are used to determine developmental standards by which they are judged and consequently included or excluded (Dahlberg and Lenz Taguchi, 1994). Placing children in the category of 'at risk', for example, attempts to normalize and divide. The language used problematizes certain children because of the inherent bias and power of definition. Such classifications as 'at risk' are part of the legitimizing processes that embed a particular construction of children as incapable, dependent and weak. Here, agency is profiled and any structural context, at best, marginalized. An ecological perspective that embraces a notion of social justice for children, however, advocates for the child as a social actor in continual, reciprocal interaction with the environment. Structural analysis and subjective account can both be acknowledged through this perspective.

The meaning ascribed to child abuse can be overwhelmingly confusing. This can only be reduced if the broad definitions of abuse that concern themselves with institutional and societal processes directly or indirectly 'harming' children, and narrow professional definitions which attempt to provide 'working categories' of abuse, are deconstructed in the context of power and purpose. The operationalization of definitions of abuse at professional and policy levels demonstrates the subjectivity of micro-constructions of the problem. Consideration of this is of critical importance.

An ecological approach to child abuse focused on the constant and reciprocal interaction of the child, family and environment (Belsky, 1993). In a move away from the traditional pathologizing model of child abuse, here, meaning and definition rest within the characteristics of the environments in which child abuse occurs. The balance between risk and protective factors within the environment is of critical importance (Jack, 2001). Adopting a largely reactive position, child protection within the United Kingdom has not met the needs of children and families in its purview. Policy developments including, Sure Start and Quality Protects have begun to consider the influence on behaviour of social, economic and community circumstance yet retain a problematizing discourse that still stresses parental inadequacy and family pathology. As Jack argued, the economic and preventative implications of adopting a developed ecological approach have not been embraced.

There is emerging evidence of the influence of inequality and levels of social cohesion on levels of child abuse. The social capital and social support available in communities bears investigation as an ecological perspective drives forward a critical appraisal of structural inequalities within society (Jack and Jordan, 1999). Community level prevention is the likely prescription here and early years settings clearly offer a context for community strategies where partnership, collaboration, multi-professional involvement and an integrated systemic approach would be required.

Summary box

- The issue of child abuse is a complex phenomenon. The sources and disciplines that inform the academic debate in this arena are numerous.
- It is extremely important for early years studies to evaluate the variety of contributions to this subject.

Emerging themes and future research

It is not simplistic to continue to argue that a deconstruction of the 'taken-for-granted' in early childhood studies must still be pursued. It is important that the debate about its curriculum and all academic research is not consigned to an exclusive or élite group. Much has been made of the importance of hearing 'multiple voices' within the research task and academic critiques of the early years field also need to be accessible to multiple audiences. There is a need to challenge the construction of childhood as separate from adulthood and to problematize adult power in the context of structural relations and social arrangements (Scraton, 1997). There is a further need to examine understandings of child abuse and child protection and to deepen the debate about ecological responses to this social problem.

The fundamental early development needs of children are becoming increasingly clear as great emphasis begins to be placed on societal support for children and families from conception to 6 or 7 years of age. Neuroscience leads the way in our understanding of the disposition of the young brain to develop multiplicities of brain cell connections, thus highlighting the significance of 'brain wiring' and 'brain sculpture' in the early years in influencing behaviour, learning and 'quality of life' through the life cycle. The promotion of both early child development and parenting potential has major impact on early brain development (The Children's Secretariat, 1999). The opportunity presented by the brain's malleability, most importantly from conception to 3 years, has to be grasped by national and international communities. The study of young children should provide wide and complex analysis. Critical analysis and reflection steer us towards the revelation and problematization of dominant discourses. Early childhood studies can engage with a breadth of academic discipline including sociological enquiry that is concerned with structural causality in relation to the child (Jenks, 1996); with ideas that disengage the child from simple constructs of 'adults-in-the-making', immoral and therefore potentially dangerousness beings, or romanticized innocents (Stainton-Rogers, 2001); with a critique of the impact of Western psychological developmentalism; and with issues concerning historical, comparative and phenomenological approaches to the study of childhood.

In the context of the above knowledge base there has to be an overall requirement to maintain the struggle for social justice within an early years context. Here lies the research aim: to deconstruct the themes, discourses, theories and practices within early childhood education and care. It must be acknowledged that deconstructing a discourse requires the construction of a discourse of deconstruction (Derrida, 1991; Cannella, 1997). As Cannella argued, in seeking for hidden meaning, post-structuralist critiques require assumptions about structuralist, modern discourse. Deconstruction can be viewed as its own grand narrative. Nevertheless, research needs to continue to critique ideas about universalism, progress and grand narration and in so doing analyse the meaning of social justice itself for the youngest of children. The 'post-modernist project' in moving away from totalizing systems enables an embrace of diversity and stresses the importance of subjective multiple voices (Goldstein, 1997). The starting point should be an assumed potential position of social justice for children. This allows for the challenge of dominant discourses of childhood but also for the self-examination of 'social justice' as a context-bound political discourse.

Early childhood studies ought to examine the assumptions underpinning the world of educational and child care practice. The organizational replication of cultural bias and dominant ideologies must be mediated through hearing and heeding the voices of both children, families and professionals. Learning about power structures and power differences and the processes and principles of empowerment must be a part of young children's educational experience. Knowledge, research and curriculum in the early years carry political bias. A political position clearly addressing an anti-oppressive practice base should be acknowledged by the 'early years world' (Delair and Erwin, 2000). The impact on early childhood of national and international politics and economics begins to be examined. Discourses of early childhood must function within macro politico-economic realities. Established curricula can be rejected for their oppressive policy functions in terms of problematizing and dominating particular groups of children and families (Pence and Ball, 2000).

The early years curriculum, either locally, nationally or internationally, cannot be assessed in simplistic terms of poor or good quality. The very use made of the construct of childhood within these contexts has to be explored. Critical appraisal is always needed of underlying knowledge, policy and practice issues and their interrelationship in a micro- and macro-political context.

Summary box

- Early childhood studies requires a critical engagement with the knowledge that underpins early years theory, policy and practice.
- The realities of children's lives need to be explored in global, social, cultural and familial contexts.
- Concepts of children, childhood and child-rearing must be examined as historically and culturally specific social constructs.

- Early childhood studies critically examines the way societies promote children's welfare, development, learning and their rights to protection, provision and participation (United Nations, 1989).
- There is increasing need to research and understand the needs of young children in a global context and the impact on them of national and international politics and economics.

Task

(1) Read Woodhead (2000)
- summarize his critique of child development globally.
- What are the advantages of a 'socio-cultural developmental psychology'?
- How does Woodhead assert young children's 'central status as principal stakeholders' in the processes of education and welfare?
(2) See Corby (1993) for a comprehensive examination of the knowledge base underpinning the issue of child abuse.
(3) See Jack (2001) for an overview of an ecological perspective on child abuse.

Indicative reading

Corsaro, W.A. (1997) *The Sociology of Childhood*. Thousand Oaks: Pine Forge Press.

James, A. and Prout, A. (eds.) (2001) *Constructing and Reconstructing Childhood* (2nd edn). London: RoutledgeFalmer.

Messer, D. and Millar, S. (eds.) (1999) *Exploring Developmental Psychology*. London: Arnold.

Penn, H. (ed.) (2000) *Early Childhood Services: theory, policy and practice*. Buckingham: OUP.

Pugh, G. (ed.) (2001) *Contemporary Issues in the Early Years: working collaboratively for children* (3rd edn). London: Sage.

Chapter 4

Towards Firmer Foundations?
An Exploration of Developments
in Early Years Education and Care

Ian Barron

F ROM the beginning of the twentieth century appropriate early years education had been called for by school inspectors and by the pioneers of early years education. Very little progress had been achieved, however, in advancing their cause throughout the greater part of the century, for early years education and care had not always been understood by the public at large and had often been treated with seeming suspicion by politicians, who tended to see early years provision as requiring few skills and being the responsibility of parents. This chapter will highlight some major issues since the 1990s and explore the political, societal and educational issues and beliefs that have affected its development.

The end of the twentieth century and the beginning of the twenty-first can be characterized by a number of significant themes in relation to early years education. The first centred on whether parents or the state should be responsible for its provision. Related to this debate was a continuing lack of clarity (or agreement, perhaps) about the purpose of early years provision: should it primarily be concerned with care (provided either to meet the needs of working parents or of children living with issues such as poverty, abuse, difficult family circumstances or disability) or the early education of young children? An awareness began to grow that perhaps it should be about both and more besides. The 1990s had also been marked by a vigorous debate: should early years education be defined in a curriculum? if so, in what form?

Alongside this debate there was also a slow re-defining of the age group covered by early years education. Until the early to mid-1990s, the early years had usually meant the time up to the age of 7 or 8; later, they tended to refer to children below statutory school age. However, children of 6 and 7 are now subject to the provisions of Key Stage 1 of the National Curriculum and, thus, have become clearly separated from younger children who are not subject to any statutory curriculum requirements. The 1990s were also marked by widespread concern about how early years services were being provided, with growing awareness of the need for greater co-ordination and integration of services. With increasing acceptance of the difference that early experiences can make to the later development and learning of young children and with growing awareness that the education and training of staff is a key factor in the quality of early years services, there has been an on-going debate about the level and appropriateness of current training of early years workers and about poor levels of pay and lack of status, especially for those working with very young children.

Social and political construction of education and care services

The provision that any country makes for the care and education of young children will reflect both the way in which it constructs children and how it structures society. As David (1990), and Anning and Edwards (1999) pointed out, the history of early childhood provision had been one of fragmentation of services, being provided by education authorities, health authorities, social services departments, or by the private or the voluntary sector. In general terms, where early years education and care was provided, it tended to be in response to some need to compensate for certain factors in children's lives, rather than the result of a genuine commitment to the importance of education in the early years. Early years education and care was located in some state-funded nursery schools and primary school nursery classes but there was no obligation on local education authorities to provide these. In general terms, Labour-controlled authorities, usually in places with higher levels of social deprivation, tended to provide more nursery education places than those controlled by the Conservatives, and urban areas were better provided for than rural ones. Playgroups, usually formed by parents, childminders and private nurseries had to fill the gap where no state provision was available. A smaller number of places, essentially provided to meet what were perceived as care needs, where children were viewed as at risk of harm, were also provided by local authority and voluntary sector day nurseries and family centres.

This fragmentation of services could be said to reflect the ways in which children and childhood had been understood: the child seen as having separate needs in terms of welfare, education and health. Regulation of services has traditionally been divided between the departments for education and health and social security, reflecting a perceived distinction between education on the one hand and care and welfare on the other. The Children Act (1989), the Rumbold Report (DES, 1990) and the Start Right Report (Ball, 1994) pointed to the confused picture of provision and called for the co-ordination of services for young children and their families. All too often, parents found it very difficult to gain information on what services were available, and provision consisted of a patchy array of school nurseries, a few day nurseries and family centres, playgroups, child-minders and private nurseries. It could be argued that such co-ordination would require, fundamentally, a far more holistic view of the nature, needs and rights of young children, in short a different construction of who and what children are.

A more holistic and co-ordinated approach was, however, difficult to achieve in an early years sector increasingly subject to a political ideology that did not support it. For the larger part of the 1990s, Conservative governments had held power in the United Kingdom and the dominant ideology had been that of 'the market' in the provision of services. Alongside this market approach, which could be seen to devolve power to the users of the services, was, as Bartlett *et al.* (2001) noted, a government concern to centralize and control what was provided. This was a period in which the centralist concern was with re-establishing traditional methods in education, which were seen as basic 'common sense'. Education was, essentially, de-professionalized, both in the early years and far beyond, and the best way to re-establish common sense, in what was believed to be a field dogged by unsuitable 'left wing' ideology, was to put power in the hands of parents, who would ensure a return to traditional approaches.

Thus parents were to be empowered as consumers and, in so doing, would come to be the major stakeholders in controlling quality in early years education. A market approach, with competing services from different providers, made it difficult for coherent and continuous services to be available. No account was taken, either, of the fact that the children were actually the consumers of the services and children appeared to be constructed as having few rights. Parental choice could also be seen as an expression of an ideological concern that the state should not be seen to be deciding what was best for families and young children, again a notion strangely at odds with the centralizing concern of the government. The period was one, essentially, of rather muddled thinking with little clarity about whether services were concerned with benefiting children or meeting the needs of working parents.

The nursery voucher scheme, introduced by the Conservative government in 1996 (providing a part-time place for all 4-year-olds whose parents wanted one) was the key to the operation of market forces in a 'mixed economy' of provision, responsive to parental preference. The voucher could be spent with the maintained sector but also with the private and voluntary sectors, including playgroups. Choice was seen to be somewhat illusory as, with falling school rolls and money at stake, primary schools swept 4-year-olds into Reception classes and large numbers of playgroups closed. Besides the already established Children Act, anyone in receipt of this money was now subject to inspection by OFSTED and was expected to work towards the desirable learning outcomes (SCAA, 1996). Whilst there was some expansion of places for 4-year-olds, the United Kingdom remained a poor provider of services for younger children, with an apparent belief that provision for children of 3 and under was concerned with care (falsely separated from education), the responsibility of parents and best met by the private sector.

Summary box

- Early education and care reflects the ways in which society constructs young children and their needs.
- Historically, provision for young children has been unco-ordinated and provided and regulated by different government departments, reflecting the ways in which children's needs have been constructed.
- This fragmentation was exacerbated in the 1990s, by a belief that early education and care should be made subject to market forces.
- This commitment to market forces, responsive to local needs, was not wholly consistent with government concerns to centralize and control what was provided.
- Whilst there was some increase in the number of early education places provided for 4-year-olds, there was little expansion of provision for younger children.

The struggle for the early years curriculum

Some would argue that nothing that could be described as an early years curriculum existed even in the 1980s. Certainly, written planning of learning experiences was relatively rare and it was only with the introduction of OFSTED inspections that some early years settings began to carry out formal planning. It could not be argued, however, that the early years tradition, grounded in the work of Froebel, Montessori, the McMillans and Isaacs did not comprise some form of curriculum, one based on the importance of children making choices and having first hand and real play experiences. As David (2001) noted, there was a tendency for those who opposed the idea of a curriculum perhaps to confuse the notion of curriculum with that of syllabus. Few of those associated with the early years would be happy to follow a narrow and rigid syllabus setting out precisely what all children should know, understand and do. However, if a curriculum for young children were understood in much broader terms as encompassing all that they did, all that was provided for them, all the people with whom they interacted and all the aspirations that children and their significant adults had regarding what they might do, be and achieve, then the notion of a curriculum would not be such a problematic matter.

The introduction of the desirable learning outcomes (SCAA, 1996) marked a point of keen debate in the history of early years education and care about whether a curriculum for the early years was appropriate and, if so, whether the curriculum promoted by the desirable learning outcomes was one to be welcomed. Just as the National Curriculum had marked a move to a more subject and knowledge-based curriculum for children of statutory school age, so the desirable learning outcomes marked a similar move in the education of children under 5, with less emphasis on play and more emphasis on 'structured learning', especially in literacy and numeracy.

Whilst these learning outcomes were never meant to be a curriculum in themselves but, rather, an indication of what children should achieve by the start of statutory schooling in the term following their fifth birthday, they became used as a curriculum and applied to children as young as 3, particularly where interpreted by less well qualified staff. The result was that, in some settings, children were expected to engage in some highly structured and inappropriate learning experiences. Whilst the desirable learning outcomes were meant to be followed by private and voluntary settings in receipt of state funding, as some measure of quality and value for money, there was also a growing expectation from OFSTED that state nursery schools and classes should follow them, even though they had no statutory basis. They may have provided a framework from which to work and inspect in the first cycle of OFSTED inspections (from 1994 to 1998) when many OFSTED inspectors lacked knowledge of the early years but it was also a sign of a government wish, personified by the then Chief Inspector of Schools, to regulate the form of curriculum provided for young children. This tendency for guidance to take on the status of requirement has not been limited to the early years: neither the national literacy nor the national numeracy strategy, introduced in the late 1990s, is a statutory requirement but the lines of statute and guidance have become increasingly blurred.

Concern began to be expressed, however, about this very early emphasis on such structured learning and about whether all forms of pre-school provision were equally effective. The approach to early learning promoted by the desirable learning outcomes was strangely at odds with the approaches to the curriculum being developed in other countries. The philosophy of the Reggio Emilia early childhood centres in Italy emphasized autonomy, culture, thinking and expressive skills, the richness of children's ways of living and learning (their 'hundred languages'), rather than literacy or numeracy learning, and derided the notion of a fixed curriculum – though, as David (2001) noted, these elements do suggest a curriculum, even if they did not comprise a syllabus. The New Zealand *Te Whariki* curriculum struck a chord with many British early years specialists, with its emphasis on empowerment, holistic development, family and community and relationships and it found expression in the Early Childhood Education Research Forum (1998) curriculum, which adapted the model to reflect British priorities.

Further concerns about the desirable learning outcomes were reflected in a growing body of research evidence which pointed to significant differences between different forms of early years education. Longitudinal evidence from the High Scope research project in the United States of America (Schweinhart and Weikart, 1997) and European research (see, for example, Sylva, 1999) were suggesting a close relationship between the type of early childhood provision and later success in education and life. Models that promoted autonomy, responsibility, social and language skills and a play-based approach to learning appeared to be closely associated with greater academic and social success later in life. Concern to explore the relationship between early experience and later learning was reflected in the decision to commission the Effective Provision of Pre-school Education Project (Sylva *et al.*, 1999) begun in 1997, which studied the progress of 3,000 children who attended a range of pre-school settings, from the age of 3 to the end of Key Stage 1 at the age of 7. It is, perhaps, interesting to note, however, that whilst studies focused on the relationship between different forms of early years education and later success, very few studies indeed concerned themselves with children's well-being and happiness, so much at the heart of the Reggio Emilia approach to early years education.

> **Summary box**
>
> - The early 1990s were marked by a debate over whether is was appropriate to have a formally recorded early years curriculum.
> - The desirable learning outcomes (SCAA, 1996) were introduced essentially as guidance for the private and voluntary sectors, which became eligible for state funding for the provision of nursery places for 4-year-olds, but came to be used as a curriculum, and were then applied to both private and voluntary and state sectors.
> - Concerns quickly emerged over what became, in many cases, a very structured curriculum, in contrast to the approaches to early education and care in other countries.
> - Research from the United States of America (Schweinhart and Weikart, 1997) and from a number of European countries, including Portugal (Sylva, 1999) points very clearly to long-term detrimental consequences of early education becoming too formal too soon.

Reframing early years education and care

After the election of the United Kingdom Labour administration in 1997, early years issues became a much more significant government priority. Once again, it is important to recognize that such a priority reflects government constructs of children and society. Early years initiatives were concerned to raise standards and to identify appropriate practice in work with young children. They were also, critically, related to a political concern to remove children and families from poverty by raising achievement and expectations. It is unclear at times whether the care and education of children are being addressed or the poverty and unemployment of families but, overall, there is greater clarity about the ways in which early years provision can benefit both children and parents: reducing poverty and improving early experiences for children are seen as enabling them to be more successful in academic terms and greater educational success is seen as a route out of poverty.

The curriculum guidance (DfEE/QCA, 2000), which replaced the desirable learning outcomes, sought to make much clearer what would be appropriate provision for children from the age of 3 to the end of the Reception year. What it did not make clearer was where this provision should be provided: the wide variety of provision still remains and children may still attend three types of provision in the same day, combining education and care. The guidance reflected the research findings (Schweinhart and Weikart, 1997; Sylva, 1999) that a less formal start to education seems to have more beneficial long-term consequences. The introduction of a Foundation Stage (from the age of 3 until the end of the Reception year) and related curriculum guidance was intended to make a clear statement that the more formal learning of the National Curriculum should not begin until Year 1 and not in Reception classes as was common previously. It is not unusual that educational policy and practice should reflect the findings of research. The Plowden Report (DES, 1967a) had been influenced by the ideas of Piaget, seeing children's development as essentially the maturational unfolding of latent skills and abilities that could not be hurried by teaching before the child was ready. The report also constructed the child along the Romantic era lines of natural goodness, dating back to Rousseau. The curriculum guidance (DfEE/QCA, 2000) reflected the influence of Vygotsky (1978), Bruner (1966; 1977), and Bruner and Haste (1987) and constructed the child as an apprentice, learning about what matters in the culture along-side significant adults, and influencing them in turn. Play and structured learning, with effective adult support (referred to as 'scaffolding'), were seen as key means of moving children on to understandings, skills and knowledge just out of sight. Equally important was the greater recognition that interests, wishes and desires of children themselves should be considered and that such an approach would benefit children's learning and development.

Despite a greater emphasis on provision for personal, social and emotional development, as laying the foundations for positive attitudes towards learning, the decision that the national literacy and numeracy strategies should still apply to Reception class children has tended to skew the balance in the curriculum and create some tensions between the English and mathematics specialists, supporting the development of the literacy and numeracy strategies, and the early years specialists, providing advice and training in respect of the Foundation Stage. Strong emphasis has also remained on preparing children for the future, but this future is, of course, very uncertain. As Claxton noted (1997) the only certainty about what 3-year-olds will need to know when they are 18 is that it is uncertain. Yet political considerations dictate that, whatever the research might suggest about the importance of life-long learning skills and the dangers of the curriculum being too formal too early, the government still has a short-term need to meet its targets for literacy and numeracy standards for 11-year-olds and this tends to lead to pressure for an early start to literacy and numeracy learning. Areas of learning such as creative and physical development, so important for young children, and knowledge and understanding of the world, covering the vast areas of science, design and information technology, and history and geography, have been relegated to secondary importance, especially in OFSTED inspections.

It is not being argued that literacy and numeracy are unimportant, far from it. There is, however, a need to ensure that arrangements for teaching and learning reflect what we know about young children and effective ways of scaffolding their development as learners and meaning makers. Play remains one of the most effective ways of equipping children as readers, writers and mathematicians, but, during the consultation period, following the publication of the draft early learning goals (QCA, 1999), incorporated into the curriculum guidance (DfEE/QCA, 2000), there was a need to lobby for the inclusion of the term 'play', which had not featured in the original proposals. Despite success in ensuring that play was referred to in the document, mixed messages were given by including a separate section on play. There is still a long way to go before it is understood that distinctions between work and play are not helpful and not real to the young child.

There is even further to go before it is understood that scaffolding the learning of the apprentice is not just concerned with the reconstruction of predetermined meanings. As Dahlberg (1999) noted, scaffolding is concerned, fundamentally, with appropriate active experiences that would enable the child genuinely to construct, negotiate and make sense of the world, thereby creating new meanings, in co-operation with peers and adults. This understanding is the key to equipping children for an uncertain future, as it gives them the skills to make sense of whatever they encounter. In Claxton's terms (1997), it provides children with the skills of 'learnacy', rather more important in a fast changing world than those of 'knowacy'.

Summary box

- Curriculum guidance (DfEE/QCA, 2000) gained more wide-spread acceptance than the previous desirable learning outcomes (SCAA, 1996), in large measure because it heeded the messages from research and because it was more responsive to the opinions of early years practitioners and academics.
- Despite greater attention to personal, social and emotional development and recognition of the significance of play, the curriculum guidance could be seen still to lack balance, with a heavy emphasis on literacy and numeracy learning and much less attention to areas of learning that are very significant in the lives of young children, such as physical development, creativity and understanding the world in which they live.
- Challenges remain in persuading policy-makers that it is just as important that children are equipped with the skills to find out for themselves, as it is that they acquire certain areas of knowledge.

Constructing the early years profession

Good quality early years education and care depends upon well trained and professional workers. However, such workers have often not been well trained or educated, and early years work has been seen as the natural refuge of the unsuccessful. Yet, to paraphrase Webb (1974), early years educators are the élite of an élite profession. Good quality early years provision is not something that can be provided by just any parent. As previously noted, at the time of writing government concerns are also to remove children from poverty through early years education. Considerable challenges remain in terms of staff being appropriately trained. A third of early years teachers are not trained to work in the sector; others have qualifications below degree level or no qualifications. Private and voluntary settings in receipt of nursery grants are required to have 'involvement' from a teacher but early childhood workers in these settings still have lower level qualifications than those in the maintained sector.

There are signs, however, of a genuine commitment to improving the quality of early years services. Early Excellence centres, so designated by the DfES, have been created in order to disseminate good practice, to act as a training and research resource and to provide co-ordinated education, care, welfare and health services under one roof. Early Years Development and Childcare Partnerships (EYDCPs) have been established in each local authority area to co-ordinate services for children and their families and to co-ordinate provision of good quality education and care in each local authority area. However, this could still be seen as the co-ordination of a range of patchy services, which might or might not involve children in lengthy journeys around different forms of education and care. The situation is beginning to improve with more nurseries providing both education and care over an extended day. Concern to provide a more integrated service for young children and their families was reflected in the Care Standards Act (2000). This transferred the responsibility for regulation, registration and inspection of early education and care from local authorities to OFSTED. The present bipolar arrangements, with separate 'care' and 'education' inspections still taking place, except in a few pilot joint inspections, do little more, however, than to co-ordinate the two regulation and inspection régimes. The decision to keep the care and education inspection régimes separate, for the time being, reinforces the unhelpful notion that care and education are somehow separate from each other.

At the time of writing there have been increasing signs of encouragement, however, in that the government, for the first time, is beginning to recognize that a highly significant period of development for children is before they are 3-years-old. This recognition is reflected in the Sure Start programme and in the Manchester Metropolitan University (MMU) project, commissioned by the DfES, to develop a Framework of effective practice for work with children under 3. The Department of Health and DfES Sure Start programme has been designed for children under 4 and their families who are perceived as being in particular need of help and support. Whilst it is true that the programmes are currently only available to those in the greatest need and there is anecdotal evidence that Sure Start programmes provide services that all parents say they want, progress is being made with extending the provision to more parts of the United Kingdom. Such projects reflect growing attention to recent brain studies (Shore, 1997; Shonkoff and Phillips, 2000), which suggested that brain synapses are fed and strengthened or weakened and eliminated by the quality of early childhood experiences and this has led to a recognition that what happens to children before they are 3-years-old may have a very significant effect on children's future educational and life chances. The discovery of support in the world of neuroscience for what early years workers always believed may prove effective in redressing the issue of lack of status for those working in the early years sector.

Sure Start and the MMU project reflect a growing recognition at national level, long established in Bronfenbrenner's (1979) ecological model, that children develop as their biology interacts with their immediate environment, with their families and with their communities. As such, the MMU framework takes as its starting point that learning and development for young children are not confined to traditional academic subjects, or even to be thought of in those terms, and are a great deal more than the usual areas of physical, intellectual, linguistic, emotional and social development. Learning and development are conceived as much more holistic and as involving a dynamic interplay as children learn who and what they are and how they feel about themselves and others, as they learn where they belong and as they seek to make meanings, in partnership with significant others, in the world in which they find themselves.

Despite considerable evidence (Pascal and Bertram, 1997; Abbott and Pugh, 1998) that the qualifications of staff are a key factor in the quality of provision, worrying signs remain that working with children is still not being seen as a high status graduate profession. Sure Start faces particular challenges in recruiting sufficient appropriately qualified staff and in ensuring that its workers, drawn from the fields of health, social work and education develop the skills needed to work effectively together. Whilst it is encouraging that government ministers seek to work towards all early childhood settings being led by an early childhood worker who has achieved level 4 of the National Qualifications Framework (NQF), concerns remain about the level of education and training of other staff working in the setting. The commitment is only to half of other staff attaining level 2 of the NQF. As noted earlier, the government is committed only to teacher 'involvement' in private and voluntary early childhood settings. A concern for state-maintained early childhood settings is that these minimum requirements will also be applied to them, in an effort to cut costs. These concerns, however, may be to misjudge the motives of the government and to under-estimate the difficulty of what it is attempting to achieve. The large numbers of untrained staff and staff with relatively low level qualifications is not the point from which any government with a commitment to good quality early years provision would wish to start. The scale of the task involved in ensuring that all staff have appropriate qualifications is not to be under-estimated. As the government programme of funding more places for 3-year-olds and of expanding the number of Sure Start programmes unfolds, there will be considerable challenges in finding enough staff of any description, let alone enough appropriately qualified staff.

Summary box

- There is now considerable evidence (see, for example, Pascal and Bertram, 1997, Abbott and Pugh, 1998) that the quality of early years education and care depends critically on the quality and training of staff, yet the early years sector remains one in which staff have relatively low level qualifications. Improving the qualifications and training of staff will require time and considerable investment.
- Early years development and childcare partnerships have made some progress with meeting the training needs of early years practitioners and with improving the co-ordination of education and care services provided to children and families but a great deal remains to be done.
- There is growing recognition that appropriate provision is also needed for children under the age of 3 and that early experiences play a critical role in the way in which the brain develops.
- The growing recognition of the significance of the early years, together with better pay and training, are the keys to improving the status of early years work.

Early childhood education reframed

Many positive signs are emerging in relation to the provision of good quality early years education and care. Until the late 1990s, a specialism in early years education was not regarded as appropriate to initial teacher education. Early years practitioners with a great deal of experience and with an early years qualification at NQF level 3 but without a qualification in a traditional academic subject were not eligible for entry to teacher training programmes. However, advanced study of early years was established as a specialism alongside more traditional subjects in 1998 and, although the 2002 teacher training requirements no longer required a subject specialism, it is still possible to enter training with an early years qualification at level 3 of the NQF and to specialize in the Foundation Stage and Key Stage 1, covering the age range 3-7. Progress is even being made with persuading the Teacher Training Agency (TTA) and DfES that teachers need to have detailed knowledge of the learning, development and care needs of children under 3 years of age.

The early years sector-endorsed foundation degree and senior practitioner qualification, intended for practitioners with existing NQF level 3 qualifications, and the development of new routes to qualified teacher status for experienced early years workers suggest that the status and training of all such workers is being seen as being of importance. The government Green Paper (2001) stated:

> It is critical that those working with young children are trained to high professional standards, and that qualifications support the development of an integrated sector ... we also want more early education specialists to come through teacher training. We will work on new routes into teaching and other senior practitioner posts so as to make the best of the skills and experience of the very large early years and childcare work force.

It remains true, however, that there is further work to be done in order to secure the long-held beliefs of this sector that graduate early years workers do not all want or need to be teachers, despite the Green Paper commitment that 'qualifications support the development of an integrated sector'. There is still a need for the graduates of early childhood studies degrees to be recognized as a new breed of professionals with a range of skills that cross the boundaries of education, welfare, health and the law, reflecting a construct of the child as many-faceted. This construct also means that it is important to develop the notion of the senior practitioner within the new early years foundation degree in order that the senior practitioner is seen as something more than someone who has not quite reached teacher status. This may involve further study in order to achieve the new professional role envisaged for early childhood studies graduates. It may involve new work-based and flexible routes to qualified social worker and health visitor status.

In conclusion, there are considerable grounds for optimism in current developments in early childhood education and care in the twenty-first century. A formulating and constructing, or perhaps a re-shaping and re-aligning of priorities in relation to childhood appears to be occurring. Whilst there remains a construction of childhood that sees the early years sector as being concerned only with equipping children for later life and for a profitable economic future, there seems to be emerging a realization that preparation for the future cannot be measured only in terms of productivity and academic success. Preparation for the future is also about social and emotional well-being and about ensuring that needs are being met in the present, as children. These beliefs have, finally, found some expression in the curriculum guidance (DfEE/QCA, 2000). The work of early years development and childcare partnerships, especially as they begin to listen to children themselves, also point to a genuine commitment to providing children and families with the services that they need now. Relief from the merry-go-round of travel around different forms of education and care provision for children below statutory school age is slow to emerge and remains a major challenge. As David (1999) noted, if secondary school pupils had to travel between lessons in the same way, it would be considered a national scandal. Co-ordination of education and care services is emerging but more integrated services, responsive to children, will be the true mark of a re-framed construction of education and care in early childhood. Finally, there appears to be a commitment to making this happen.

Summary box

- The 1990s saw a great many changes in early years education and care, involving debates over who should be responsible for provision and funding, the form that the early years curriculum should take (and whether it should be written down), growing concern over poor co-ordination of education, care and health services for young children and continuing debates about the education, training, status and pay of early years practitioners.

- The 1990s were marked by a continuing partnership between the public and private sectors in providing education and care for young children. Parents were seen as the consumers of early education and care and market forces were seen as the key to improving quality.
- Only at the end of the 1990s did early education and care services expand and become better co-ordinated, with the creation of early years development and childcare partnerships.
- The mid-1990s witnessed a debate about the form that an early years curriculum should take, and the very formal approaches that emerged from the desirable learning outcomes (SCAA, 1996) became a cause of growing concern in the light of more play-based approaches in other countries and of research which suggested that formal learning approaches could damage children's later educational and life chances.
- For much of the 1990s education and care for children under 3 years of age continued to be seen as essentially the responsibility of parents, and little attention was paid to the needs or rights of young children.
- The end of the 1990s and the beginning of the twenty-first century have been marked by an expansion in early education and care for 3-year-olds and a needs-led expansion of provision for children under 3.
- Removing children from poverty and an emphasis on the significance of children's early experiences have come to be seen as the keys to improving children's educational attainment and their life chances.
- The education, training and status of early years workers have finally been recognized as having a direct impact on the quality of early years education and care.
- There are encouraging signs that early years education and care are grounded in a genuine concern for children but preparation for the future must be grounded in careful reflection on what is appropriate for children in the present.

Task

(1) Identify what you consider to be the characteristics and needs of young children (for example, playfulness, naivety, inventiveness, time to explore and investigate).
(2) Read Tina Bruce's (1997) bedrock principles. How far do you agree with these principles?
(3) Now read about the curriculum guidance (QCA/DfEE, 2000).
  - How far is the curriculum guidance consistent with the way you have described the characteristics and needs of young children?
  - How far is the curriculum guidance consistent with Bruce's bedrock principles?

- Do you feel that there are any tensions between the requirements of the curriculum guidance, the ways in which you have described the characteristics and needs of young children and the bedrock principles? If so, what are they and what do you see as being the causes of the tensions?

Indicative reading

Abbott, L. and Moylett, H. (eds.) (1999) *Early Education Transformed.* London: Routledge. This books reviews the status of early years education at the end of the twentieth century and highlights key trends for the new millennium.

Dahlberg, G., Moss, P. and Pence, A. (1999) *Beyond Quality in Early Childhood Education and Care.* London: Routledge. This is, perhaps, the most challenging of these texts, drawing upon a post-modern perspective that challenges 'child-centred' orthodoxy and the notion that quality is an absolute and measurable commodity and suggests that quality must be a construct that considers children, families, employment and community development.

Penn, H. (1999) *Early Childhood Services.* Buckingham: OUP. This book has some challenging and interesting chapters concerned with the links between theory, policy and practice. Notions such as the natural nature of children's play are challenged and an overview is given of developments in early education and care in various countries.

Pugh, G. (ed.) (2001) *Contemporary Issues in the Early Years* (3rd edn). London: Paul Chapman. This book offers an accessible and thoughtful overview of the key policy and practice issues in contemporary early years education and care. Chapters deal with key concerns, such as the learning and care environment, equality of opportunity, children's rights, supporting children's learning and staff education and training.

Chapter 5

The Politics of Identity and Schooling

Cedric Cullingford

W HAT do pupils really learn in school? At one level the answer to this question is obvious, especially if the word 'really' is omitted. Pupils learn what they are supposed to learn – the prescribed National Curriculum carefully constructed and structured into a series of key stages in which the content is planned centrally and delivered by teachers. To ensure compliance with the requirements of the 1988 Education Reform Act, a powerful inspection régime (OFSTED) monitors what takes place inside schools to check whether a 'broad and balanced' curriculum which is the 'entitlement' of all pupils is being delivered. OFSTED has the power to take special measures and in some cases close schools.

Behind the question of what pupils really learn lies a continuing contemporary debate. It focuses upon three issues:

- Who is in control of the curriculum?
- What has the most powerful influence on learning, home or school?
- What is being learned in school beyond the National Curriculum?

The National Curriculum was introduced partly because of the suspicion that teachers were following their own individual judgements about what children should study and learn. The control of subject matter was out of the power even of governors and local education authorities. The 1944 Education Act while insisting upon religious (Christian) education actually celebrated the freedom of the curriculum and gave considerable power to teachers to shape it. Indeed, the curriculum was considered to be the responsibility of the professional judgement of teachers. The Plowden Report of 1967 was seen as the apotheosis of a new spirit of individual exploration by pupils, fostered, in particular, by primary school teachers.

Education policy is usually created more by myth and anecdote than by empirical evidence. This should be borne in mind when we explore educational issues, themes and problems. Just as the 1960s have become a period held up for vilification and turned, with hindsight, into a kind of self-parody, the very strength of the primary tradition has been turned into a self-indulgent free-for-all where double-mounted pictures and easels for decoration were supposed to hide an absence of discipline. It only needed a unique case, that of the William Tyndale Primary School in London, to give some substance to support this argument. In this particular school, the teachers were found to be ignoring the discipline of work subjects with a resulting lack of standards in reading and writing and, worse still, some teachers appeared to engaged in socialist thinking. This was exactly the ammunition needed to support the case for more centralized control over what should be learnt.

The development of the core curriculum ensuring exactly what should and must be taught was one phase in the populist and governmental reaction against the autonomy of schools. The underlying assumption was that what was taught was actually being learned and that one could be certain that if the right subject areas were being delivered then standards in schools would rise. The control of the individual teacher, even that of the powerful, now almost mythical, figure of the chief education officer was to be curtailed.

Such a philosophy of curriculum control raises the second issue. To what extent is it the home or the school which actually in practice influences what pupils learn? Are socio-economic factors significant variables? The starting point for this debate was not so much the deep-seated and hereditary assumptions such as belief in innate intelligence in individuals that characterized school selection in the post-war period. The argument tended to move in a direction which suggested that the complex influence of home and neighbourhood did indeed have a substantial impact upon children's learning. In addition, since the work of Rutter and Mortimer (1990) and their colleagues, it was an accepted fact that schools also made a difference even allowing for the variables of home background and economic status.

This particular approach informs that adopted by OFSTED. Schools are approached as if they are hermetically sealed units in which all that is worth inspecting is readily observable in the interchange between teacher and pupil which can be measured in the standard assessment test (SAT) results. It is very clear that this assumption is not supported by the facts. School league tables demonstrate the advantages enjoyed by particular communities and not enjoyed by other communities. Nevertheless, the argument underpinning the inspection approach to education is that all schools could be the same, that with the same rigorous approach to management educational achievement set against national targets would not depend on other factors. Indeed, even suggesting that poverty and socio-economic disadvantage has a substantial impact upon school performance is considered an excuse for poor perform-ance in schools. If schools are so powerful they are also far easier to control than the many lived realities of wider society with its complexities of the inter-relationship between private and public spheres of influence. The belief in the significance of the school is linked to that of the power of central control.

The third debate about what actually happens inside schools is the most complex. The formal curriculum is clearly laid down and while there may be minor adjustments, like the addition of citizenship education in September 2002, the central structure seems immutable. Not only is the content prescrib-ed but the teaching methods, such as in the literacy and numeracy initiatives, are also laid down. Ever since the report of the 'three wise men' (Alexander *et al.*, 1992) centralized control has entered into the area of teacher pro-fessionalism, something that would have been unheard of before the 1990s.

The formal curriculum is what is taught. The aim is to produce a skilled work force equipped to compete in a globalized economy that believes in a system in which children will concentrate upon the acquisition of knowledge and skills necessary for employment. At one level this both is and ought to be the case and yet any close analysis of school subjects reveals that the 'hidden curriculum' is just as important. The creation of a compliant work force and citizenary might be an acceptable aim but it might also come about for quite different reasons. The use of the political terms 'Left' and 'Right' are not very helpful since they imply that debate at the level of theoretical and empirical depth is being high-jacked by party policy-makers. It is, however, clear that those who have analysed schooling for its support of social norms have tended to be associated with more radical traditions. Those who, for example, explore the personal circumstances of individual pupils provide a different insight into the experience of schooling (Willis, 1977). Whilst they might well agree that what is learnt results in some kind of compliance they do not necessarily accept that this is either advisable or a good thing.

Let us take four examples of research that suggest that the inner realities of schooling contain multiple levels of complexity and contradiction. Gramsci (1973), for example, analysed the experience of school in terms of presenting a view of the world as an unchanging 'hegemony' where pupils learned that there was little they could do to affect radical change. Both King (1978) and Sharp and Green (1975) explored the differences between the rhetoric of schooling and its realities. They were particularly interested in the liberal statements made by teachers and the way that teachers described how they promoted and demonstrated these values through their classroom practice. What was discovered was a complete distinction between good intentions and the actual, detailed and powerful control exerted by teachers. The values of hierarchy and control were very much in evidence.

Such an unexpected or, perhaps, unintentional conveying of conservative values was also explored by Bowles and Gintis (1976) who suggested that the messages schools were conveying were closely related to the needs of the economic system. Far from being sites of critical enquiry, schools were very much the bastions of economic capitalism. Schools are hegemonies of clear values, creating order and discipline, and the need for compliance and acceptance of core values decided within powerful, structural, contexts of influence.

Whether we approve of the fact or not, schools are seen to impose values on their pupils. There are certain elements of the National Curriculum, such as citizenship education, which expressly address issues connected with ethical and moral positions. Many parts of the curriculum, such as history, have their philosophical basis in the moral and social understandings they convey. Even the formal curriculum is at times not completely tied to academic knowledge. The national debate about curriculum is partly about the extent to which schools ought to promote consciously certain standards and behaviour not taught elsewhere. Compared to other European cultures a great deal of emphasis in the United Kingdom is placed upon the social aspects of schooling. Teachers see themselves *in loco parentis*, responsible for all aspects of pupil learning both inside and outside the formal curriculum. There is then a side of schooling that is aware that all pupils learn much beyond the core curriculum and the requirements of each key stage.

If schools have a moral and ethical role to play, to what extent does it compare with the role of parents? Many argue that the idea of teaching citizenship education is in fact dangerous, partly because it could be interpreted as the deliberate manipulation of children or because it acts against the values of parents and others outside schools who should be responsible for social learning outside the formal curriculum. Pupils inside the classrooms do learn something of social expectation but the question remains whether they learn much more from home than from school.

Despite this analysis of the social context of schooling many would argue that essential attitudes towards politics and society are formed in the home. The comparatively recent interest in early childhood, revealing far greater powers of observation and analysis than those suggested by Piaget, concluded that the early years of a child's life are vital in the formation of social understanding. Attitudes, motivations and the ability to relate to others are well formed before a child enters school. This is why early socio-economic and cultural factors are so important. Schooling then is a matter of the accumulation of knowledge and skills, the National Curriculum providing all that is necessary. The key stages and the testing régime verify that all that should be learned is being learned and makes schools accountable for this process.

Schools are, however, social institutions. However much it might seem appropriate to view schools as depositories of knowledge or centres for the acquisition of factual knowledge, they are also social arenas. For many a young child they represent the first experience of a society larger than that provided by the home. All who have been to school will recognize the influence of the peer group and of school ethos in shaping attitudes; schools have their hierarchies and their rules.

Studies of early childhood point out how important social relationships are and how they influence learning. It is easy to forget this. In the Headstart programme in the United States of America there was a concerted effort to make up for any intellectual deficiencies in young children. The idea was that a special programme of academic attainment would make a significant difference to the growth of children. There was an equal measure of satisfaction and disappointment when the programme concluded that it had made little difference to the development of children's capabilities. Intervention appeared not to be successful. A closer inspection of the evidence however reveals changes more subtle and longer lasting. What had been influenced were children's social attitudes, their self-esteem and their relationships with their peers. Academically, the participants appeared to make little substantial progress but their social outlook had changed and this had a profound effect on their futures. The learning of facts and the learning of attitudes have a close symbolic relationship. How can one distinguish between the accumulated skills and the manipulation of knowledge and critical thinking skills?

What then is really learned in school? Or to put it differently where do young people learn the social attitudes which so deeply inform their lives? 'September 11', like all genocidal wars across the globe, makes it imperative that educators seek answers to this question. What makes some people turn into fanatics; why do some people join fascist groups and become racist; why do people develop malignant prejudices towards others? These are not theoretical or abstract questions but they are rarely part of the school experience. Some people, in some groups, unleash their sense of personal identity on others in a destructive manner. Such questions seem grandiose for schools and they tend not to inform the National Curriculum at a significant level. This is not the place to suggest how they might be better integrated into the formal curriculum but it is appropriate to question where such attitudes originate. These questions are not rhetorical even if they are rarely addressed. If we study the experience of pupils in school it is clear that they learn much about themselves and about each other that might be accidental and unexpected but which is crucial for their development.

Summary box

- Pupils do not only learn within the school environment. There exists a range of environments outside the boundaries of formal schooling which contribute significantly to children's learning.
- In school pupils do not only learn facts and skills which are part of the formal National Curriculum, the hidden curriculum of schools provides a myriad of learning opportunities.
- Schools are a formative social influence in a variety of cultural and social contexts within which children interact with other children and with adults.

What follows now is an attempt to sum up what is really learned through the experience of schooling. At one level schools disseminate and test knowledge. Schools also inform attitudes and create an emotional outlook which pervades what pupils do but also what they learn about.

One of the fundamentalist insights that have emerged from the study of childhood is the vulnerability of young children. They are easily hurt. There is no deliberate intent to cause children such emotional trauma. Much of what happens in the social life of the school happens by chance, certainly outside official hierarchies of school organization and management. Young children are also vulnerable to a variety of influences largely because broader and more fundamental issues to do with society and politics are rarely a part of their experience formally or informally. They often learn, instead, through overheard remarks, individual observation, through anecdote and conversations with their peers. Such learning is difficult to control or to predict but it does not make it any the less real. Understanding society and their place in it, the way in which politics works and the place of the individual in both small communities and larger ones such as nations can be seen to be formed in three ways:

- media representation;
- school evaluations of core issues, themes and problems;
- the powerful influence of peer group pressure.

Studying contemporary issues by following the news media or pursuing understanding through the study of history is not the favourite occupation of young people. However, this certainly does not prevent them from following debates, forming prejudice and acquiring firmly held beliefs about individuals and groups. Young children have been shown to prefer some nations to others and have demonstrated a distaste for a particular culture or language (Cullingford, 2000). Such discriminations are not created formally, based upon careful judgment and reasoning, rather they are based upon glimpses that flash upon the inward eye in the form of images and stories. The media operates at a variety of different levels. The news might not be a preferred option for television viewing among children but very few are totally unaware of what is going on in the world. The most powerful media of communication among children is that of gossip, the overheard remark on a bus, train or in a school queue. We only have to remind ourselves where we were when we heard a particular piece of news to acknowledge that fact.

The media present a complex, direct and consistent image of society. Whatever children take from all the snippets of information to which they are exposed they have little choice but to try and make sense of it, whether it be wars or crimes, glittering occasions or sport. Such news reflects the differences, the contrasts and the hierarchies of the social world. Some people are clearly viewed as being more important than others and some have more power, power that they wield over others. All this is obvious but it also applies to the social world of the school. The headteacher is responsible to the governing body and, in turn, teachers are responsible to the headteacher – both are also responsible to outside agencies who impact upon the running of the school. There exist formal and informal distinctions, crime and punishment. There are groups being formed, deliberately for the purposes of learning and discipline, and informally for reasons of subjective taste.

Many of the ways in which societies run themselves, for good or bad, are enacted in school. Even if schools were hermetically sealed from the real world they would still provide crucial learning experiences about the way people learn to live together. There exists inside schools authority and disobedience; the influence of power impacts upon personal relationships, behaviour and status. The fact that pupils are also learning informally about society makes crucial the messages which schools, informally, convey about wider society. The connection between school and wider society lies in peer groups who not only demonstrate the application of power and control but pass on social values, whether it is the latest film or news event. Contemporary issues might not always, if ever, be part of the formal curriculum but they represent an essential part of gossip, the general social chatter of the school.

The vulnerability of young children makes them open to all kinds of difficulties in schools. There are particular matters about which pupils feel strongly in their personal and social lives. One emotion experienced from an early age is shame, exposure to humiliation. That feeling of exposure, of being viewed with contempt is one of the deepest and most marked in childhood. The lack of confidence that can result from remembered hurt is a potential formative influence. School environments present ample opportunities for such experiences. There are few children who do not cite moments when they are exposed to the humiliation of not knowing the answer to a question or of simply not knowing what is expected from them in a given situation. If the teacher does not provide the context for exposure, the peer group will. The concept of being 'picked upon' is not just a matter of failure in a lesson but of peer group interaction. One of the underlying concerns among young people is 'fairness', both a personal and social concept. Feeling that something is unfair can easily turn into resentment, an attitude antipathetic to society.

A second pain experienced in childhood is that of being ignored. This can be a matter of lack of interest from parents and a sibling rivalry where others seem to attract all the attention. This sense of marginalization can be bitterly resented. Again, schools are perfect sites for the fostering of feelings of this kind. In a crowded classroom with busy teachers some children are bound not to receive enough attention. Deeper than the sense of anonymity is resentment when teachers do not show concern over bullying, when they have no time to intervene in daily relationship problems. The scars of being ignored run deep and can have lasting influences upon attitudes towards what might be judged as appropriate behaviour. Some can nurture thoughts of revenge.

The third resentment or potential pain of childhood is less psychologically damaging but also an essential element of the school experience. It is being caught up in purposeless activity, which is not the same as being bored. Children tend not to mind too much about being bored. Boredom can even be associated with pleasure, filling time with distractions and games which do not tax the mind. The routines of school can, however, be resented not so much because they might seem boring but because they might seem meaningless. Certain tasks are created in such a way that it appears to the pupils carrying them out that their only purpose is to keep them occupied. It is not so much drudgery and hard work which is resented but the repetition of routine. Work can then be associated with anonymous and sometimes seemingly humiliating tasks that are both taxing and meaningless, a waste of talent. Emotional and intellectual energy can be turned in a positive direction.

If one wants to understand the causes of prejudice and discomfort within society, schools are in a difficult position since they provide all the social opportunities for the very problems which children face emotionally. Schools are, in the way in which children attend them, not just micro-societies but sites for trials of strength and weakness in many relationships. All this is not deliberate but a reflection of the demands of the formal curriculum.

Schools are also contradictory places because they have conflicting purposes. Schools are expected to fit their pupils for the role they will occupy in society. This general expectation is usually accepted without question even if the manner in which it is pursued is far more subtle than the mere conveying of transparently agreed messages. This view is paralleled by another, that schools are academic sites. This latter aim seems incompatible with the first. The third purpose of schooling is supposed to be the fulfilment of individual potential, the development of personal needs and the emotional satisfaction of the child. This suggests that in some respects children can explore their own development, that what they need is to discover for themselves and enjoy the unfettered satisfaction that schools might offer. We recognize this aim when we visit schools and when we read their mission statements. The academic, the social and the personal are all considered to be central aims – the question is whether they are compatible.

To return for a moment to the first question, what do pupils really learn in school? Well, they learn about their own identity and its meaning in relation to others and they form very clear views on society which, given their vulnerability, can easily be tribalistic, informed by resentment against others and the warmth of group belonging. So, what are the views and outlooks acquired by pupils; on this we have clear and consistent evidence.

Schools help pupils form views of the world. Such information that is useful for pupils is gathered in a variety of ways. The normal way of acquiring a sense of identity and understanding of society can be through a series of accidental processes, such as the accumulation of disconnected facts, ideas and insights. Many would argue that the development of the individual must remain accidental if they are not to face the accusation of manipulation. Yet, the absence of attention given to this central part of learning, how to be a person, means that young children are vulnerable to prejudice and extremism. There are many controversial and political issues attached to citizenship or economic understanding but there is little fuss about these subjects.

Pupils piece together their understanding of the world from a variety of sources; images are then reinforced by schools. When pupils talk about their understanding of the world and their place in it they constantly express the thought that increased nationalism and regionalism can result in alienation. There are three distinct bases for the forming of prejudice and stereotyping: a sense of the world as a whole; the way in which politics impacts upon the social world and the place of individuals as themselves.

Young people understand their world in terms of contrasts between countries. Whilst there is a variety of distinctions to be made, the crucial one is between rich and poor. Many researchers have demonstrated how early in their lives young people form prejudices against other countries, usually traditional enemies such as Germany. They are far less clear about the origins of these perspectives. Underlying antipathies emerge from the realization that the world is deeply divided and unfair. On the one hand are the clear manifestations that the United States of America is a world power, rich, powerful and dominant in consumer terms. Young people know that money counts. On the other hand is the image of Africa as a whole, of the malnourished and the poor. This impoverishment is not viewed simply as a matter of chance but is a matter of concern and distaste. However, although images of destitution keep appearing, nothing diminishes admiration for richer countries.

Such contrasts between rich and poor are of great importance since they also apply to pupils' own experience. Whilst they delineate the conflicting images of different nations clearly, they also point out two other levels of experience, the visual impact of television and personal confrontation with people they meet. The way in which programmes on television can celebrate the lifestyles of those who can afford possessions, and the abject poverty of the disadvantaged is pointed out to pupils. This contrast can be reinforced through personal experience. All pupils have seen the homeless and the destitute. The contrasts between those who have and those who have not are not abstract or theoretical in the social world of the child; they go beyond prejudice against certain groups. They represent an ontological basis for the world in which pupils live and work.

The media are particularly important in pupils' understanding of politics where contrasts between rich and poor are closely linked to issues of who has power and who is powerless. There is a strong awareness that power lies in the hands of the minority long before there is any understanding regarding differences between party doctrines. Whether it is the way in which a political style is presented, or whether it is because of the dominance of the media by a particular group, the perception that merges is that the world of politics involves an enclosed élite. The result of this is a strong underlying sense of normality and of helplessness. This suggests a certain cynicism but it is a far more complex issue. It appears to be part of a picture of the world as being deeply divided. 'The rich are not like you and me' is one lesson that pupils learn at an early stage in their lives. The media constantly point out that they can make little tangible difference to, for example, government decisions, even if they have a strong local context.

Much is made of a sense of personal helplessness and the estrangement of the disaffected. That children should feel disenfranchized is not surprising, ontological insecurity is expressed by pupils not in terms of despair, instead what they demonstrate is a sense of ambivalence and neutrality. When pupils talk about their own nation they do so in terms of it strengths and weakness-es, there are clearly countries which they admire and where they might like to live but they accept that such feelings are beside the point – they accept where they are and have a sense of belonging to that place. The same applies to their homes and environments. They would prefer to live in larger homes and have bigger gardens, and they would appreciate being in a safer and less polluted environment. Yet pupils are also pragmatic and realistic, appreciating that, friends and family, those aspects of their lives that matter most, surround them, wherever they live. The way in which pupils understand their circum-stances and those of others is complex. The sense of personal helplessness is applied not only to themselves but also to what they know, understand and see in others. Pupils possess a latent sense of outrage but they also submit to the world as they know it. There is a deep sense that they are who they are because of chance, characterized by their class, ethnicity and their language.

These perceptions of the world combine to produce a coherent view, reinforced in the school; the same contrasts, the same submissions and the same mentality represent the essential experience of school. Let us take them in reverse order from mentality to contrast. When pupils summarize their im-pressions of school and cultural impressions of school life, they demonstrate a submissive frame of mind. They 'put up' with school because it is there; they have no choice, school is a rite of passage. In this experience the sense that they are of any particular individual importance is absent. For all the em-phasis which schools place on mission statements, pupils emerge from their schooling thinking it is something they may have endured but certainly over-come. Schooling acts out and embodies the essential culture of society and re-inforces its message in the individual, even if that message remains neutral. Schools also place individuals in context. Part of that context involves the use of power through the hierarchical structures that schools promote and main-tain. At this level this hierarchy is simplistic through which pupils learn the complexities of the organization and the implications of challenging authority.

The command structure of schools is very clear. It reinforces the sense of differences which exists between people in that community. It is similar in some sense to the contrast between rich and poor but it is more volatile and more complex. Pupils are certainly aware of two kinds of power struggle: one existing between teachers and pupils, the other operating within peer groups. Both give the impression of a society seething with potential tensions. The contrast can be exhibited in two ways: in competition and bullying. Competi-tion is for the teacher's attention and for the need to be seen to do well, if not too well which runs the risk of alienating individuals from the group. Bullying is against anyone who stands out from the group as being different; here a pupil can be quickly deflated or suddenly forced out of a friendship group. The contrast between success and failure is powerful and constant. The friendship patterns between groups, incidents of bullying and the complex relationship that exist with teachers are all too well documented.

The results of the experiences of schooling and the observations made of the world present a certain outlook on life, a pattern of behaviour and an expectation of what could happen. Learning takes place at the level of culturally acquired instincts that lie beneath the formal curriculum of facts and knowledge. When the world is experienced as a whole, and its essential unfairness is lived through inside schools, then a certain outlook will be held by all the products of the system despite their individual differences and the degrees of vulnerability they possess.

To understand the forming of personal and national identity in which schooling plays such a crucial part we need to be aware of the vulnerability of pupils to a variety of influences. Children are not impervious to personal insights, what they learn is often inadvertent, so that even the best of intentions do not always work as they are intended. One cross-cultural example illustrates this point. European ministers focus upon their citizens learning about different cultures and languages, and cultural interchange is encouraged. Yet one does not need to witness groups of young people wandering the streets of their towns, and the other European towns which they may visit, talking to each other in their native language, hating the local food and seeing the locals as being very different, and possible inferior, to understand the huge problems that issues to do with intercultural integration hold. Do holiday-makers on the southern coast of Spain eating fish and chips and watching football matches on 'Sky TV' really appreciate the nuances of local culture? Is a visitation of English football fans a friendly interchange of understanding? Culture and identity are complex ideas. The same distinctions between tokens of difference and genuine understanding can be applied to racism. Images of difference lead not so much to pity as to distaste.

Children imbibe ideologies from an early age and their general receptiveness and curiosity is formed long before it might manifest itself in prejudice. Schooling has a tendency to close rather than open the mind and make sure that early encounters with culture are firmly located in the consciousness. What is learnt through observation is a narrow structure of understanding, of constraints and power, of fear and the avoidance of trouble. This is obviously not the intention of schooling. At school children learn the distinction between social and personal rights. They understand the importance of the former, but are aware, however, that society is all too obvious but in a way which sees it manifest not so much in community but in ways of doing things. There is a need to fight for personal rights against others, many of whom occupy positions of greater power and influence.

Schooling helps give pupils a strong sense of resilience. Whilst it might not be its primary aim to get children to stand against all the social problems of relationships, such as bullying and unfairness, this is what actually happens. The sense of personal independence and the need for self-aversion is the outcome of a particularly weighted education system. Schooling clearly does makes a difference to the lives of children, but an under-developed area is that fact that such differences might not have much to do with academic achievement but are a question of social and moral outlook. Pupils are ready to learn, they need to learn. We do not focus enough energies on what they actually learn outside the formal curriculum – in the absence of anything better the danger is that they can learn prejudice.

Task

(1) Explore the contention that the hidden curriculum which operates inside schools has far more influence upon children's learning than the National Curriculum.
(2) Is the home more influential in shaping children's sense of identity?
(3) Who are the most powerful and influential social groups inside schools, teachers or peer groups?
(4) What might the relationship be between the command structures of schools, e.g. managerialism and personal autonomy e.g. ownership?
(5) How might an understanding of children's vulnerability to the social world help in developing coherent understandings of how they form a sense of identity?
(6) How are group identities formed among children?

Indicative reading

Alexander R.J., Rose J., and Woodhead, C. (1992) *Curriculum Organisation and Classroom Practice in Primary Schools.* London: HMSO.

Cullingford, C. (2000) *Prejudice: from Individual Identity to Nationalism in Young People.* London: Kogan Page.

King, R. (1978) *All Things Bright and Beautiful? A Sociological Study of Infant Classrooms.* Chichester: Wiley.

Chapter 6

Children's Rights

Dominic Wyse

I N this chapter the idea that childhood can be viewed not as a fixed definition but as a construct is explored by analysing the tragic case of the murder of James Bulger. This provides the basis for further exploration of legal issues which are such a strong motivating force in relation to rights. The impact of the UN Convention on the Rights of the Child is also examined in relation to children's participation in schools. One of the problems that British society has faced in moving towards greater recognition of children's rights is the way in which children and childhood are viewed. Old ideas such as children *should be seen and not heard* or that they *should not speak unless they are spoken to* still pervade our society. The idea that children's immaturity makes them incapable of making rational decisions about their lives is another impediment to recognition of rights. However, these ideas have not remained static and one of the significant movements in childhood theory has been the recognition that childhood can be viewed as a construct.

One of the early constructs of childhood that continues to the present day was the idea of childhood innocence. The French philosopher Jean Jacques Rousseau (1712-78) felt that when children were born they were pure and un-influenced by the negative aspects of their society – this is the idea of the *tabula rasa* or blank slate. For this reason Rousseau felt that adults should not be in a hurry to imprint their versions of the world on children, rather that they should be encouraged to discover the world for themselves, and that their innate positive characteristics would guide them in the early stages.

Rousseau used the fictional character Emil as a means to explain his theories about childhood. Early independence is stressed as an important way to encourage the child to learn at his or her own pace. He refused to accept the idea that children were lazy and suggested that they actively thought about their lives. However, like the ideas of Jean Piaget, whose work was written much later, he seemed to suggest that children were egocentric: that is, they tended to think more about their own concerns than those of others. This last idea perhaps needs some careful thought since many children are capable of thinking which goes beyond their own concerns. Children, for instance, who act as sole carers for sick relatives show high levels of awareness.

Although the idea of childhood as a period of innocence has a long track record, periodically this view is challenged by events in society. One of the most serious aspects of this is when children kill other people. Adults find this very difficult to deal with. On a straightforward level we are all shocked by any kind of killing but we are more shocked if children are killed. For example, in the United Kingdom the murders of children carried out by Fred and Rosemary West and the earlier murders by Ian Brady and Myra Hindley were widely reported and these reports reflected society's revulsion. The reactions to these kinds of killings was partly made stronger by the feeling that, as I have explained, childhood is seen as a period of innocence. The killing of vulnerable innocent children is seen as much worse than the killing of adults who are supposedly less vulnerable. In part this is because adults are assumed to have greater responsibility for their actions. However, the generalization that all adults are capable of being responsible for their actions and all children are not is a contentious one. Many adults in society repeatedly show an inability to think before they act and often regret the consequences afterwards, something to which some children are also prone.

The emotions generated by adults killing children are magnified when children kill children. The murdering child has lost his or her innocence through the act. The victim has also had his or her innocence irrevocably taken away. This clashes very strongly with our perceptions of how children should behave and how childhood should be characterized, and results in much greater shock from adults. This contrasts markedly with the response to the weekly killing of thousands of adults across the world, for example in wars, to which we can almost become desensitized.

Although child killings are rare, unfortunately they do happen. Society's concern for children means that whenever there is a child death there is usually much soul-searching. In recent years one case of children killing another child was the subject of much debate and is interesting because it reveals messages about the ways in which society views children.

In 1993 the 2-year-old James Bulger was killed by Robert Thompson and Jon Venebles. One of the most powerful images of the case was an extract of CCTV footage which was repeatedly featured in television news bulletins following the trial. In the extract two 10-year-old boys are seen holding the hand of a 2-year-old boy and leading him away from the shopping centre where he had been with his mother. It is not difficult to imagine the awful consequences for the family that such an event must have created even if it is impossible for us to understand fully the extreme emotions which were generated.

The case provoked a furore of media activity particularly once the guilty verdict was reached:

'How do you feel now you little bastards?' (*Daily Star*)

'Born to Murder' (*Today*)

'Freaks of Nature: The faces of normal boys but they had hearts of unparalleled evil. Killing James gave them a buzz' (Daily Mirror)

The first thing to say about these headlines and the *Daily Star* headline in particular is how inappropriate the vindictive tone was. Criticisms continue to grow about the standard of some sections of the British press compared with other European countries. Editors of such papers have an ethical responsibility to think carefully about the impact of the language of their newspapers. The extreme language almost incites violent reactions to the killers without due regard for the possible circumstances that may have contributed to their act. One outcome of such reporting was the fact that even when the killers had finished their sentences they had to be given new identities because it was feared that they might be killed.

Franklin and Horwath (1996) made the point that specific reporting about the two killers quickly became generalized into suggestions that all children had the dangerous potential to be 'evil'. Right wing-leaning papers such as the *Daily Mail* and *The Times* often blame the alleged freedom of the 1960s as the cause of a whole range of problems in society. Rousseau's ideas and those of others that children are inherently innocent was challenged in particular by the Editorial in *The Times* (quoted in Franklin and Horwath, 1996: 139):

Popular reaction to the behaviour of James' youthful killers has been conditioned by the belief, prevalent since the Victorian era, that childhood is a time of innocence ... But childhood has a darker side which past societies perhaps understood better than our own ... children should not be presumed to be innately good. In the lexicon of crime there is metaphysical evil, the imperfection of all mankind; there is physical evil, the suffering that humans cause each other; and there is moral evil, the choice of vice over virtue. Children are separated by necessity of age from none of these.

One of the factors that contributed to the demonization of the two killers was the lack of attention to the possible causes or explanation of what led them to carry out such an act. There were a number of factors (Franklin and Petley, 1996: 142) that, while they do not in any way amount to a reason for the killing, do need to be taken into consideration:

- Jon Venebles had been referred to a psychologist by a primary teacher because he harmed himself, including banging his head against a wall, cutting himself and hanging himself upside down on a coat peg.
- He was bullied at school.
- Robert Thompson's family lived in poverty.
- Mother and father had separated and mother drank heavily.
- The house was destroyed by fire.
- His brother was taken into care having been threatened with a knife by another brother. When he returned the brother took an overdose to pressure social services to take him back.

In addition to specific circumstances there are a number of general charact-eristics of children who kill, as Wolff and McCall Smith (2001) pointed out. Most children who kill have serious neuropsychological abnormalities; they find it difficult to control their impulses; they are failures at school which leads to truancy. All have experienced severe problems in their families such as domestic violence, abuse, drug misuse, mothers who are depressed and the absence of fathers. These factors show that we must be very careful before we start labelling all children as evil, particularly in view of the fact that many of the mitigating circumstances can be attributed to the failings of adults. It is perhaps this which is at the root of our unease about children who kill, because we all feel a deep sense of responsibility and failure.

It is easy to assume that the way in which problems are dealt with in the country you live in, is the only way. Of course this is not the case and the more experience and understanding you gain of other countries the more you see that there are many ways of addressing problems. Franklin and Petley (1996) compared the Bulger case with a child murder in Norway.

In 1994 a 5-year-old Norwegian girl was found dead in the snow near her home. The police asked parents in the area to discuss this with their children. Two days later they determined that the girl had died of hypothermia having been kicked unconscious by three 6-year-old boys. One of the boys told the police that they kicked the girl until she stopped crying. Another of the boys was upset by the events and had taken his mother to the place where the girl was lying but she was already dead. The age of the children meant that further investigation was carried out by health and welfare authorities rather than the police. The sensational and vengeful tone of the British press was not a feature of the Norwegian press who took care not to prejudice the views of witnesses. They also reported an extraordinarily compassionate attitude by the parents concerned. The mother of the dead girl was reported as saying

> 'I FORGIVE THEM. I forgive those who killed my daughter. It is not possible to hate small children. They do not understand the consequences of what they have done ... I can sympathise with the boys' parents. They must be going through a lot now. I do not know all of them yet, but they are welcome to contact me if they so wish.' (Franklin and Petley, 1996: 150)

Norway's track record on human rights resulted in a much more compassionate and thoughtful response to such a dreadful event. Of course it also needs to be born in mind that the two killings are not identical. In particular the ages of the children could be regarded as significant. The law in the United Kingdom places importance on the child's ability to understand that what they did was wrong. The quote above from the Norwegian mother indicates that the children who killed the girl may not have properly understood their actions.

The consequences of British society's response to the Bulger trial as portrayed in the media were serious. The Home Secretary of the day intervened in the case and ensured that Venebles and Thompson were given much harsher sentences than would normally have been the case. Because of this, lawyers representing the boys appealed to the European Court of Human Rights. The judgement found that because of the context of an adult court complete with hostile crowds and press, the boys had been intimidated, which resulted in them not understanding the implications of the court process as well as they might have. It was also found that the Home Secretary had breached human rights law because he had intervened in a way that was unfair, since sentencing decisions should be made by judges who are independent and not subject to political pressures to the same extent. Wolff and McCall Smith (2001) argued that children should be treated differently from adults in the courts. They gave evidence which showed that adolescents who had committed murder had a better chance of rehabilitation than adults partly because they were still developing. They also argued that the age of criminal responsibility should be raised from 10 to 12 or 14, which is something that was also recommended by the European Court judgement.

Summary box

- The Bulger case illustrates the way that childhood is a construct and one that continues to change, sometimes for the worse.
- If we accept that childhood is a construct then we need to challenge our preconceptions of childhood if we are to interact with children positively and productively.

Legal issues

The Factory Acts of the nineteenth century were motivated by a desire to improve children's working conditions and to ensure that they received a basic education. The motivation of the reformers came through a sense of altruism which had been prompted by the poor conditions in which children worked and lived. There was an understanding that children had the right to safe and healthy lives and that they also had the right to an education. Since that time there have been many significant Education Acts. However, in recent times educational legislation has been more strongly driven by the questionable idea that there is a direct correlation between educational standards and national economic prosperity rather than a concern for children's rights.

British educational legislation does not give rights to children, but to the parents who have to ensure that their children attend school and to local education authorities who have to provide schooling. There is no practical way for children to enforce their rights to education although the courts have been used to try to argue that children with special educational needs have not been given an adequate education by local education authorities. However, legislation in Scotland, the Standards in Scotland's Schools, Etc. Act 2000, offered an important step forward in the battle for children's rights. For the first time children have a right in national law to be consulted on their education.

Of greater significance arguably is section 2(2) which provides that:

> In carrying out their duty under this section, an education authority shall have due regard, so far as is reasonably practicable, to the views (if there is a wish to express them) of the child or young person in

decisions that significantly affect that child or young person, taking account of the child or young person's age and maturity.

Although this section is open to widely divergent interpretations ... and is highly qualified in its terms ... it remains true that the imposition of a duty on education authorities to consult children and young persons over educational decisions of any sort – with its correlative right in the child or young person to be consulted – is unique in education legislation within the UK. (Meredith, 2001: 5)

It is not only Scotland that has made positive changes to its legislation. The devolved powers for the countries of the United Kingdom have increasingly led to the education systems developing in different ways. Northern Ireland has proposed a national curriculum that is radically different from the curriculum in England; the inspection system has undergone reform in Wales; statutory testing processes in Scotland do not include league tables and the system allows children to be tested when they are ready, not at a set time in the year.

Further afield, Norway has led the world in its record on rights. It was the first, in 1981, to establish an ombudsman for children. Flekkøy (1995: 182; my italics) argued that the ombudsman achieved some notable gains for children and their rights:

- legislation prohibiting physical punishment and physical and psychological treatment threatening the physical or psychological development of children, a prohibition which *includes* parents;
- raising the age at which young people can be tried and sentenced by adult courts and imprisoned in adult prisons;
- the establishment of national, governmental guidelines to incorporate the needs of children into all urban and rural planning considerations.

Hague's (1998) analysis of the role suggested that the ombudsman had also had considerable impact on the process of school reform. Equality, participation, appropriate environment and the need to take account of children's interests have all been enhanced by the work of the ombudsman.

Another source of legal evidence is an international one which was made possible by the establishment of the UN Convention on the Rights of the Child (CRC). On the 2nd of September 1990 the CRC became part of international law. It is instructive to examine the United Kingdom's progress with what was a radical and internationally popular treaty.

The UN Convention on the Rights of the Child

The United Kingdom like other countries was required to submit a report to the UN Committee on the Rights of the Child, on the progress of implementation of the CRC after two years. It is interesting to examine some of the recommendations of the UN. The concluding observations of the committee were initiated with some positive comments. For example there was praise for the 'working together' initiative. This came from the Children Act 1989 which encouraged multi-professional and inter-disciplinary approaches to child welfare. The committee also took note of the government's intention to extend the provision of pre-school education.

The committee had fifteen areas of concern in relation to the report submitted by the United Kingdom. First on this list was their worry that the United Kingdom registered six reservations about the UN Convention. The committee considered that the most serious of these was the reservation that the United Kingdom might not apply the Convention in the case of refugees. The committee felt that this breached articles 2, 3, 9 and 10 on non-discrimination, the best interests of the child, separation from parents, and family re-unification. The second concern registered by the committee was the lack of an independent means to co-ordinate and monitor the implementation of children's rights. It was in the light of this problem that the Children's Rights Development Unit (CRDU) produced their *UK Agenda for Children* in 1994 which was an analysis of the extent to which law, policy and practice in the United Kingdom complied with the principles and standards contained in the Convention. The CRDU consulted more than 180 voluntary, statutory and/or professional organizations who worked with children and held 40 consultation sessions with children and young people throughout the United Kingdom. The introduction to the Agenda provides a stark contrast to the rosy picture portrayed by the United Kingdom report to the UN.

> The UK's initial report to the UN Committee illustrates not progress but complacency. It is dishonest by omission, highlighting particular laws and statistics that indicate compliance, without adequate recognition of gaps, inconsistencies and blatant breaches.

This situation underlines the importance of pushing for meaningful involvement of children in political processes. The United Kingdom government felt a political necessity to present a report that showed their progress in a positive light. However, if British society was structured to give children greater political rights this would include a contribution to such reports perhaps resulting in a less biased picture. The Agenda is divided into fourteen reports, covering personal freedoms, care of children, physical and personal integrity, an adequate standard of living, health and health care services, environment, education, play and leisure, youth justice, child labour, immigration and nationality, children and violent conflict in Northern Ireland, abduction, and international obligations to promote children's rights.

The first question that 'an adequate standard of living' deals with is 'does poverty exist?' The answer to the question is not so obviously self-evident, as most governments tend to downplay the existence of poverty. Questions of finance get to the nub of the political agenda and as such are fought strongly by governments. For example, whereas to much of the population the payment of very high wages to significant segments of society is obscene and represents an indication of inequality, governments tend to argue that a lack of incentive to earn large sums of money would have a number of negative consequences. In the context of strong resistance by government it is difficult to argue that a) poverty does exist and b) children are suffering. Statistical claims and counter-claims are often used to frustrate positive action. CRDU suggested that the two best definitions of poverty include the level of income support, or to define the poverty line as 50 per cent of average full-time income after housing costs, widely used in many European countries. In the European Community between 1957 and 1985 the United Kingdom had the largest increase in the incidence of poverty where the percentage of children living in poverty had increased from 9 per cent in 1980 to 18 per cent in 1985. Government figures published in July 1993 revealed there were 13.5 million people including 3.9 million children living in poverty; one in three of all children. Small gains have since been made in reducing poverty but the picture is still bleak.

Article 31 of the UN CRC safeguards children's rights to play and leisure. However 'an adequate standard of living' indicates that poverty interferes with that basic right. In modern British society the expectations on parents go far beyond the basics necessary for survival, (although this is not to minimize the importance of the fact that thousands of children do not have these basics) parents are expected to provide a range of toys, outings, holidays, etc. Poverty restricts the parents' ability to provide the increasing range of experiences that are deemed necessary.

The following quote from the CRDU (1994: 87) gives some idea of the seriousness of poverty and its implication for children's rights:

A survey of poor families in the North East of England concludes: 'The picture that emerges ... is one of constant restriction in almost every aspect of people's activities … The lives of these families and perhaps most seriously the lives of children within them, are marked by the unrelieved struggle to manage with dreary diets and drab clothing. They also suffer what amounts to cultural imprisonment in their homes in our society in which getting out with money to spend on recreation and leisure is normal at every other income level.

More recent work by the UN committee concentrated on some of the dependent territories not covered in the first report from the United Kingdom. These reports are of interest because they point towards problems that still exist on the mainland. The UN Committee on the Rights of the Child (2000a) generated issues still to be addressed by the United Kingdom government.

> 6. Please provide information on the measures taken and/or envisaged to ensure that the principles and provisions of the Convention on the Rights of the Child are disseminated at all levels of society. Additionally, please indicate whether training on children's rights has been provided for professionals working with and for children.

> 10. Please provide updated information on the ways the principle of 'respect for the views of the child' (art. 12) is reflected in legislation or actions undertaken by social welfare institutions, courts of law and administrative authorities. Please also provide some examples of implementation of this principle by courts and/or administrative bodies at both central and local levels.

> 18. Please also indicate whether human rights, including the rights of the child, have been incorporated into the school curricula, and training made available for school managers, administrators and teachers on the principles and provisions of the Convention on the Rights of the Child. In this context, please also indicate whether a complaints procedure has been established within the school system for students whose rights have been violated. Additionally, please indicate whether there is a concern with respect to violence in school.

Following the response from government the final conclusions of the committee recommended that greater effort be made to ensure that adults and children were aware of the Convention; in particular there was a need for professionals to receive training in this area. Analysis of the Bulger case above illustrated serious problems with the legal system in relation to children's rights, something which the UN Committee on the Rights of the Child (2000b) also picked up:

> 18. The Committee notes with concern that the Children and Young Persons Bill proposes to abolish the presumption that children between the ages of 10 and 14 years are *doli incapax* (incapable of committing a criminal offence), which means that legally the minimum age of full criminal responsibility is lowered from 14 to 10 years. The Committee expresses concern regarding the low legal age for criminal responsibility in the Isle of Man (10 years). Additionally, the Committee is concerned that the law does not adequately provide for the special protection and care of children who have attained the age of 17 years.

The evidence from the UN committee suggested that there were still many areas that had to be improved if children were to achieve the rights given to them in the CRC. Participation rights, including the necessity to be informed about the Convention are key to future development. Evaluating the extent and nature of children's participation is difficult. Ochaíta and Espinosa (1997: 294) did some work in this area, concluding that 'new studies are needed which would analyse, quantitatively and qualitatively, the actual participation of European children and adolescents in their families and schools'. There have been a significant number of quantitative studies attempting to address children's participation including the work of Alderson (1999).

Summary box

- There is much that the United Kingdom can learn from other countries such as Norway in order to improve children's access to rights.
- The lack of knowledge of the UN Convention on the Rights of the Child by teachers and their pupils is very worrying. It is difficult to uphold your rights if you have no knowledge of what they are.

School councils

The use of school councils is fairly well established in secondary schools in England but less so in primary schools. Alderson (2000) suggested that the numbers of school councils in the United Kingdom may be higher than the previous literature suggested but recognized that her survey may have included a high percentage of unusually 'enthusiastic' schools in what was a low response rate. Alderson also made the important point that 'only councils provide a formal, democratic, transparent, accountable, whole-school policy forum' (124). My own research was the first published qualitative work to examine children's participation in English schools, focusing on two primary and two secondary schools. Greater detail about this work can be found in Wyse (2001), but here I wish to focus on the roles school councils played in the lives of the secondary pupils. The two primary schools in my research did not have school councils; the two secondary schools did. (Names of schools and pupils used below are fictitious.)

At Graysham Secondary School the children agreed that a school council was a good idea 'if it worked, but it wouldn't always work'. The use of the future tense here was interesting in view of the fact that I had been told that the council was still operational. It was also explained that the process of gathering information from the form representatives was inadequate, 'we're put on the spot, we don't get time to think about what we're going to say or make notes, we just get told'. The head girl at Graysham articulated with clarity some of the reasons for the school council not being effective. She felt that although it had not been deliberately disbanded it had been neglected. One obstacle to the effective working was that 'they [the teachers] need to listen to what people say, they have our views but they don't listen to them'. It was agreed that the fact that the council secured some lockers was a good thing but relatively unimportant. There was a perception that most issues raised by the school council members resulted in a lack of action combined with a lack of communication over the reasons for it.

In addition to the school councils both secondary schools also had a prefect system with a head boy and girl. As it became clear that the children thought the schools councils were not working I wondered if the head boy and girl might offer a useful means of communicating the children's wishes.

> **Researcher:** 'Do you think the head boy and girl, because they're pupils the same as you, do you think they could be useful for you in helping to express your views, is that how it might work?'

> **Child:** 'We used to … when we used to go to him every week, he used to write everything down and give it to Mr Norden and Mr Norden passed it on to Mr Coole but he never does anything like that, the only thing he's done is lockers, which everyone knew we were getting anyway.'

> **Researcher:** 'So if you don't feel that the head boy and girl can help you, what's the answer then, because they're like the teachers aren't they, if

they can't be advocates for you – do you know what an advocate is? Someone who speaks on your behalf, somebody that takes your side of the argument and puts it forward to someone else.'

Child: 'I don't think it's really their fault, I think it's Mr Norden, he doesn't do anything about it.'

Child: 'We were asking about our class ... we wanted to change it but he hasn't got back to us.'

The children's difficulties with the participation systems could in part be attributed to the theories of the headteachers. At Graysham any notion that the boundaries between child and adult might be problematic were clinically dispatched: 'Children are children: adults are adults. Children are different ... We love the children in a way but we are in control. As they get older they get more responsibility. They have rights and responsibilities.' The headteacher at Railton Secondary School also conceptualized rights with their corresponding responsibilities and like the headteacher at Graysham emphasized the responsibilities. In an interview he felt that rights on their own could cause confrontation and felt that in the recent past the pendulum had swung too far in favour of rights:

'A right is an idea which has to be balanced; counterweights – I am in the middle ground ... Ideally there should be an audit of what happens but schools have been asked to do colossal amounts – almost like everything the Church used to do schools now have to do. We are not as cohesive as we used to be. This rights thing does not bring about citizenship. Nobody should use the term "right" until the next [this] millennium'.

Meaningful participation is clearly difficult if you are not sufficiently aware of your rights. The requirement to inform children and adults about the CRC itself (article 42) was not being adopted in the schools that participated in the research. On completion of the data collection the headteacher from one of the primary schools was the only person from all the children and teachers we met who was aware of the Convention. However, when asked to define what rights were, most of the children articulated significant principles:

what children think they should do;
what children want;
people should ask children what they want;

adults should ask instead of adults getting their own way;
have the responsibility to go where the mums don't want them to go;
save children on their own.

The issues such as the potential conflict between children's rights and adults' responsibilities; differentiating between mothers' and children's rights; and an undue emphasis on protection rights came through in the children's statements. An assembly at one of the primary schools illustrated how discussion of rights could emphasize protection of children. During the assembly the headteacher reminded the children that they had talked about rights in the past by referring to the 'stranger danger' work that they had done.

As part of her dissertation for a degree in childhood studies an undergraduate Williams (2002) extended an aspect of the work described above by investigating the work of two school councils, one a primary school and the other a secondary school. St Matthew's Primary School is based in the middle of a small semi-rural village, with one hundred and fifty-five children in the school and thirty in the pre-school nursery. It is in a predominately white, working class area. Woodland High School, with about six hundred pupils, also has predominantly white working class pupils and is located in a semi-rural traditional farming area where over half the children use school buses. The participants were all school council members voted for by their peers, eight St Matthew's pupils taken from Year 3 to 6 and ten Woodland High School pupils taken from Year 7 and 8. Two school council meetings were attended in each school and during this time Williams wrote field notes to record the conversations that took place. A semi-structured interview schedule was used to record the meetings that Williams held with the pupils after the school council meetings. Another schedule was used to record the interviews with the headteacher of the primary school and the senior teacher from the high school who co-ordinated the school council meetings. Although this was a small scale study some significant issues arose which need to be investigated further.

The pupils welcomed the opportunity for greater involvement in the running of their schools. There was considerable optimism that things could be changed. For example, in one of the schools a water fountain was requested and this was duly installed. However, both councils were in the early stages of development and the optimism may partly have been a product of the novelty of the experience. Both councils suffered from a lack of systematic organization. The meetings did not appear to have as high a priority so tended to be postponed at short notice. The reasons for this included impending OFSTED inspections or even simply that staff were too busy. Systems were not in place to encourage the council members to gather formally the opinions of their peers and this resulted in them tending to rely on their own. For example they did not have any documentation with them at the time of the meetings. Issues of power and control are always interesting as part of democratic processes: the headteacher at St Matthew's Primary School chaired the meetings and also set part of the agenda; pupil council members had some responsibility for behaviour management during lunch breaks.

> **Arran:** 'We have some problems controlling some boys' behaviour at lunchtime. The behaviour has improved slightly over the last few weeks because one of the teachers has intervened.'
>
> **Brian:** 'Some children are still running around the classroom, and it's not safe.'
>
> **Headteacher:** 'It's not safe for children to run around. They need to be aware of health and safety, and others. As school council members you need to push on other children to control behaviour. Any problems the school council must report to the teachers.'
>
> **Rebecca and Terry:** 'When the teacher asks the class to put away the equipment there is some people who don't help.'
>
> **Gemma and Terry:** 'The same in our class, some people don't help putting the items away at the end of class.'
>
> **Brian:** 'The turn-taking of the playstation could cause problems.'
>
> **Headteacher:** 'In the warmer weather we need playground patrol by pupils as there is more area with the field being used.'
>
> **Brian:** 'Yes, we tell teacher and the dinner ladies if we see something that's not allowed.'
>
> **Headteacher:** 'I'll be meeting the dinner ladies tomorrow to see if the system of patrolling is working. Do you think it's working?'
>
> **Rebecca:** 'Mostly working.'
>
> **Brian:** 'Not many people know about the patrol.'
>
> **Milly:** 'Need to remind every one [all the children] about the playtime rules, they don't listen to the patrol by Year sixes.'
>
> **Brian:** 'We need to stop children and make children aware of the patrol duties and remind them of the rules.'

Whether the use of council members for these duties supported their rights or not is one of the key questions. The headteacher saw this as a positive initiative because the children were 'taking responsibility for their own lunch time.' However, it is necessary to ask what the real benefits were for the children. It is possible to argue that a structure designed to be democratic has been subverted in order to use the children as unpaid helpers. There is a tradition in primary schools of Year 6 children being given various practical tasks to support the running of the school but this is quite different from the behaviour management roles that the children are being asked to take on. Another question is to what extent the children were properly informed about the initiative and genuinely consulted on whether they would like to take part. Will there be an evaluation by the children not just about the effectiveness of the scheme from the teachers' point of view but its benefit to the school council members and the children in the school generally? The difficulties of power and status is apparent in the following exchange which came after the headteacher had been trying to improve 'door duty'.

> **Milly and Arran:** 'We've had enough of the school council.'
> **Headteacher:** 'Can you stick with it 'till after Easter? What is the reason that you don't want to continue?'
> **Milly:** 'I'm missing my friends at lunch time.'

Arran looked disheartened, but decided to stay, possibly because of the headteacher's comment and the fact that all the other children were looking at him.

Both school councils were in the early stages of development and sometimes this leads to children offering fairly safe requests about school resources, such as equipment at playtime. Unless the adults who are supporting the children encourage them to combine straightforward issues with more complex ones, children may lose interest. In contrast to Williams' findings the school council website (School Councils UK, 2002) gives examples where children have had significantly more responsibility, but these schools are very much in the minority:

In Colby County Primary School, Norwich, the children:

- have been asked by the local education authority to help in training pupils from other schools on an in-service training day;
- run their own school bank, have set up a tuck shop and are responsible for dealing with suppliers;
- have been involved in evaluating lessons.

In Grove Junior School, Essex, the children:

- have been involved in selecting teachers;

- will be involved in making the new school development plan;
- are responsible for the organization of fundraising, in particular they support a child in Nepal and are responsible for making sure that enough money is raised.

This chapter has analysed children's rights in three ways: how society defines children and childhood; the legal issues; and the extent to which rights are manifest in schools. This analysis has shown the difficulties that the United Kingdom faces. However, one of the more positive developments in England was the appointment of a Minister for Children in 2000, and the establishment of the Children and Young People's Unit. This unit sent out for consultation a strategy for children and young people. This strategy includes some welcome principles (2002: 3-4):

The Government believes that all policies and services for children and young people should be centred on the needs of the young person. (The best interests of the child or young person should be paramount, taking into account their wishes and feelings.)

- high quality;
- family oriented;
- equitable and non-discriminatory;
- inclusive;
- empowering.

Children and young people should have opportunities to play an effective role in the design and delivery of policies and services

- Results oriented and evidence based
- Coherent in design and delivery
- Supportive and respectful
- Community enhancing

This strategy will provide a challenge for the education system because historically England has a poor record in involving children in meaningful ways. The child-centred education movement is one example of an attempt by some educators to engage children's interests through the structure of the curriculum. However even this limited form of participatory education was systematically and repeatedly attacked by educational policy-makers in the last ten years of the twentieth century. The growth of school councils does provide a very promising twenty-first century mechanism to involve children in their education but more research is needed to suggest how such councils can work effectively in their best interests. As a basic starting point every school in the country should have a pupil council.

Summary box

- Participation by children is required by international law but is not a feature of most schools. This urgently needs to change.
- Government should raise expectations that all schools should have pupil councils and that schools should take steps to evaluate their effectiveness.

Task

(1) Reflect on your own schooling, then talk to one of your peers about any examples of participation.

(2) Locate the Save the Children website (http://www.savethechildren. org.uk/) and read about some of the recent developments in support of children's rights.

(3) Attend a series of school council meetings and think about the way that decisions are made. Use a list of issues in this chapter to explore the council's effectiveness.

(4) Discuss with groups of children their knowledge about the UN Convention on the Rights of the Child. If they are unaware, offer them information and discuss their response.

Indicative reading

Children and Young People's Unit (CYPU) (2002) *Young People and Politics: a report on the YVote/YNot? Project by the Children and Young People's Unit.* London: CYPU. The full report enables you to check the methodology of the survey which is reported on the CYPU website. Does not include reference to children under 14.

Ochaíta, E. and Espinosa, A. (1997) "Children's participation in family and school life: a psychological and developmental approach", *The International Journal of Children's Rights*, 5: 279-97. Persuasively argues that proper use of child development research to inform practice can lead to better participation from children.

UN Committee on the Rights of the Child (2000a) *List of Issues (Isle of Man): United Kingdom of Great Britain and Northern Ireland. 26/06/2000.* Geneva: Office of the United Nations High Commissioner for Human Rights. Available from http://www.unhchr.ch/data.htm (accessed 9th July 2002). This is a list of issues in connection with the consideration of the initial report of the United Kingdom.

UN Committee on the Rights of the Child (2000b) *Concluding Observations of the Committee on the Rights of the Child (Isle of Man): United Kingdom of Great Britain and Northern Ireland. 16/10/2000.* Geneva: Office of the United Nations High Commissioner for Human Rights. Available from http://www.unhchr.ch/data.htm (accessed 9th July 2002).

Wyse, D. (ed.) (Forthcoming 2003) *An Introduction to Childhood Studies.* London: Blackwell. Many of the issues in this chapter revolve around an understanding of children's lives as a whole not just in relation to education. This book gives a readable introduction to many more childhood issues.

Chapter 7

The School Curriculum

Keith Crawford

THE purpose of this chapter is to provide an analytical narrative which explores the major issues, themes and problems associated with the development of the school curriculum in the period 1976 to 2000. This timeframe has been selected because during this period the school curriculum experienced radical and permanent changes which have exerted a profound effect on what pupils are taught, how they are taught and their knowledge and understanding assessed. The chapter is divided into three sections. The first section describes and discusses curriculum developments in the period 1976 to 1986, the second focuses upon the development of the National Curriculum in the period 1986 to 1997 and the third explores New Labour's approaches to the school curriculum.

1976-86: re-constructing the curriculum

One of the myths formed concerning the construction of the national curriculum is that it represented a revolutionary and original change of direction by a radical Conservative Party determined to reverse generations of failure and declining standards. The truth is different. The 1988 National Curriculum was the culmination of a decade and more of curriculum policy-making. The origins of the 1988 National Curriculum can be traced back to the mid-1970s and to what has become known as The Great Debate initiated by the Labour government of Prime Minister James Callaghan. Black Paper criticisms of education were significant in shaping populist views of education, schools and teachers (Knight, 1990). Black Papers' writers targeted what they saw as the dangers of an education system which they claimed was in the hands of politicized experts, and a decline in basic skills, self-discipline and moral values. Black Papers introduced the concept of a 'crisis' in education into populist discourse (Cox and Dyson, 1969a), identifying three targets. The first claimed a decline in educational standards and attacked comprehensive education (Cox and Dyson, 1969b). The second was on militant and subversive teachers. In teaching curriculum courses focusing upon equal opportunities, social education and multi-cultural education, some teachers were accused of promoting social disorder leading to a loss of authority and a challenge to the state's legitimacy and power (Cox and Dyson, 1969b; Cox and Boyson, 1977). The third target was social indiscipline. Juvenile crime, vandalism and ill-discipline were blamed upon 'progressive' educational practices said to be damaging children's life chances (Cox and Dyson, 1969a; 1969b).

Newspaper headlines such as 'The Wild Men of the Classroom' (*The Times*, 10th October, 1976: 6); 'Political Fanatics' (*The Daily Mail*, 10th November, 1976: 2) and 'Please Sir, Don't Be Trendy' (*The Daily Mirror*, 7th February, 1975: 7) fuelled popular disquiet. Accusations were made that 'literacy in Britain is marching backwards' (*The Daily Mirror*, 7th February, 1975: 7). Parents were said to be '... increasingly frustrated by the lack of discipline and low standards of State schools' (*The Daily Mail*, 18th January, 1975: 4).

Educational experts were subjected to what Ball (1990: 18) called a discourse of derision which:

acted to debunk and displace not only specific words and meanings – progressivism and comprehensivism, for example – but also the speakers of those words, those 'experts', 'specialists' and 'professionals' referred to as the 'educational establishment'.

The following passage from the second Black Paper (Cox and Dyson, 1969b: 15) offers a potent example of a discourse of crisis.

In this Black Paper, we again suggest that if informed, civilised, mature and well-balanced citizens are wanted for the future, we must scrutinise most carefully those educationalists who teach hatred of authority and contempt of tradition; who nurture ignorance and self-indulgence as a point of principle; and who disregard the claims or indeed the realities of the social world ... The Black Paper has encouraged parents, teachers, MPs to speak out on the present day abuses in education. There are many signs that the trend is now back to more balanced and tried views, the best of old methods and new. We believe that everyone who agrees with this has a duty to fight for education, and that Parliament has particular responsibilities in the coming year.

Black Paper writers offered commonsense remedies for the renaissance of educational, social and moral integrity. What was required was that schools and teachers should function within clear guidelines, with constraints and controls shaped by agencies and groups outside the secretive and uncommunicative world of the educational professional; that there should be educational aims and objectives which rejected an egalitarian focus and embraced traditional, academic conceptions of teaching and learning, and educational competition and choice essential to learning as it was to economic growth, firmer controls and accountability (Cox and Dyson, 1969a; 1969b; 1970).

The growth of a populist critique of education posed acute problems for the Labour government which had taken office in 1974. A populist groundswell of opinion created a climate of crisis which no government interested in retaining power could afford to ignore. To counter accusations of incompetence and complacency Callaghan's Labour government found itself compelled into a response to the Black Paper critique, but the Labour Party had lost the initiative and the government's response could do little but colonize the territory of right-wing criticism.

Callaghan's response was to request DES civil servants to produce a memorandum which covered literacy and numeracy, secondary education, the examination system and the problems of 16 to 19 year-olds who would not enter higher education and who did not have the skills thought necessary for employment. The so-called 'Yellow Book' (DES, 1976) was presented to Callaghan in July 1976.

On 18th October 1976, Callaghan re-stated the Yellow Book's themes at Ruskin College, Oxford. Two themes dominated the Ruskin speech: first, the need to re-define educational objectives around improved standards, basic skills and the needs of the economy; second, the intention to widen the scope of educational debate beyond the professional educator to include the consumer, parents and employers (Donoughue, 1987; *Times Educational Supplement*, 15th October 1976; 22nd October 1976;).

The Ruskin speech was a prelude to the Great Debate, a series of regional invitation conferences chaired by ministers and DES civil servants during which the invited audience of educationalists, employers and other interested parties discussed the issues identified in Callaghan's speech. The Great Debate was followed by the publication of a Green Paper (DES, 1977). Central in the Green Paper's discourse was the claim that the curriculum was not matched to life in a modern industrial society and did not reflect Britain's industrial needs: By 1981 Britain's economic base, locked into heavy industries such as coal, iron and steel and ship building, had shrunk considerably (Gilmour, 1992). Mass unemployment, rising to over 3,000,000, 11.3 per cent of the total work force, was the fundamental political issue in 1981. Nearly 50 per cent of the labour force under 18 were unemployed; it was projected that by 1982 nearly 800,000 under 18 year-olds would be without work.

Curriculum documents reflected this context. The DES (1980: 59-60) published a framework for the school curriculum, seeking agreement between government, employers, parents and teachers on curriculum content, and emphasizing the need for traditional teaching methods. This framework also claimed that 'a good deal of support has been found for the idea of identifying a "core" or essential part of the curriculum which should be followed by all pupils according to their ability' and was followed the year after by a second document on the curriculum (DES, 1981).

Two further important documents were written during the mid-1980s, first in an HMI (DES, 1985) document and second in a White Paper, *Better Schools* (DES, 1985). Both bore the hallmark of continuity in curriculum aims set out in the consultative document (DES, 1977) and in terms of providing the basis of what was to constitute a national curriculum framework. The HMI document recognized that British society in the mid-1980s was in a state of flux, 'teachers and pupils in all schools live in a society in which many of the moral reference points are now less clear or less widely agreed' (para. 64). British society was multi-cultural, a society in which ethnic minority pupils 'should be helped to enter into a British society which recognizes, respects and draws upon their own culture and traditions within a context which emphasizes that which is common to and shared by all'.

The HMI document also argued that 'that which is taught should be worth knowing, comprehensible, capable of sustaining pupils' interest and be useful to them at their particular stage of development and in the future' (para. 92). A balanced curriculum was required, one that gave each curriculum area appropriate time. This meant ensuring, for example, the avoidance of 'an undue emphasis on the mechanical aspects of language or mathematics, or in writing ... given over to note-taking or summarising' (para. 112). It also argued that there were some 'essential issues which are not necessarily contained in subjects, but which need to be included in the curriculum. Whatever the arrangements for cross-curricular issues, they should not be left to chance or to individual initiatives' (para. 26). Paragraph 27 listed environmental education, health education, information technology, political education and 'education in economic understanding' as being important 'in helping pupils come to understand the economic system and the general factors which influence it, some of them contentious' (para. 27).

This framework was endorsed in the White Paper (DES, 1985). This was a key document because it represented a synthesis of government's views on education which had developed from 1977. The White Paper argued that education was a national concern, a public service and an investment in the nation's future. What was required was a curriculum framework which reflected the demands of a changing society and a modern capitalist economy:

> economic, social and demographic trends have profoundly altered the circumstances under which schools have to do their work. Britain's place in the world has changed and our membership of the European Community is increasingly influencing our society and our economic opportunities. British society has become more complex and diverse; values and institutions are increasingly called into question; the pace of technological change has quickened; and unemployment has added to the pressures of a daily life which has become more precarious and sometimes turbulent. (para. 2)

There was included a focus upon literacy and numeracy, the centrality of religion and morality, the importance of national culture and a call for a nationally agreed curriculum framework. Standards appropriate to 'protect the nation's prosperity' were strongly emphasized. The White Paper claimed that there should be 'substantial emphasises' on 'competence in language and maths' together with an understanding of 'the nature and values of British society' [which were not defined] and 'moral education' (para. 61).

Schools should provide an education designed to serve pupils and the United Kingdom's needs (para. 10). Curriculum 'clutter' had prevented the proper study of important content because of repetition and the study of outdated courses, of which science was mentioned (para. 56). There was a direct attack on a restorationist target in the claim that discrete courses in peace studies were unnecessary, because it 'unbalances the curriculum and oversimplifies the issues involved', and a strong focus on improving educational standards and criticism that expectations of pupils were 'insufficiently demanding' (para. 20).

The main emphasis in the White Paper was upon curriculum relevance, arguing in paragraph 46 (my italics) that:

> It is vital that schools should always remember that *preparation for working life* is one of their principal functions ... The economic stresses of our

time and *the pressures of international competition* make it more necessary than ever before that Britain's work force should possess the skills and attitudes, and display the understanding, the *enterprise and adaptability* that the pervasive impact of *technological advance* will increasingly demand ... The balance within the curriculum and the emphasis in teaching it now needs to alter accordingly.

Summary box

- Debates about the school curriculum during the 1970s and 1980s were dominated by images of an education system in crisis characterized by claims of a decline in basic skills, self-discipline and moral values. A 'discourse of derision' (Ball, 1990) targeted the practices of the teaching profession which was said to be militant and subversive. Ideologically and politically, criticisms of this kind originated from supporters of conservative educational values anxious to restore traditional approaches to curriculum, teaching and learning.
- Pressure group activity fuelled by the populist press created a political climate within which government was forced to respond to complaints that the curriculum did not reflect the demands of parents and employers nor Britain's industrial needs within a changing global technological market.
- One outcome in the period 1976-86 was increasing government involvement in contributing to the debate over what ought to be included in the curriculum, although this stopped short of direct and centrally controlled initiatives designed to take curriculum control away from local education authorities, schools and teachers.

1986-97: the National Curriculum

Kenneth Baker's arrival at the DES in 1986 marked a concerted move in the direction of centralism as a key plank of Conservative education policy. The social background at this time also played its part in the decision to legislate for a national curriculum. In the mid-1980s this included urban violence in Brixton, London, Handsworth in Birmingham, inner city deprivation, unemployment and racial tension (Marwick, 1990) all of which was vividly and emotively reported in the tabloid press promoting a feeling that once again Britain was becoming ungovernable. The impact of a long-running teachers' strike was still being felt and the education system was thought to lack purpose, direction and structure, (Morris and Griggs, 1988). The education policies of certain Labour London boroughs were popular targets. In October 1986 *The Mail on Sunday* reported that in Brent 'Race Commissars in a left-wing borough are recruiting 180 Thought Police to patrol schools for pre-judice' Baker expressed concern in a television interview and the *Daily Express* led with 'Flushing out the fanatics'. The Association of London Authorities was forced into publishing 'It's the way they tell 'em', which attacked the manner in which the press distorted anti-racist policies in some boroughs.

Baker announced the decision to legislate for a national curriculum in a television interview in late 1986 citing the variety and local determination of curriculum structures as one of its weaknesses. Six months later, the DES (1987) published a consultation document explaining and justifying the national curriculum proposals. The document listed ten subjects which it was intended would form the curriculum entitlement of all children and described the assessment procedures as being an integral feature of those subjects. This was poorly received and widely attacked as being representative of a curriculum better at home in the late nineteenth century than the late twentieth century. The continuity with earlier curriculum is striking. In the *Times Educational Supplement* (1987) it was complained that 'the 8-10 subject timetable which the discussion paper draws upon has as academic a look to it as anything Sir Robert Morant could have dreamed up'. Goodson (1988) pointed out the similarity of the 1988 National Curriculum with the 1904 Secondary Regulations.

The focus of attack by Neo-Conservatives such as the Hillgate Group, was social welfarism, the spectre of cultural relativism, particularly multi-culturalism, anti-racism, the fragmentation of a common culture and the threat of a postmodern world which, it was claimed, led to lawlessness, disorder and anarchy. Quicke (1988: 8) described how the aim of Neo-Conservative pressure groups was to use education to re-assert the cultural dominance of Conservatism 'to conquer the hearts and minds via a slow drip feed into the nation's consciousness'.

The Hillgate Group (1986: 3), claimed that the educational system was corrupt, dominated by progressive theory and practice the product of 'egali-tarian propaganda' peddled by departments of education in universities. The traditional curriculum had been rejected in favour of a 'politicized' alternative which consisted of 'artificial' or 'soft' subjects. The outcome had been a decline in educational standards as a result of attempts to undermine 'the pre-cious heritage of our culture, replacing tried and lasting subjects with spurious alternatives'. State intervention into the curriculum and closer management of professional practice was required to ensure 'the survival of knowledge and culture'. A national curriculum was needed, one which would protect and have at its heart 'the values of a traditional education' with a core of reading, writing and arithmetic and 'proven' subjects such as foreign languages, history and literature, part of the 'lore and tradition of our country'.

Other demands included an 'exacting' examination system which would 'test children's knowledge and aptitudes' and replace the 'dangerous and unjustified' GCSE, a product of 'egalitarian thinking'. Examination results should be published allowing parents the opportunity to 'choose' which school they wished their child to attend. Schools should be inspected, not by Her Majesty's Inspectors whose credibility as independent arbiters of educational standards had been 'subverted by the bureaucratic self-interest and fashionable ideology of the educational establishment', but by independent inspection teams who were subject to parliamentary accountability.

In a further publication The Hillgate Group (1987: 3) offered further justification of their nation building intentions. Without central control and state monitoring of the curriculum 'the knowledge, skill and culture upon which our society has been founded' will be 'irretrievably lost' as a consequence of the 'misguided relativism' of multi-culturalism which threatened the 'traditional values of Western societies'. The aim of the curriculum was to integrate all children, regardless of ethnic heritage, into 'the national culture' and to ensure a 'common political loyalty' (4).

The images were well established in restorationist discourse: the justification and legitimization of popular concern; parents and employers as consumers; educational standards, traditional values, basic skills, attacks upon politically motivated teachers and curriculum areas outside an academic model. This was a discourse which expressed a wide range of popular discontents and added a powerful element of popular cultural appeal. The National Curriculum was designed to play its part in a general revival of traditional conservative values.

Complaints were made that the document ignored important areas of human experience and that absent was a consideration of a focus upon the humanities, social studies and environmental studies (Haviland, 1988). Subject areas such as sociology, politics and economics, for example, were ignored. Bash and Coulby (1989) accused the National Curriculum of being academic, of avoiding curriculum relevance, political, economic and social thinking and of treating initiatives, such as TVEI, as if they had never happened. Goodson (1998) argued that in the late 1980s and the early 1990s those with curriculum power were attempting to rehabilitate, re-invent and re-constitute a traditional subject-based curriculum and to ignore the fact that curriculum projects in the 1960s were developed in response to the failures of an academic curriculum.

Johnson (1991:71) used the phrase 'an astonishing silence' to describe the claimed absence of a focus upon multi-cultural education, social studies, personal and social education, political education and cross-curricular themes within the framework for the National Curriculum, which he claimed cut out a 'whole generation of innovations'. Their 'deliberate' rejection reflected the National Curriculum's origins as a Neo-Conservative response to discredited educational practices and to a 'sense of loss' (Apple, 1993). For Johnson (1991) the National Curriculum structure was a calculated attempt to resurrect and reinforce Neo-Conservative hegemonic aims mediated through a traditional curriculum.

Hatcher and Troyna (1994) also argued that the intention of those responsible for constructing the National Curriculum was to re-assert and reinforce the dominant position of a traditional, subject-based, curriculum. In their review essay which explored Ball's (1990) post-structuralist account of policy sociology, Hatcher and Troyna were critical of Ball's claim that an 'unintended' consequence of the National Curriculum was the re-inforcement of traditional subject boundaries. On the contrary, they argued, the government's intention was 'clearly towards reinforcing subject boundaries' (165). Goodson (1989: 157) had suggested that the National Curriculum could be interpreted 'as a political statement of the victory of the forces and intentions' of the Neo-Conservative New Right. The 1988 National Curriculum was a curriculum built upon precedent and practice which ignored a decade or more of curriculum development and alternative approaches to organizing and describing the curriculum, and it was a curriculum which ignored those new initiatives which had been a response to the changing socio-economic and cultural shape of the nation.

Summary box

- This is a period when government was becoming closely involved in curriculum and when pressure group activity was at its most vociferous. It makes a move in terms of curriculum control from a local administered to a nationally administered and determined system characterized by the introduction of the ten subject National Curriculum.
- At the heart of the introduction of a National Curriculum was an attempt to ensure higher educational standards, traditional values, an emphasis upon basic skills designed to support traditional conservative values.
- Curriculum initiatives stemming from the 1970s which had focused upon Schools Council initiatives such as social studies, and humanities were marginalized in the construction of a subject-based National Curriculum as where issues to do with technical and vocational education.

1997-2000: New Labour and the National Curriculum

In the run-up to the 1997 general election the Labour Party's strategy was to narrow the gap between themselves and the Conservatives on key educational issues. Sutcliffe (1994) had written three years before the general election that:

> The year 1994 may come to be seen by educational historians as the time when the political weather changed; when six years of Tory radicalism came to an end and the Labour party, under a new leader, embraced much of the Government's agenda, promising consumer choice and talking tough on standards. A new political consensus, based on a mutual desire to woo the parent vote, seems to be emerging.

In a speech published in the *Times Educational Supplement*, 23rd June 1995, Blair stressed that many Conservative education reforms until then opposed by Labour would be supported in some form if the Labour Party came to power. He suggested that:

> While the old Left emphasised support for schools without sufficient pressure on them to succeed, and the new Right thought that the solution was pressure without support, we need both. Pressure means pupils, teachers, schools and LEAs setting targets for improvement, it means the publication of meaningful performance data, proper school inspection and teacher appraisal, rigorous pupil assessment, and intervention when schools are failing ... Support means not just proper funding, but valued teachers, professional development, extra-curricular activity, flow-through from inspections, parental and community involvement and national leadership. All are vital.

A leader in the *Times Educational Supplement* (1997: 8) suggested that while Blair might attempt to distance himself from the accusation that he was colonizing Conservative values there was little doubt that he was targeting 'light-blue Tories who might consider defecting, and Labour voters who want to know the rationale behind the emphasis on "duty" in the new Clause 4'.

If we had any doubts about the direction of Labour's education policy then Young (1997) reminded us that in September 1995 Blunkett had said: 'In general I am left-wing and radical on economic policy but conservative on social matters. This is the very reverse of the attitudes and actions of the

Labour Party throughout the eighties and early nineties.'

The Labour government developed the previous administration's view that standards of literacy needed to rise, setting targets for the year 2002. David Blunkett, then Secretary of State for Education and Employment, spelt out in the introduction to the national literacy strategy (DfEE, 1998) how the government intended to raise literacy standards – indicating that 80 per cent of 11-year-olds would be expected to reach level 4 or above in the Key Stage 2 English tests by the year 2002. This was the logical result, in the government's eyes, of the literacy task force they set up when in opposition in May, 1996. The aim of the task force, chaired by Professor Michael Barber, was to develop a strategy for 'substantially raising standards of literacy in primary schools over a five-to-ten-year period'.

The government's concerns over literacy standards at the end of Key Stage 2 led to a 'slimming down' of the content of foundation subjects at Key Stage 1 and 2. This effect could already be seen in many local education authority schools where the morning was taken up with numeracy and literacy and the afternoons were devoted to the remaining National Curriculum subjects.

The then Schools Minister Estelle Morris (*Times Educational Supplement*, 13th June, 1997) called for daily literacy and numeracy hours in every classroom, 'teachers need to learn a balance of teaching methods, including phonics, in teaching reading – and whole-class interactive methods in teaching maths'. Michael Barber (*Times Educational Supplement*, 9th May, 1997), chair of Labour's literacy task force, expressed himself convinced that the focus on literacy must be increased to combat the 'lottery' of learning how to read so that the reading standards of 11-year-olds in the United Kingdom were internationally comparable. 'We are living in a global economy and our children will all be competing in the same jobs market.'

The national literacy strategy set out a clear and precise framework for teaching literacy. The framework document (DfEE, 1998) set out teaching objectives from Reception to Year 6. The structure was laid out with graphical representation as to how the literacy hour 'is to be divided between a range of learning situations'. The work to be covered in Reception was spelled out and each school year covered with detailed advice/instruction for each term. The aim whilst clearly to improve literacy for all children was also to enable the government to reach its targets for the year 2002. Already in place were tests at Key Stage 1 and 2 and baseline assessments were introduced. The structure of the literacy hour, together with the testing and assessment procedures already in place, suggested that there was a systematic framework designed to ensure that all children would become literate – or at least meet the target of level 4 by 2002.

New Labour, new citizens?

Following a pledge to strengthen education for citizenship and the teaching of democracy in schools, it was anticipated that New Labour's promise to tackle social fragmentation through the education system would be realized. The need to address this problem had become an urgent pre-occupation of New Labour policy-makers, given public concern over the continuing breakdown of social norms and values.

The first three years of New Labour's administration were marked by constitutional radicalism. Devolution of power to Scotland, Wales and Northern Ireland, the avocation of regional assemblies, reform of the House of Lords, modernization of the monarchy, the potential of a Freedom of Information Act and a commission to investigate the possibility of electoral reform were intrinsic to the New Labour vision of citizenship.

Citizenship was seen by New labour as a concept with which they could address society's widespread disillusionment with most forms of conventional civic and political activity. In May 1998, the government ordered a comprehensive review of the school curriculum to allow more time for classes in citizenship and parenting, and the QCA were asked to consider what schools should be doing to prepare young people 'for the opportunities, responsibilities and experiences of adult life', including training in citizenship; personal, social and health education; and '... the spiritual, moral and cultural dimension' (*The Guardian*, 15th May, 1998).

The QCA (1998) published a report on citizenship with the recommendation that citizenship should be taught as a statutory entitlement for all pupils aged 5-16 from the year 2000. The tone of the document was resolute in its diagnosis and emphatic in its prescription, the sense of urgency for 'citizenship education being a vital and distinct statutory part of the curriculum'. This was justified by reference to data that had profound consequences for traditional forms of democracy in Britain. The document asserted that 'we aim at no less than a change in the political culture of this country both nationally and locally'. The teaching of citizenship and democracy was said to be of such critical importance to schools and the 'life of the nation' that 'there must be a statutory requirement on schools to ensure that it is part of the entitlement of all pupils'.

The report offered definitions of citizenship and the needs and aims of the area based upon the rejuvenation of participatory democracy through the inculcation of civic virtues. The contemporary importance of utilizing the National Curriculum for such an undertaking was asserted and implications of proceeding with, or ignoring, such a project were prominently stated. The document defined citizenship as having three strands:

- Social and moral responsibility: children learning from the very beginning self-confidence and socially and morally responsible behaviour both in and beyond the classroom, towards those in authority and towards each other. Social and moral responsibility was claimed to be a pre-condition for the other two strands and a strand which has implications for other areas and aspects of the curriculum beyond citizenship.
- Community involvement: children learning about and becoming helpfully involved in the life and concerns of their communities, including learning through community involvement and service to the community.
- Political literacy: pupils learning about making themselves effective in public life through knowledge, skills and values. The term 'public life' is used in its broadest sense to encompass knowledge of, and preparation for, conflict resolution and decision-making, whether involving issues in local, regional, national, European or international affairs.

Summary box

- New Labour's educational policy could be said to bear similarities with that of previous Conservative administrations. Curriculum policy-making was marked largely by continuity not by change.
- There was an increased emphasis in the curriculum upon the core skills of literacy and numeracy; curriculum time and content in other areas was reduced to take account of this priority.
- In response to social and political concerns regarding the alienation of young people from society citizenship education was added to the National Curriculum from September 2002 onwards.

Conclusion

This chapter has illustrated that curriculum innovation in the United Kingdom during the past twenty years has been subjected to far reaching and widespread changes. The school curriculum is essentially the knowledge system of a society incorporating its values and its dominant ideology. The curriculum is not 'our knowledge' born of a broad hegemonic consensus, rather it is a battleground in which cultural authority and the right to define what is labelled legitimate knowledge is fought over and where particular knowledge and selected organizing principles receive the official stamp of approval. Much curricular content is the outcome of compromise and will, if we choose to look hard enough, reveal signs of conflict. A crucial context for such analyses is the politics of the social movements that create the need for compromises over school knowledge and an investigation of the larger crisis in the economy, in ideology, and in authority relations, adds a structural sense to our analysis and interpretations.

The content of the curriculum is always a source of social conflict. The pedagogy that accompanies the curriculum and the allied assessment procedures are subject to analysis and comment by competing groups who invariably hold distinctly different educational and ideological visions. This should not surprise us. Curriculum as theory and practice has never been, and can never be, divorced from the ethical, economic, political, and cultural conflicts of society which impact so deeply upon curriculum construction. We cannot escape the clear implication that questions about what knowledge is of most worth and about how it should be organized and taught is problematic, contentious and very serious.

Task

(1) Read the article by Crawford (1998) in *Research Papers in Education*.

(2) Read Ross (2000) chapter ten (an excellent analysis of curriculum change in the twentieth century).

- What are the historical and political origins of the National Curriculum?

- How has political power been exercised, who has decided what the National Curriculum would contain?

- Were there disagreements over the content and structure of the National Curriculum and where did they come from?

- Why was the National Curriculum framed in terms of subjects?

Indicative reading

Apple, M. (1996) *Cultural Politics and Education*. London: OUP. Chapter two "The politics of official knowledge: does a national curriculum make sense?" This is a more challenging and discursive chapter but is well worth the effort in examining the ideology and politics of curriculum construction.

Ball, S.J. (1993a) "Education, majorism and the dead", *Curriculum Studies*, 1 (2): 195-214. A useful article about the National Curriculum. A critique of the development of the National Curriculum from a political perspective.

Graham, D. and Tytler, D. (1993) *A Lesson for Us All: the making of the national curriculum.* London: Routledge. Duncan Graham was Chief Executive of the National Curriculum Council. This is an entertaining but partial account of his time in office.

Taylor, T. (1995) "Movers and shakers: high politics and the origins of the National Curriculum", *The Curriculum Journal*, 6 (2): 161-84. This is a useful narrative which explores the development of the National Curriculum during the 1980s in terms of the interaction between powerful interest groups.

Chapter 8

The Politics of Effective Schooling

Graham Boyes and Adrian Smith

THE impetus towards the study of effective schools began with the publication of *Fifteen Thousand Hours* by Rutter *et al.* in 1979. Since then there has been a plethora of publications and ideas about what constitutes school effectiveness, who drives this forward, and indeed how to measure progress. In addition, schools have to consider other aspects such as where the drive for effectiveness originated. Was this an internal or an external pressure? Who should be involved in the search? Is this a leadership activity or are other staff involved? Does the drive for effectiveness stop with the professionals or are other people stakeholders in the process? This chapter examines some of the questions raised above and puts forward ideas for discussion.

It is vital to make clear at this point that there can be no overall policy. Schools, even within one particular phase, differ so much that each has to work out its own solution to the question. This does not give licence to headteachers to run their own course. On the contrary there must be within each school's approach some central elements common to all. Without these, the all-important aspects of inter-school comparisons could not be made. Outside inspections must take this on board to be fair and equitable to all. Equality of opportunity does not mean a 'one-size-fits all' technique. If the inspection of individuality is lost then the service as a whole loses its perspective.

The search for effectiveness

In the search for the essence of effectiveness there is one crucial aspect to consider: can schools achieve that balance between taking on board any requirements for externally driven change and the maintaining of the *status quo*? There seems to be an acceptance that school effectiveness is measured by indicators imposed from outside rather than focusing on the internal mechanisms. Proponents of the two extremes are wary of the opposing view, seeing it as some kind of betrayal of purpose. They see the end product as justifying the purpose and ignore the values held by others. If education is seen as a public service, with huge amounts of public money spent on it, then external inspection is the only way to ensure value for money and a service delivery which can be accountable, a view opposed by the self-evaluation lobby who see education as a profession which, if not entirely self-regulatory, should be at least allowed to offer indicators for success. An examination of the main aspects should produce for us some common ground which unites the strengths and beliefs of the extremes.

School improvement versus school development

While change occurs at different rates and paces, its omnipresence is now a constant feature of our lives. Attitudinal change may lag behind technological and scientific change, thus creating difficulties in reconciling old values to new circumstances (Whitaker, 1993). It is worth considering at this point the esoteric concerns of both camps. Presumably both sides are looking at the same situation but from a different perspective. In practical terms this does, however, put into focus for us the dilemma facing schools attempting to re-concile the many and varied initiatives designed to lead to school effective-ness. In other words where schools are concerned, whatever the arena for debate, they, on a daily basis, are operating in a practical manner which some-times hides loftier considerations.

Proponents of school improvement see the process as some kind of ex-ternally driven process. All the considerations as to leadership come from a national or at least a regional perception of need and direction. Change is im-posed from outside by people who by being in that position have an ability to see the whole, and, therefore, clearer picture. The aims of education are seen in terms of national requirements in a rapidly globalized world where only those nations will survive, who have an educated work force directed to those aspects which can improve the national lot.

Improvement implies that there are some kinds of measures by which the service is already judged to be lacking. The remedy for this lies in the im-posing of nationally agreed indicators which will reverse the decline of standards and bring results up to an acceptable level. Opponents of this approach claim two mains areas of contention.

- There seems to be no agreed criteria for having accepted a decline in the first place. Moreover, they maintain that even if results of international comparisons rise there is no guarantee in our rapidly changing world that these results will bring practical benefits to society.
- To follow this approach limits the purpose of education to the practical and even mundane. It fails to answer some of the fundamental problems of society and in any case does not serve the human need for an expansive and all encompassing education.

It lacks 'soul', and has at its heart some kind of methodology which does not take into account any kind of individuality.

Development is seen in terms of accepting that all is not perfect but that there is sufficient acceptable methodology in place for leadership to take a strategic view, identifying good points and those that need some development. School development has, at its core, the self-appraisal systems which seek to suggest that those in the locality know best what is right. Central to this argument is the acceptance that no institution can act totally independently and must be aware of national requirements. The control, however, of the timescale and direction lies in the hands of the people on the ground. Development suggests a less confrontational approach where changes are taken on board at a rate dependent on local perceptions and where judgments are supportive rather than imposed.

Most schools do not operate solely in one camp or the other. In practice, requirements of daily running for schools ensures that purely esoteric beliefs are over-ridden by the need to comply with providing an education service of value. Yet, the ethos by which schools operate is influenced by some movement along the continuum. Those schools aware of their philosophy should be able to marry this with the internal and external pressures and produce a move towards effectiveness which reflects genuine leadership and vision.

Managing change: the critical role of the headteacher

> Good heads are crucial to the success of schools. We need to develop strong leaders, reward them well and give them the freedom to manage, without losing accountability. (DfEE, 1998)

The key to unlocking the full potential in our schools lies in the expertise

of teachers and headteachers. Research and inspection evidence demonstrate the close correlation between the quality of teaching and the
achievement of pupils and between the quality of leadership and the
quality of teaching. (Teacher Training Agency, 1998)

The undoubted sentiment here is that leadership is crucial to school improvement. Although there was an acknowledgment of the part others had to play,
without firm and purposeful leadership there could be no progress. This was
focused on headteachers as leader and manager. Indeed, the DfEE comment
made it clear that initiatives about to be made known would develop the
headteacher's ability to manage, presumably within some sort of guidelines.

Whether improvement was engendered inside or outside school, the headteacher would be expected to implement change, or oversee others imple-
menting the change. Whichever it was the headteacher was to become the
recipient of initiatives which he or she would have to ensure were made
known to all involved and properly carried out. It is worth remembering that
this was at the time of an enormous shift in the duties and responsibilities of
headteachers. It was suddenly essential that headteachers became aware of the
distinctions between leadership and management actions. Even more acute
was the need to accept that on occasions the two are intertwined in such a
way that the action concerned falls into both areas. Headteachers had to learn
how to acclimatize themselves to the new way of working. The responsibility
for leadership and management imposed a review of working practices not
only on a daily basis but in relation to others involved in the life of the school.

School improvement during the 1990s became the responsibility of
leaders and managers. This meant that while the DfEE and Teacher Training
Agency sought to empower headteachers, it was obvious that improvement
could not come overnight, nor could it come by addressing one area of school
life alone. All aspects of running a school are linked and therefore any change
to one affects another. Careful leadership with its propensity for vision, the
long-term view, strategic planning and a somewhat daring approach to change
are needed in full measure. If an expansive foresight is the crux of leadership
then wise stewardship is the mien of management. Management's role is to
ensure that strategic policies are operated on a daily basis, accounted for and
measured. There is no opportunity for allowing the existence of any aspect
which cannot be said to lead to school improvement. This is not to say that
non-core activities should not happen. It merely indicates that *whatever*
happens should be against the background of working for school improvement. It is rather like suggesting that as the Key Stage 2 standard assessment
tests only concern English, mathematics and science there should be no other

subjects taught. Despite schools' desire to post good results no one would suggest a curriculum solely comprising these three subjects.

Leadership and management are focused on the headteacher, but are actually seen in a much wider context than the simple operation of school. As school life is made up of a myriad of actions over a year, involving a host of people with widely differing agenda it is the role of leadership to unite these in the search for improvement by fulfilling seemingly ever-expanding aspects of leadership. Krech *et al.* (1962) identified fourteen 'Functions of Leadership' – the leader as:

- executive;
- planner;
- policy-maker;
- expert;
- external group representative;
- controller of internal relations;
- purveyor of rewards and punishments;
- arbitrator and mediator;
- exemplar;
- symbol of the group;
- substitute for individual responsibility;
- ideologist;
- father figure;
- scapegoat.

Although this list was compiled some time ago, and even if others were to re-define some aspects, the central tenets still ring true. Leadership has a wide brief. Headteachers working towards improvement do at some point play all of those roles. Indeed, the National Professional Qualification for Headship (NPQH) has at its roots the need for men and women to display competencies drawn from such lists in order to fulfil *all* the necessities of headship.

Leadership's other players

While very few would deny the crucial role that headteachers play in the drive for improvement, there is nonetheless a leadership role for other people, both inside and outside the school (Figure 8.1). Leadership is invested in a variety of people who all come to the issue of improvement from differing stand-points, with a differing comprehension and level of understanding the task.

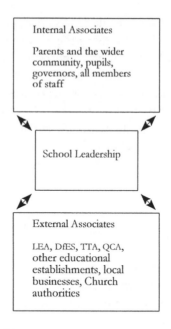

Figure 8.1:   School leadership

It must be an essential criterion of school improvement that training is given in leadership to all people at all levels. School then becomes truly a learning society by investing time, money and other resources in leadership for improvement. It also becomes incumbent on those involved that they play the leadership role; they cannot opt out. If this is part of a job description then it follows that resources will be available in some proportioned way. If those concerned act in a voluntary capacity then they must understand the niceties *before* commitment to action.

Assessment and evaluation

'Assessment' and 'evaluation' are terms which have become interchangeable in general parlance. Yet to comprehend fully their role in school improvement we must distinguish between the two to clarify their use in the process.

Assessment

The process of assessment is concerned with *measures*, mostly those which are objective and recorded. It has at the heart of the process a direct link between the planning stage and the final assessed stage. Therefore, the assessor has criteria available at his or her disposal. Assessment has built into it the expectation of success and seeks to measure how far the action has moved along the road to success. Assessment is therefore concerned with:

- objectivity;
- validity;
- reliability;
- fairness;
- success criteria;
- a knowledge of the planning cycle.

In schools assessment is used in a variety of ways. It serves the relationship between *teacher* and *pupil*, between *teaching* and *learning*, and between *planning* and *knowledge* of the success (or not) of that planning. All those connected with school have some part to play in the process, but sometimes in differing roles. Thus a pupil having a piece of work marked is part of the assessment process. The work was set to a prescribed parameter and duly assessed against those measures. This brings to the process ideas of quality. Reward or not is the result, whether this is some immediate reward of verbal praise, or a certificate of societal importance. On a wider front the leaders in a school will assess annually whether the school's budget was indeed spent on the intended targets.

Assessment allows for objective comment on the period of time covered and allows for explanation of interim changes of direction. Assessment for the most part is an element of the in-house process of school improvement. It manifests itself in the form of plans and reports, available for the most part to anyone interested. The best kind of assessment leads to future planning and is therefore vital to the improvement process. Assessment is at best capable of producing statements of success set against previously agreed criteria; but it is far from a complete process. Assessment explaining the *what*, but not the *why* and *how* is too objective and lacks interpretation and 'soul'. This is the role of evaluation.

Evaluation

Evaluation gives cultural credence to assessment and sets it in the world of justification and accountability. If schools were seen by OFSTED in terms of assessment alone no great moves to improvement would follow. It is evaluation that gives the process life and, therefore, a vitality to improve and develop genuinely. Evaluation (like assessment) *can* be summative, but may also be formative, that is, used at the beginning of a process. Indeed, if the improvement movement is seen as cyclical than the best evaluation *must* be formative as well as summative. It is only the uses to which it is put that require us to distinguish between the two. It is also worth remembering that evaluation does not happen in one go, at one time. Evaluation is carried out *formally* and *informally* in a range of ways and for a range of reasons – the end of a lesson, after a building project or following the introduction of a national initiative. What then is at the heart of evaluation? What causes evaluation to 'rise above' assessment alone and produce for schools a working tool for improvement which assessment could not? If assessment is about the measure of events and individual actions, evaluation expands the process into systems and procedures. Evaluation looks at effects and inter-relationships. It may be that work produced in classes is assessed at one level, whether that be good or bad. The improvement technique would be to ask *why* that level was achieved. This may expect to use teacher assessment but would also include some kind of statistical data, the *interpretation* of which becomes the evaluation process. Evaluation then contains the following elements:

- both objective and subjective judgment;
- the use of formal statistical data;
- a measure against a whole context;
- some kind of desire to prove the *worth* of the process.

One might ask who takes notice of evaluation. At its worst use evaluation is a process which merely records comments about some event or idea. The purpose is justification by the provider that the whole event was worthwhile, or a burgeoning desire to produce evidence that an event has taken place. The problem is that this is to deny evaluation its real value, that of informing the future and making vital judgments on the past. It would be to live in some kind of naïve world *not* to expect judgment of effort. No body, public or otherwise, could exist without judgment. A retailer of goods stays in business because that business provides goods or a service which the public need or want. Over the course of history many trades have ceased to exist, or have become viable only in a niche market, because of the changes, usually techno-logical, within society. In education there is no reason to believe that such judgments should not exist. The question that is posed most often is *who* should be the arbiters of success. With the publication of league tables, the extended coverage in the press and broadcast media, and the loosening of re-strictions on choice of school, the evaluation of individual schools is a real and living concern. The devolving of responsibilities for running schools to the local level, governors and headteachers, has only served to sharpen up the need for effective evaluation.

Creative thinking and the evaluation process

Our present systems in school require leadership from a wide variety of participants. It has been mooted that headteachers have become a manager of leaders. That is, they not only lead *per se* but utilize leadership qualities in others. This complex system of role descriptions has a drawback which is inherent in any hierarchy, that leadership may not be exerted or seen to be used. With the number of daily and long-term actions going on in schools, derived from a number of sources, it is very easy to lose track of one strand within a whole range. As presumably each single action is part of a whole to work towards improvement, it follows that the leadership and construction of each action has been thought out to good effect, with proper evaluation to follow.

Any such approach therefore requires creativity (see Figures 8.2 and 8.3), not only for that one strand, but in its fit to the whole. This creativity shows itself in two main forms:

- the ability to plan all resources for that one act, to draw them to a meaningful process, and to have planned the timetable so that the action has the right passage through the potential quagmire;
- the ability to resolve competing strands into a coherent and planned process over a given timescale which makes sense to those who are involved.

It has to be accepted that not all levels of leadership will require all aspects of creativity. The essential element is that at least *one* person has the higher level creativity. It is also true that while it would be a bonus to have more than one person with such abilities, schools can suffer from a crisis of direction if too many people exert this aspect of leadership at the same time in some kind of unco-ordinated jumble.

West-Burnham (1997) listed twelve characteristics of the creative thinker, amongst which were:

- being at ease with complexity;
- being relaxed with abstract concepts, and;
- synthesising rather than describing data.

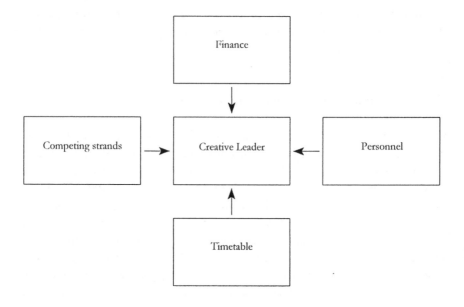

Figure 8.2:   Creativity at the single strand level

These characteristics have to be present not only in those in leadership positions but have to be built into the evaluation process. The processes shown in Figures 8.2 and 8.3 have very little meaning if the movement from planning to evaluation is not lubricated by the very characteristics in West-Burnham's list. School improvement is a living entity in that during the life of one action creative thinking must reveal itself. Each action has before it a rough road to travel. The ability of leaders to provide the action with the relevant requirements for success is the essence of creative thinking and action.

Who is school improvement for?

It would seem at first hand self-explanatory that school improvement is for the good of the school. However, that is too simplistic. Schools do not operate in a vacuum. In so many ways schools operate in a world of inter-related needs and expectations, relying on partnerships and networks. The external aspects of school improvement exert a pressure to conform to the requirements put on all schools. The need to influence the behaviour of pupils for good, the expectation of good results in examinations, and the need for the breadth of education are some examples of society's view of schools.

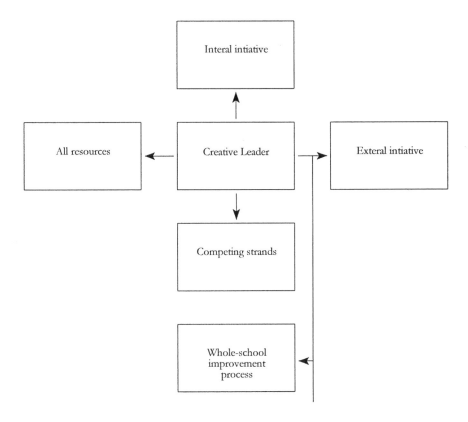

Figure 8.3: Creativity at whole-school level

Therefore, it could be claimed that school improvement is for the good of society as a whole. Indeed various politicians have expressed the opinion that an education service publicly funded has a fundamental duty to provide for society's perceived needs.

On a more introspective side the various players have some claim to benefit from improvement. Each player, whether pupil, parent or teacher, has differing needs to be satisfied. Those who school improvement serves may be seen on a continuum, beginning with the headteacher as the crucial leader and stretching outwards to some perception of society as a whole. At each stage each player takes from improvement those expectations which were the original reasons for their participation. This exemplifies yet again the need for the crucial leader to exert not only their own reasons but to bring together those of all the other players – a skill to be developed and cherished in headteachers.

All the players have some part to play in improvement and all have expectations to success, or otherwise. From headteacher to governors, these may be seen as stakeholders. That is, the health of the school is of direct concern to them. To some degree it is not always apparent to them that the health of the service as a whole actually matters. Headteachers, staff and governors want first and foremost for their school to be seen to provide an effective and efficient service. Parents and pupils see a narrower view – that of their progress. On the other hand the 'outside' players can find it difficult to reduce their view *from* the global *to* the specific. Once again then there is demonstrated the imperative for someone to tie together the different visions for school improvement. The answer to the original question then is that school improvement is for all players but each player takes from the process what he or she sees as relevant.

The case for evaluation

Evaluation is the key to school improvement. Whatever is driving improvement some appreciation of a school's worth informs future planning. All schools are expected to combine the relevant merits of both internal and external evaluation processes (Figure 8.4). The difficulty for schools is to ensure that what comes out of the evaluation process is actually *of relevance*.

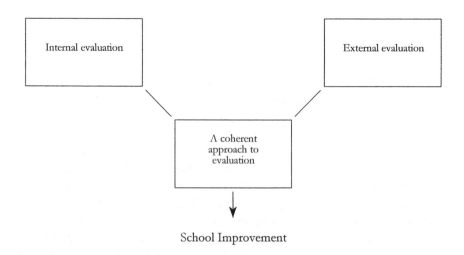

Figure 8.4:   A balanced approach to evaluation

What there is to commend internal evaluation will be discussed later. The problem is that self-evaluation can lead to self-delusion. A huge amount of statistical data is engendered, and together with other self-evaluation techniques schools can be overwhelmed with information. The development of self-delusion arises for two reasons. First, making sense year-on-year of such data is difficult. It is necessary to establish *which* data will be examined. Having done this for particular cohorts other data may be relevant. Schools therefore need to establish a two-pronged attack using data which will be used to show trends over time, and data which for a particular year had some relevance to priorities which were highlighted. In addition, schools have to be aware of the audience for this information and the agenda that audience may have. A number of audiences can be seen:

- school staff;
- governors;
- parents of the school;
- parents applying to school;
- local education authority;
- DfES;
- OFSTED;
- the community at large.

Each audience brings a different understanding of school data and takes only that data which is useful to them. Explaining and interpreting data has become part of the job description of teaching staff, whether this is to parents, governors or local education authority officers and advisers. It therefore becomes apparent that a leadership task is to ensure that the dissemination of data and other information is valid, useful and equitable.

Self-delusion can develop for another reason, that of introspection. It is all to easy to develop the idea that the school is progressing well (or otherwise) because no view is taken of external comparisons. A view which is too narrow focuses on certain issues which report well to various audiences but may in fact mask problems or indeed not address the real issues. The case therefore for internal evaluation is clear – schools know best their own status – but it does bring its attendant difficulties. The antidote to this is external evaluation.

External evaluation is carried out in a variety of ways mainly through OFSTED inspections, but there are others. The question is: what do external inspections do to balance the internal approach? More than anything external evaluation brings:

- the outside, overall perception from local education authorities or OFSTED; and
- they encourage schools to adopt a wider view.

It may be thought that these two points are in effect the same, but this would be to miss one vital factor. External evaluations are at the same time imposing an external perspective *and* developing the use of an external view by school. In other words schools are taught to 'look both ways'. The use of evaluation information *is* useful as a focused internal tool. It is also the starting point for a comparison with schools *as a whole*.

Caution must however be brought to any external evaluation. It is often seen as pure and objective, but this may not always be the case. One example of this is the statistical data published in schools' performance and assessment (PANDA) documents. While its facts are valid and true the interpretation on them is open to various agenda and therefore can be as unreliable as school generated information. The real authority in evaluation is a proper use of both methods to represent views from inside and outside the establishment.

School improvement and accountability

Much has been made of the need for public institutions to be accountable. It is claimed that an open and accessible system for all aspects of public life, not just evaluation in schools, will lead to a fair system, and therefore accountability will become 'built into' the way institutions operate. Accountability will become something taken as a right and expressed in what is done. It will no longer be something which is done to others.

Accountability has then a dual role: it is on the one hand a source of control over what schools do, on the other it is a safeguard for schools in that it sets boundaries within which schools should be expected to operate. The clear message for schools is that evaluation inevitably incorporates accountability. It is not sensible to set up ways of working which do not have as an automatic expectation of the role of evaluation, whether that is self-evaluation or acceptance of some kind of external judgment.

It is worth noting at this point that external evaluations are seen as judgmental. They can weigh heavily on the collective conscience. This is mainly due to the fact that those evaluated feel a certain lack of control over the process and its outcome. Even where the success criteria is published the parameters of external evaluations are extensive and staff feel that outcomes from beyond their control will still have an affect on them. There is no shirking the responsibility of evaluation from outside, but the process is at its best when both sides play an equal role and the process, while still judgmental, is a learning process carried out by professionals accepting not only the worth of the process but of each other. One way in which this is achieved is by working to equate the actions of internal and external evaluation. Only when adequate knowledge of both systems feeds useful information to all players can some of the fears and inadequacies of the system be eliminated.

Target-setting is seen as a valuable method of the first part of the evaluation process. After all if a school can state its aims objectively will the evaluation not be all the easier to assess? At the various phases of compulsory education there are requirements to set targets from which judgments will later be made. There is however a fundamental question to ask prior to any targets being set. What are targets? They may be seen in one of two ways:

- statements of the *status quo*; or
- statements of the intentions of the school.

They form two sides of the same facts or figures. Take, for example, attendance figures in a school. The school might be informed that its attendance figures are not as good as they might be; they are seen as lower than the national average and possibly lower than schools in the area, or schools of a similar nature. What should the school do? If it is seen to do nothing more than previously, the claim is made that it has not reacted to this piece of evaluation information. Presumably the school already has some sort of system in place for measuring and encouraging good attendance. Moreover it may work with other agencies and parents to good effect. So why should it set targets *higher* than its present position? Is it to comply with the requirements of the larger body, the local education authority, or the national average? Can the school actually have a positive change on the attendance figures by setting targets? Are there factors out of its control, which adversely affect its efforts? Setting targets alone will not improve the situation. Yet here are the two perspectives. There are so many variables affecting attendance that whatever the school does it cannot guarantee improvement. Indeed certain indisputably uncontrollable variables may occur which result in a worse attendance figure. However by setting targets there is something to aim for; the concept is fixed in the minds of all the players. This brings us to the final point about target-setting as a means to improvement. Driven from either inside or out it is impossible to maintain a year-on-year increase in figures. Education is not an exact science nor is it a production line where variables can all be eliminated. All concerned have to accept targets as *aims* not *ends*. Target-setting is often an exercise of hope and wishful thinking, at its best a method of shared expectations. Its meaning only has validity if a proper examination of the results is made and tied to realistic comments.

What should be part of the improvement process?

How do you judge the worth of a school? This will depend on the position you find yourself in. Are you a parent, prospective parent, governor, applicant for a post in school, an adviser or inspector? Many others make judgments on schools. Each category of judgment-maker has their own agenda. Some are genuine; some mischievous. In general there are several aspects which can be used to ascertain what a school is like. Evaluations can be applied to:

- the learning which takes place;
- the teaching that occurs;
- the policy for admissions;
- the financial arrangements and its tracking;
- the school's ethos and culture;
- its recruitment policy;
- its policy on liaison with parents and the community;
- its examination data;
- its pastoral systems;
- its care for, and development of, the building.

The problem is that each area has its own indicators for evaluation and so for improvement. Schools working actively towards improvement have not only to identify the areas of responsibility but also the success criteria. That all the differing perceptions of the areas for evaluation are brought together under one umbrella is a matter of good public relations.

If the *what* of improvement is generally easy to agree, it is somewhat more difficult to find a *vehicle* to express this, especially bearing in mind the differing perceptions. Most vehicles are both a simple method of publicity and a statement of that year's priorities. Often this information is expressed in:

- school/department budgets;
- school development plans;
- mission/ethos statements;
- curriculum policy documents;
- non-curricular policy documents.

Useful information can be gleaned from:

- governors agenda and minutes;
- details of staff development exercises;
- school events.

Each of these documents builds with others to produce an overall picture of how the school operates. Each category of person looking at this information brings with them certain knowledge not only about that school but schools in general. Herein lies the main problem for communication – the vehicle used has to address the needs of its audience. Without that correlation there can be no full understanding. Leadership of school improvement has therefore to ensure that this aspect is catered for and provided with status.

The who and the how of school improvement

We have seen earlier that school improvement is judged both from within and without, and at very differing levels. If we take the internal and external perspectives separately, we see that each agency has various duties to perform (see Table 8.1). Drawing on them schools can find valuable information for school improvement whether this is locally or nationally based. The true value is to ensure that this is included in the change mechanisms within school (Table 8.2). That means having a planning cycle which informs future action.

The smooth running of internal systems requires a concerted effort to orchestrate all aspects of the improvement process. It is an essential element of leadership to ensure that each strand is able to contribute to the whole. It would be folly to suggest that once having incorporated a particular strand into the process it would always be in place; each strand has to 'earn its place'.

Table 8.1:   External school improvement

Agency	Tools for improvement
LEA as a whole unit	SATs
Community	Examination results
DfES	PIPs data
Parents of potential pupils	PANDA and inspection data
OFSTED	Attendance figures
Other LEA agencies	PLASC information
Other establishments	

Table 8.2:   Internal school improvement

Internal systems (Key players)	Mechanisms (Tools)
Teaching staff	PANDA and inspection information
Support staff	Scrutiny of planning and work
Parents	Pupil assessment material
Pupils	SATS, PIPS and exam material
Governors	Lesson observations
	School target-setting
	Attendance measures
	Co-ordinator/HOD techniques
	SEN focus
	Staff development/induction issues

The mix of methods is fluid and therefore those charged with carrying out the process have to blend each input with other aspects. Leaders then have to make sense of the information which is presented. A balance of internal and external methods provides a host of information which directs the way to school improvement.

Conclusion

School improvement is a nebulous concept. Much is said about the *content* and *methods*, but to define school improvement is fraught with problems. How do you agree that a school has improved? At one point are you satisfied that a level of improvement has been achieved? By whose definition is improvement measured? Indicators are capable of differing interpretations. Those schools which are non-selective on academic grounds, for example, educate the pupils who are enrolled at that time. It is therefore very likely that examination scores will, when measured as a percentage of the pupils, rise *and* fall. This requires a longer-term view of such indicators. Even at this stage there has to be a point when the natural maximum for that school is reached. Another difficulty is that of continuance. With the amount of information available improvement indicators can swamp those charged with their interpretation. While no one would deny that the aim of working towards school improvement is important, it is vital to remember that it is a constant job to make sense of the information, and in particular that which falls outside the area of school data.

School improvement is both internal and external. It is the balance of the two that drives the impetus forward. Leadership co-ordinates the efforts and interprets the information. The real skill is being aware of *where* the school is going and *how* it is going to get there. As school improvement is illusive, it takes a cool head to stay on track when indicators do not always provide the information a school would like. Fitting school improvement into the daily events in school is a philosophical issue. It is much more than raw data and in-built systems. It is part of the ethos of school, and by that token has to be integrated into thinking and planning. On the other hand it should not be allowed to take over events and create a monster that dominates all that the school does. At best school improvement techniques add to a school's armoury of systems at their disposal, at worst it becomes a burden which adds nothing to knowledge and betterment of the school.

Summary box

- Questions concerning school improvement focus upon who should be involved. Is this merely a leadership activity or are other staff involved; does the drive for effectiveness stop with professionals or are other stakeholders involved in the process?

- Can schools achieve that balance between taking on board any requirements for externally driven change and maintaining the status? Schools face a number of dilemmas when attempting to reconcile the many and varied initiatives designed to lead to school effectiveness.

- 'The key to unlocking the full potential in our schools lies in the expertise of teachers and headteachers. Research and inspection evidence demonstrate the close correlation between the quality of teaching and the achievement of pupils and between the quality of leadership and the quality of teaching.' (Teacher Training Agency, 1998: 1)

- Leadership is invested in a variety of people who all come to the issue of improvement from differing standpoints, and with a differing comprehension and level of understanding of the task. It must be an essential criterion of school improvement that training is given in leadership to all people at all levels.

- The question that most often is posed is *who* should be the arbiters of success. With the publication of league tables, the extended coverage in the press and broadcast media, and the loosening of restrictions on choice of school, the evaluation of individual schools is a real and living concern. The devolving of responsibilities for running schools to the local level – governors and headteachers – has only served to sharpen up the need for effective evaluation.

Task

(1) The aims of school improvement are said to be to improve the quality of the school environment, teaching and learning experiences and to aid a drive towards higher professionalism and standards. However, this is a complex task involving a number of key stakeholders. Who are these stakeholders and what is their legitimate role in moving towards these aims?

(2) Where should power and control lie in issues to do with school improvement, with those functioning within schools or with those outside schools, responsible, for example, with school funding?

Indicative reading

DfEE (1998) *Teachers – meeting the challenge of change*. London: HMSO.
Teacher Training Agency (1998) *National Standards*. London: HMSO.
West-Burnham, J. (1997) *Managing Quality in Schools*. London: Pitman.
Whitaker, P. (1993) *The Primary Head*. London: Heinemann.

Chapter 9

Inclusive Education: principles and practices

Brenda Judge

> We are all of equal value, we are all of equal worth.
> We should not be divided by the difference of our birth.
> (Hardman, 2002: 43)

The origins of inclusive education

FEW areas of education have undergone such a rapid development as that which characterized special education over the last twenty-five years of the twentieth century. Indeed the present government's seemingly headlong rush for inclusion, of all pupils into mainstream schools is one example of that development, where philosophical thought outpaces practice.

Differences in children have in the past precluded some of them accessing mainstream schools and have served to perpetuate the continuation of a segregated system. However, it must be clearly remembered that segregated schools on the basis of disability, that is, special schools, were created to provide for those who were categorized as being unable to be accommodated in mainstream schools. As such, to suggest that elimination of this separate system will only necessitate the development of a more responsive mainstream system is a suggestion which could be considered naïve. Many barriers, not just those of a physical nature, such as a building layout for example, stand to block the path towards inclusion for all.

If we begin from a premise that the antithesis of inclusion is segregation then it is possible to begin to understand why, initially, inclusion was focused upon those whom it was possible to identify as having separate and different provision, that is to say, those who were educated away from the mainstream. This is where the inclusion movement began, and is what I will refer to for ease from now on as 'mainstreaming'. The Warnock Report (DES, 1978) identified that at any one time 20 per cent of the school population would have a need, which would require special and additional assistance, and of these only 2 per cent would have severe physical, sensory intellectual and/or emotional difficulties. It becomes obvious, therefore, even to the least untrained eye, that the integration movement first started its campaigning and pressurizing for this easily identified group, the 2 per cent. Most of these children were excluded from mainstream schooling because of their differences. Children with illnesses were sometimes sent to open-air schools, deaf children to schools for the deaf, blind children to schools for the blind etc. Children were labelled and categorized, and dispatched to special schools without ever having the opportunity to discover whether they could exist in a mainstream setting. In recent years there have been increasing demands, not only from the wider community at large, but also from adults who have experienced the system of segregation, that the idea of segregated special schools is unjust. They argue that as a society we should have an inclusive education system as a matter of basic human right.

However, although fundamentally agreeing that an inclusive education is a fundamental human right, I would argue that such a view of 'inclusion' is very narrow and is why I refer to it as 'mainstreaming'. Inclusive education goes beyond mainstreaming, which is founded on the assumption that all that is needed is to merge two separate school systems and permit those who are 'differently able' to be provided for in the mainstream setting. Lipsky and Gartner (1996) argued that integration could not be achieved by 'allowing' people of differing skin colour, for example, into an existing white society, but only by fundamentally changing that society so that diversity was genuinely valued and what was 'normal' was not solely defined by one group. Logically then, if this argument is accepted, inclusive education must go beyond the integration of a single pupil or groups of pupils who have specifically different needs (mainstreaming), to that of a cultural re-structuring of the present education system which ensures that the norms and cultural values which are defined respect the diversity of the wider community. The philosophy underpinning mainstreaming is one based upon the fact that the inequality of provision stems from the individual differences of the respective pupils, whereas the philosophy, which underpins an inclusive education, is one which believes there are processes within the education system that reproduce inequalities.

What is inclusion?

At the time of writing the concept of inclusive education enjoys a high profile not just in the United Kingdom but also around the world. It has been embodied in many United Nations conventions as well as in domestic statutes (Sex Discrimination Act of 1975 and 1978; Race Relations Act 1976; Education Act of 1981, 1996 and 1997; Disability Discrimination Act 1995; Special Educational Needs and Disability Act 2001). In order to inform our debate about the development of inclusive education further it may be pertinent to look at some definitions based on the literature and government documents.

In United Kingdom government documents of the 1980s and 1990s inclusive education was promoted as *disabled and non-disabled* children and young people learning together in ordinary pre-school provision, schools, colleges and universities with appropriate networks of support. Reference can also be found in government literature and studies in the United States of America to the notion that inclusion is that all pupils in a school, regardless of their weaknesses in any area, become part of a school community. Another further definition is the notion of *full inclusion*, that is, where all children/students, regardless of condition or severity of need will be in a mainstream classroom receiving a programme of full-time study. The entire child's/student's needs will be met in that setting.

All these definitions are based upon a deficit model, which is then modified to meet the needs of the individual; it is mainstreaming not inclusion. Also by their very nature these definitions are patronizing and degrading although well intentioned. For example, if Professor Stephen Hawkins and anyone of us were placed together in a room to debate the relative merits of quantum physics, which of us in that scenario would have the *weakness*? Also the use of terminology such as 'disabled' and 'ordinary', subscribes to a medical model of disability where people are seen as 'not able' because of impairment rather than being 'differently able'. Differences such as these have been used to label (cripple, dumb, loonies etc.) and segregate people for generations and are often used in a derogatory manner. They have contributed to a climate of distrust and fear which needs addressing. Such language is not one which instils pride and value, nor is it language which refers to any individuals I have ever taught. Throughout my teaching career I have never taught an ordinary class; in fact all my classes have been made up of extraordinary individuals.

A more appropriate definition, although by no means a definitive one, is that inclusive education values the learner as an individual. It brings support services to the learner in order to enable them to fulfil their full potential. It should aim to educate all learners and celebrate a diverse society. As Bennett *et al.* (1998) found, both in British and American education systems, if children are deemed to have particular difficulties in school they are, more often than not, grouped together with other children who have been identified as having similar needs. The philosophy behind this approach is founded in a fiscal policy of better use of resources and teaching staff. However, more often than not, these children could be found in prefabricated buildings being taught by teachers who found it difficult to manage larger numbers. The net effect for these children was segregation from pupils their own age, being branded as less able and different and experiencing restricted educational opportunities. For example Sinclair Taylor (1995) found that the pupils he spoke to in a study of integration in a multi-ethnic special needs unit of a large mainstream secondary school had a clear perception of how they were viewed by their peers. They saw themselves as *spastic, mental* and *of less value* than those in mainstream classes. Evidence such as this has informed the debate about segregation and been part of the motivation within the education system to move away from such a system.

Reynolds (1989) recognized that inclusion needed to be viewed as a cumulative process, which eventually would see pupils who had previously been excluded from mainstream schooling being included. He also argued that such segregation/exclusion from the mainstream was influenced as much by the community values about ethnicity, race, gender and language as about pupils' differing abilities. In accepting this argument we must also understand the inhibiting effect that the moves in the 1950s to integrate racially-segrated schools in the United States of America by *bussing* pupils from one geographical area to another for their schooling had upon the move towards total inclusion. The negative response to and effect of this well-intentioned policy put the inclusion movement back decades. It has to be understood that discrimination and prejudice of any form whether based on race, gender, class, sexual orientation or disability grow from the same seeds of fear and intolerance to difference. This means that making schools more inclusive will involve all in the school community in challenging their own attitudes and beliefs, a process which can be painful and damaging if not handled carefully. Inclusion demands change and change is a process which takes time, and unfortunately for some of our children time has run out.

Ainscow (1995) suggested that integration/mainstreaming was about making superficial changes, providing some restricted provision for pupils, often those with special educational needs, in schools where the communities had changed very little in attitude and values. Integration/mainstreaming means that, if Ainscow's argument is accepted, a school will assimilate a learner who has different needs but that the responsibility lies with the learner to make changes so that they can be part of the community, whereas inclusion demands that it is the learning community, the school/college/university that has to change by modifying resources and changing attitudes.

Inclusion not only has a broader perspective in terms of learners and the learning community but it has also widened its scope beyond those who have learning difficulties and/or physical and sensory disabilities. If the definition I proposed earlier is to be considered as valid, it means that all learners who have differing needs, whether they are intellectually-based, racially-based, linguistically-based, gender-based or sexually-based, have to be included in mainstream provision and their needs met within that provision. The Centre for Studies on Inclusive Education promoted ten reasons for inclusion. They started, quite appropriately from the premise that inclusive education is a human right, that it makes both good education and good social sense (Table 9.1). They argued that from a human rights perspective all children should be valued regardless of race, gender or disability and to this end children need to be together without any groups being excluded and segregated. They

Table 9.1:   Index for inclusion

Human rights	(1)	All children have the right to learn together.
	(2)	Children should not be devalued or discriminated against by being excluded because of any differing learning needs they have whether they be based in their intellectual capabilities, their physical capabilities, their gender or their race.
	(3)	Disabled adults, describing themselves as special school survivors, are demanding an end to segregation and exclusion.
	(4)	There is no legitimate reason to separate children for their education. Children belong together – with advantages and benefits for everyone. They do not need to be protected from each other.
Good education	(5)	Research shows that children achieve better both academically and socially in integrated settings.
	(6)	There is no teaching or care, which can take place in a segregated school, which cannot take place in a mainstream school.
	(7)	Given commitment and support inclusive education is a more efficient use of resources.
Social sense	(8)	Segregation teaches children to be fearful, ignorant, and breeds prejudice.
	(9)	All children need an education that will help them develop relationships and prepare them for life in the mainstream.
	(10)	Only inclusion has the potential to reduce fear and to build friendships, respect and understanding.

Source: This model is adapted from The Centre for Studies in Inclusive Education (2003) and is reproduced here with their kind permission.

promoted the belief that inclusion makes good educational sense, citing research to support their argument that children achieve better in integrated
settings, and that there is not an education or care package which cannot be
provided for in mainstream schooling. Finally they argued that inclusion
makes good social sense, stating that if inclusion is approached in an appropriate manner, fear and prejudice will be eradicated and the world will be a
much better place.

In the Index the Centre emphasized a process view of inclusion. They saw
inclusion as a never-ending process, involving specifying the direction of
change, which requires schools to engage in a critical examination of what
needs to be done within a learning community to ensure that the learning and
participation of the diversity of learners can be enhanced. Within this index
the term 'barriers to learning' was used instead of special educational needs,
thus emphasizing the role of the learning community and the responsibility
of that community in removing the barrier to learning rather than it being the
role of the individual to make accommodations themselves.

Summary box

- Inclusive education needs to go beyond the integration of a single pupil or
  groups of pupils who have specifically different needs, to that of a cultural
  re-structuring of the present education system to ensure that the norms
  and cultural values which are defined respect the diversity of the wider
  community.
- Full inclusion requires that all pupils regardless of condition or severity of
  need will be in a mainstream classroom receiving a programme of full time
  study.
- Inclusive education values the learner as an individual. It brings support
  services to the learner in order to enable them to fulfil their full potential.
  It should aim to educate all learners and celebrate a diverse society.

Another easily identified group of pupils who have been *mainstreamed*, that
is, segregated within mainstream are children who have English as an additional language (EAL). It can be seen at a glance that the segregated system
that has existed for children in special schools and the subsequent moves
towards mainstreaming has a number of similarities with the provision for
those pupils who have English as an additional language. Ortiz (1984) claimed
in a study that each of these groups could be easily identified; each had staff
who had specialized training; each developed their own teaching techniques
and resources; up to 1999 each had independent resourcing in the United
Kingdom, 75 per cent of funding for pupils with English as an additional

language came from the Home Office not the DfES; and each group experienced considerable prejudice and bias. Some would argue that teaching pupils with special educational needs does not require unique teaching techniques and resources, in fact Lewis and Norwich (2000) were unable to find any evidence to support the claim for unique teaching techniques. They did find what they referred to as a continuum of successful teaching strategies which had been adapted and adjusted to meet the needs of the particular learners, that is, good teaching.

However, if we accept the premise that there are some similarities between the two groups, even if only at the simplistic level of both groups being easily identifiable, then it is possible to begin to understand why these groups in particular have been the focus of the New Labour government's push for inclusion. Another major influence upon the government's thinking was the recommendations of the Macpherson Report (1999), published after the inquiry into Stephen Lawrence's death. After its publication the Prime Minister stated that it contained a lesson for the whole of British society, and that we should respond collectively. The government endorsed the findings of the report and agreed to set up a working party to oversee its implementation. The last few recommendations of the report centred around the role that education could play in preventing the chronic, undisputed racist attitudes of the youths suspected of Stephen's murder from infecting another generation and creating the atmosphere for another tragedy. These recommendations were:

1. That consideration be given to amendment of the National Curriculum, aimed at valuing cultural diversity and preventing racism, in order to reflect the needs of a diverse society.

2. That local education authorities and school governors have a duty to create and implement strategies in their schools to prevent and address racism. Such strategies to include:
    *   that all schools record racist incidents;
    *   that all recorded incidents are reported to the pupils' parents/ guardians, school governors and LEAs;
    *   that the number of racist incidents are published annually, on a school by school basis; that the numbers of self-defined ethnic identity of 'excluded' pupils are published annually on a school by school basis.

3. That OFSTED inspections included examination of the implementation of such strategies. (MacPherson Report, 1999)

The review of the National Curriculum in England and Wales provided a unique opportunity to address one of the key factors that will help to build a cohesive united, multi-cultural Britain for the twenty-first century. The Department for Education and Employment's own advisory committee on ethnic minority pupils (DfEE, 2000) stated that the education we deliver must meet the specific educational needs of minority ethnic pupils and prepare all pupils for life in a culturally diverse society, including their role in combating racism. However, they observed that most local educational authorities and schools lacked clarity and direction when it came to addressing inequalities in attainment between different ethnic groups. It found that most schools had equal opportunity policies; few had clear procedures for monitoring their implementation and their impact on practice as limited; and that fewer than 25 per cent of local education authorities had a clear strategy for raising the achievement of ethnic groups.

New Labour and inclusion

In a White Paper (DfEE, 1997) New Labour set the tone for the main thrust of education reforms through the late 1990s and into the twenty-first century. In his foreword the then Secretary of State for Education and Employment, David Blunkett, described the government's core commitment as equal opportunity and high standards for all. The document recognized that inequality of educational attainment is a key factor placing young people at risk of isolation, non-participation and social exclusion in later life. The term 'under-achievement' is often used to describe differences in attainment between differing social groups and unfortunately there has been confusion about this term. The notion of under-achievement has played a particularly significant role in the development of debates around ethnic diversity in British education, especially through the work of the Rampton and Swann committees in the late 1970s and early 1980s. The label 'under-achievement' has been widely used to refer to different educational outcomes among racial and ethnic minorities but the term has a long contested history. Authors/ researchers such as Gillborn (1997), Gillborn and Gipps (1996) Foster *et al.* (1996) and Gillborn and Mirza (2000) all questioned the use of the term and the danger of it undermining ethnic minority effort to succeed, seeing it all too often as being a stereotype. Emphasizing the difference in attainment between groups can be part of a necessary analysis of inequalities in educational outcomes, but care should be taken that such an approach does not lead to a hierarchy of ethnic minorities based on assumptions of inherent ability. As Gillborn and Mirza (2000) pointed out, although it is vital to identify differences in attainment it is essential to avoid being seen as supporting wider beliefs that portray either model or deficient ethnic minorities. Thus, simply replacing under-achievement with a more recent notion of differences needs to be carefully considered. The National Curriculum 2000 stated that it must

> secure for all pupils, irrespective of social background, culture, race, gender, differences in ability and disabilities an entitlement to a number of areas of learning and to develop knowledge, understanding, skills and attitudes necessary for their self-fulfilment as active and responsible citizens.

David Blunkett, when Secretary of State for Education, stated

> the education of children with special educational needs ... is vital to the creation of a fully inclusive society in which members see themselves as valued for the contribution they make. We owe it to all children – whatever their particular needs and circumstances – the opportunity to develop to their full potential and contribute economically and to play a full part as active citizens.

It is obvious from these government pronouncements that the rationale behind New Labour's 'inclusive' philosophy was not based on the rights of the individual but on the needs of the country and in particular the economic wealth of the country. It begs the questions of whether inclusion should be about producing pupils who are capable of making an economic contribution to society. Or should inclusion be about pupils fulfilling their potential for their own self-respect and personal fulfilment? These questions reflect the more general debate about education and who should benefit from it. If you share the traditionalist perspective then education is about producing the necessary work force for the benefit of the state, but if your philosophy is more in line with that of the progressives, that is, that education should be child-centred, then you would believe in education for education's sake and for the benefit of the individual. No solution is clear-cut and of course both the holders of the purse strings, the state, and the individual have a stake in the purpose and outcomes of education.

The thinking behind most of the movements involved in integration/ mainstreaming and inclusion is based upon the conception that the provision of additional resources would enable those pupils who were previously segregated to be integrated. However, the premise behind inclusion is one which may well require the profession to look at the curriculum and the manner in which it is delivered. Despite the New Labour initiative regarding inclusion there seems to be a policy practice gap, a large discrepancy between the inclusion rhetoric and the practical application on the ground. New Labour placed itself in a paradoxical position, on the one hand promoting an inclusive education, with particular emphasis on the inclusion of children with English as an additional language and those with special educational needs, and on the other hand promoting a traditional curriculum in the primary school which placed a strong emphasis on whole-class teaching of literacy and numeracy. The literacy strategy tried to address low achievement in literacy skills by the use of additional literacy teaching, but, unfortunately, a large number of schools use these resources to withdraw children and they are often taught by classroom assistants in inappropriate spaces, not unlike the scenarios painted by Bennet *et al.* in 1988, providing evidence that the policy practice gap had not been reduced very much in the years since their research.

The Labour government, in its second term of office, introduced a revised national curriculum, often referred to as the 'National Curriculum 2000'. It became statutory in August 2000 and contained a rationale, which set out the values and purposes underpinning the school curriculum. In the rationale was a stronger emphasis on inclusion, which was defined as providing effective learning opportunities for *all* children. A new statutory inclusion statement then replaced and extended the statutory statements on access. The new statement set out three key principles for inclusion, which schools should consider at all levels of curriculum planning; setting suitable learning challenges; responding to pupils' diverse learning needs; overcoming potential barriers to learning and assessment for individual and groups of pupils. It can be seen from these statements that the emphasis from the New Labour government was on institutions, schools examining their provision in order to ensure that no pupil was denied their entitlement. The rationale and introductory statement to the National Curriculum 2000 (my italics) provided the following advice:

- Information is given in *setting suitable learning challenges* about the curriculum flexibility available and the action that schools should take to ensure that all pupils are presented with learning opportunities relevant to their attainments to enable them to progress and to achieve positive outcomes.
- In responding to *pupils' diverse learning needs,* specific reference is made to the action necessary to ensure that all pupils are enabled to achieve, including boys, girls, pupils with special educational needs, pupils with disabilities, pupils from all social and cultural backgrounds, pupils of

different ethnic groups including travellers, refugees and asylum seekers, and pupils from divers linguistic backgrounds.

- In *overcoming potential barriers to learning and assessment,* specific reference is made to the provision that should be made to meet individual requirements for pupils with special educational needs, pupils with disabilities and pupils for whom English is an additional language.

The inclusion statement included non-statutory examples of the action which schools might take in order to meet pupils' particular needs and requirements, with reference to particular subjects as appropriate. Additional non-statutory information on inclusion that is specific to a subject was included in the subject areas in the Key Stage 1 and 2 booklet or specific subject booklets for Key Stage 3 and 4.

The school system and the school curriculum are not the only areas of education upon which the New Labour government imposed the need to be more inclusive. In its drive to increase the numbers of students who enjoy the advantages of higher education the government introduced a major initiative to widen access. This included monitoring students who enter higher education from different ethnic groups, penalizing institutions that do not meet targets in this area and broadening entry qualifications to enable students, who do not have traditional qualifications, the possibility of entry to higher education. This emphasis is slightly different from that which has been the focus of school inclusion, as the groups who tend, in the majority, not to have attained traditional entry qualifications for higher education are those who left school at 16 with minimal qualifications, those who had been alienated from the school system. If we examine the rhetoric of the inclusion movement within New Labour we see that it seeks to embrace all learners whatever their ethnicity, gender, race, social class, capabilities, or disabilities. Within the documentation distributed through government departments such as the DfES and the QCA the focus is primarily on meeting the needs of pupils with special educational needs and those who have English as an additional language.

As already mentioned earlier in this chapter, there is legislation on gender, race and disability in place, which has to be taken into account when considering educational provision. I would now like to consider some of that legislation in more detail.

The Sex Discrimination Act (SDA)

The Sex Discrimination Act came into force in 1975 and was amended and broadened in 1986. The Act makes it unlawful to discriminate on the grounds of sex. Specifically, sex discrimination is not allowed in employment, education, advertising or when providing housing, goods, services or facilities. It is unlawful to discriminate, in employment or advertised jobs, against someone who is married. The Act applies to two kinds of discrimination, that of treating someone unfairly because of their sex which is known as direct discrimination; or discrimination which sets unjustifiable conditions that appear to apply to everyone but in fact discriminate against one sex, that is, indirect discrimination. Co-educational schools, colleges or universities must not discriminate in the way in which they provide facilities or in the way in which they admit students. For example, all students have equal access to the National Curriculum. The schools careers service must not discriminate between boys and girls in the way they provide advice and assistance. Single-sexed schools may restrict admission to either girls or boys but they must not restrict the types of subjects they teach.

The Race Relations Act (RRA)

The Race Relations Act 1976 makes it unlawful to discriminate against anyone on the grounds of race, colour, nationality (including citizenship), or ethnic or national origins. It applies to jobs, training, housing, education and the provision of goods, facilities and services. Just as with the Sex Discrimination Act there are two kinds of discrimination under the Race Relations Act. Direct discrimination occurs when someone is treated on racial grounds less favourably than other people. When someone is segregated on racial grounds from others, this is also direct discrimination. Racial abuse and harassment is also unlawful direct discrimination if it occurs in circumstances covered by the Act. Indirect discrimination occurs when a condition or requirement is applied equally to people of all racial groups, but many people of a particular group are able to comply with it. Such indirect discrimination is unlawful when it cannot be justified other than on racial grounds. The Act applies to any schools and colleges maintained by local authorities, grant maintained schools, independent (fee paying) schools and colleges, special schools and universities. It includes the governors of a school or college and the local education authority. It is unlawful for education authorities to discriminate in the way they carry out any of their duties.

The Disability Discrimination Act (DDA)

The Disability Discrimination Act (1995) creates rights for disabled people in employment, access to goods, services and facilities, the sale and letting of property and access to transport. Education is excluded from the main provisions of the Act, but the Act does demand other duties from education providers and funding bodies in the United Kingdom. The Act requires some further and higher education institutions to provide disability statements, which will state what the college/university offers for disabled students and how accessible the facilities are.

Special Educational Needs and Disability Act (SENDA)

The Special Educational Needs and Disability Act (2001) strengthened the 1996 Education Act which explicitly set out in section 316 the conditions for educating children with special educational needs in mainstream education, stating that this should not be incompatible with:

- parental wishes;
- the children receiving the special education provision which their learning difficulties call for;
- the provision of efficient education for the children with whom the special educational needs child will be educated; and the efficient use of resources.

The Special Educational Needs and Disability Act strengthened the endorsement of inclusion, revising section 316 by removing the clause 'the children receiving the special education provision which their learning difficulties call for' and ensuring that no mainstream school could refuse a place to a child with special educational needs on the basis that the school could not meet the pupil's needs. In addition the section was re-written to give it a much more positive spin so that it read:

> If a statement is maintained under section 324 for the child, he must be educated in a mainstream school unless it is incompatible with:
>
> - the wishes of the parents;
> - the provision of efficient education for other children.

These four Acts have impacted upon the educational provision in the United Kingdom in a momentous manner and have contributed to the continuing drive to eradicate inequality in our society, but in my opinion they fail to address the biggest barrier to an inclusive education. Until any government is prepared to address the issues related to class and the differing educational opportunities, which are afforded to people who come from differing social backgrounds, then inclusion will not mean inclusion for all.

To try to combat the inherently class ridden United Kingdom society, the New Labour government also established in 2001, under the direction of the deputy prime minister's office, a social exclusion unit. This unit defined social exclusion as being a phenomenon, which occurs when a person, groups of people, or geographical areas are excluded from society because of a combination of things ranging from education to housing. This was an attempt by the New Labour government to address the fundamental issue of class. They recognized that it is a combination of issues which often come together to produce groups of individuals who are excluded from contributing to society fully and living a more fulfilled life. This unit initiated a number of educational projects concerning the education of children in care, the exclusion of pupils from school, support for children in school, and, in particular, in partnership with the DfES and the Learning City Network (LRN) a road show which focused upon the skills needed for social inclusion and, in particular, adult basic learning skills. New Labour hope to ensure that the number of people who gain experience of higher and further education increases during the twenty-first century and this unit is part of its drive to meet this target. The unit has a brief to liaise with government departments, which deal with education, housing, transport, and urban renewal. In this way the government hopes to generate a co-ordinated response to social inclusion.

Exclusion from school has been studied in a number of contexts. The differences in the exclusion rates of boys and girls were studied by Castles and Parsons (1997). They found that at secondary level around four boys for every girl were excluded and in primary schools one girl for every fourteen boys. Gillborn and Gipps (1996) found that Afro-Caribbean pupils were between four and six times more likely to be excluded from school than their white peers. This number has since been reported as falling, but it is still excessively high. OFSTED (1996) and Hayden (1997) both reported that children who were excluded from school were more likely to have experienced poverty, homelessness, parental illness and bereavement. Brodie and Berridge (1996) also identified that a disproportionate number of children in local authority care were also excluded from school. These entire findings pointed to the need to co-ordinate departments and fight social exclusion as a whole. The Department for Education and Employment (DfEE) also stated in 1999 that the rate of permanent exclusions or pupils who had statements was seven times higher than those without.

In 1999 the DfEE sent guidance to schools which stated that governing bodies and headteachers should monitor the sanctions against pupils of ethnic minority backgrounds and reassure themselves that the school's behaviour policy against racial prejudice and harassment was being fully enforced. This guidance also drew schools' attention to the fact that sometimes if schools operate policies which could be perceived as 'colour blind' this in itself could lead to persistent inequalities between ethnic groups. The Department for Education and Employment (DfEE, 1994) also found that some pupils who were in the care of the local education authority had cause to experience disproportionate exclusion. Brodie (2000) examined a number of ways this exclusion operated including the use of admission policies to exclude pupils in care.

Is social inclusion the new equality of opportunity?

If social inclusion is about ensuring that no person, group of people of geographical area is disadvantaged and thus excluded from the mainstream of society, it would seem to follow logically that in order to do that effectively everyone must be afforded equality of opportunity. If this is the case then how does inclusion differ from equality of opportunity, if it does at all?

Those who are concerned about inclusion consider the issues of equality of opportunity primarily from the perspective of the needs of society. They consider the exclusion of people from mainstream society as being economically expensive both in terms of what talents are lost to society and the cost to society in caring for those excluded from society which may manifest itself in terms of crime and punishment and/or economic and social benefits; whereas equality of opportunity would appear to be more about ensuring that everybody has an equal opportunity to succeed, that education, employment and good health care are a human right. The New Labour government recognized, along with others, that if we are to ensure that all sections of society are to be included then equality of educational opportunities has to be a human right. This in itself is recognition of the fact that education is the password to inclusion, education provides knowledge and the means to acquire knowledge, and knowledge is power. If this is to be the case then the school curriculum has to become more accessible to all groups within society. Teachers have to look at themselves and consider how they behave, and schools have to examine their procedures. Above all society as a whole and each section of society has to value all sections of that society. Without valuing each other whatever legislation is put in place, whatever initiatives governments undertake, the goal of an inclusive society a long way off. An inclusive education system is one step to that road.

Task

Using the 'index for inclusion' model on page 159, consider its principles in terms of practical issues and practices which might be implemented inside the classroom to ensure that the rhetoric of these principles can be translated into action in terms of:

- human rights;
- 'good' education;
- social sense.

Indicative reading

Brodie, I. and Berridge, D. (1996) *School Exclusion: research themes and issues*. Luton: University of Luton Press.

Castles, F. and Parsons, C. (1997) "Disruptive behaviour and exclusion from schools: re-defining and responding to the problem", *Emotional and Behavioural Difficulties*, 2 (3).

The Centre for Studies in Inclusive Education (2003) "The Index for Inclusion". Bristol: The Centre for Studies in Inclusive Education. Available from http://www.uwe.ac.uk/csie/csiehome.htm (accessed 9th April 2003). The website provides a variety of resources for the critical exploration of a number of core issues relating to social inclusion.

DfEE (1999) *Social Inclusion: pupil support* (Circular 10/99). London: DfEE Publications.

OFSTED (1996) *Exclusion from Secondary Schools 1995-1996*. London: OFSTED.

Chapter 10

Citizenship Education:
origins, challenges and possibilities

Ian Davies

I N this chapter I have three principal aims:

- to describe how citizenship education came to achieve a high status;
- to discuss the problems and challenges associated with securing a place for it in schools and other educational institutions;
- to suggest how teachers and others might work towards the effective implementation of citizenship education.

I hope that readers, by the end of the chapter, will know more about the twists and turns in the debates over citizenship education. Principally, I aim to encourage readers to understand and reflect critically upon:

- the various causes that led to the introduction of citizenship education into the National Curriculum in England and into debates surrounding post compulsory education;
- the traditions that are associated with thinking about citizenship;
- the various forms of citizenship education that can exist;
- the different ways in which citizenship education can be implemented;
- the critical challenges for citizenship education likely to appear.

Given the diversity of thought and action apparent in relation to citizenship and the necessary participatory democratic nature of the debates that take place I would not expect readers to agree with my analysis. Indeed I hope that readers will, through the development of the different sorts of understandings mentioned above, explore and then elaborate upon their own perspectives. Ultimately, I should like to encourage more people to become involved *as citizens* in the formulation of policy in relation to citizenship education and/or as actors in its implementation with teachers and learners.

The origins of citizenship education in England

Citizenship education seems, suddenly, to have achieved high status. Governments around the world keen to emphasize their commitment and projects – to advise on how it could be taught, learned and assessed – have multiplied (Torney-Purta *et al.*, 1999). This chapter focuses on the situation in England (different features and arrangements apply in various parts of Britain) where citizenship education became part of the National Curriculum for secondary schools in England in August 2002. Various authors (for example, Batho, 1990; Brennan, 1981; Davies, 1999; Crick and Heater, 1977) have explored the (rather depressing) historical background to the introduction of citizenship education. There had been some interest in political education early in the twentieth century with, for example, the League of Nations Union doing some good work. However, the Spens (1928) and Norwood (1943) reports largely neglected the area, reflecting the failure of the Association for Education in Citizenship (Whitmarsh, 1974). Although the 1944 Education Act included a clause favourable to political education (Brennan, 1981: 40) this was never implemented. Pamphlets (Ministry of Education, 1947; 1949) concentrated on the supposed importance of learning about the British Constitution and illogically suggested that a healthy democratic society could be encouraged if schools would only develop 'the old and simple virtues of humility, service, restraint and respect for personality' (1949: 41). The Crowther Report (Ministry of Education, 1959) was largely silent on the matter of political learning. The Newsom Report (Ministry of Education, 1963: 163) did make a claim about the importance of educating children so that they were not victims of the 'hidden persuaders' but there was no thorough consideration of the topic. Traditional school subjects such as history (DES, 1967b) were felt to be the area in which political education would find expression rather than through the development of any explicit and systematic approach. Some Schools Council papers (for example, 1967: para. 2) made passing references to political education but failed to give any in-depth treatment, and were themselves part of the expression of neglect which led to most pupils having 'little good to say for what they have learnt in those subjects which are concerned with the understanding of human nature and institutions'. Of course, there are exceptions that could be made within this general picture. Those interested in citizenship education before 1969 were able to draw (positively or negatively) on the work of Dewey (1966) and Oakshott (1956). Some relevant research and development work had taken place (Oliver and Shaver, 1966). The Association for the Teaching of Social Sciences had been set up in 1963. Very important has been the long-term existence of the Council for Education in World Citizenship (Heater, 1983).

However, before 1969, if any citizenship education was being promoted at all it was almost exclusively for élite students (for example, those studying at HSC or 'A' level) and based around learning information for the purposes of doing well academically and preparing for high status professions. If it was ever practised in any explicit sense for the majority it was as civics which 'may have been utopian, quietist, simplistic, indoctrinating as well as class-biased, hardly meriting the description of "education"' (Entwistle 1973: 7).

This low level of implementation continued until at least the end of the twentieth century. Stradling and Noctor (1981) and Fogelman (1991) both reported positively on what headteachers had said when faced with an official looking questionnaire but the reality was, they argued, rather more prosaic. Even Stradling and Noctor's estimate that the average pupil would receive no more than two 35-minute periods per week of political education for no more than ten weeks of the year may have been optimistic (Davies, 1993). This history of neglect needs to be explained. What caused policy-makers, schools and teachers to ignore citizenship education for so long? Crick and Heater (1977) succinctly raised the issues that kept citizenship off the agenda: a lack of tradition; few teachers who were professionally committed to the field; a belief that politics was solely an adult domain; and a fear of indoctrination. This sort of explanation shows how difficult it is for citizenship to break through into curriculum statements, schemes of work and lesson plans. We must, of course, even in the much more positive situation in which citizenship has acquired formal status of a National Curriculum subject, be aware of the possibility that implementation will not be easily achieved. Perhaps the difficulties associated with effective implementation will be clarified by reference to the reasons citizenship education became more positively regarded at three different points during the last three decades of the twentieth century. The contrast between these three different phases that involved an increased level of attention to citizenship reveal very different understandings of the nature of citizenship itself.

During the latter part of the 1970s there were three key causal factors.

- In 1970 the age of majority was lowered to 18. This meant that many in schools and colleges would be entitled to vote. It suddenly became much more difficult to sustain arguments that asserted that school students should not consider civic issues.
- Research on political socialization showed that young people were exposed (through textbooks, the media, the family) to many issues that related directly to citizenship. Furthermore, rather than being unable to understand these matters, research showed (for example, Greenstein, 1965) that young people were capable of beginning to make sense of a political world. Not to teach something that was important, omnipresent and could be understood seemed now to be unacceptable especially at a time when democratic involvement was more readily accepted as a good thing.
- Perhaps most important, there were concerns about the level of understanding held by young people (Stradling, 1977) and the possibility that their ignorance would be exploited by extremist groups. In this climate it was not difficult to secure the support of key politicians for relevant curriculum initiatives (Crick and Porter, 1978).

During the 1980s a very different set of causal factors emerged:

- There grew up a distrust of teachers who were seen by some as serving up a diet of left-wing propaganda. The Education Act (No. 2) of 1986 included clauses which banned partisan political activity in primary schools and insisted that when controversial issues were being discussed there should be a balanced presentation of opposing views. The need to remind teachers of such matters said a great deal about the low esteem in which they were held.
- The Scarman Report following the riots of the early 1980s and focusing on the need for better relations between police and young people suggested that law and order played a key role in the development of policy. There were fears that young people were becoming alienated and were potentially (or actually) dangerous.
- There were demographic factors, the growth of privatization and consumerism, which led to a perception among some that the welfare state could no longer be afforded. In this climate direction about citizenship education began to emerge from Douglas Hurd and John Patten in the Home Office and young people were encouraged to realize that they should meet their 'voluntary obligations' (Hurd, 1988: 15).

The end of the 1990s were influenced by a further set of causal factors:

- The Labour Party won the 1997 general election and the new government was determined to develop a strong communitarian approach to social policy. The 'third way' (Giddens, 1998) seemed to provide the key to the renewal of social democracy, involving forms of education that, allowing for the development of basic skills, encouraged purposeful engagement to strengthen ties between individuals and groups.
- Citizenship was seen to be a way of providing a way of establishing something that was coherent but nevertheless wide ranging. Escaping from what was seen by some as the narrowness of, for example, political education or anti-racist education, citizenship would provide an over-arching coherence that employed the three key strands of social and moral responsibility, community involvement and political literacy. Citizenship was seen as being both sufficiently flexible and robust to address matters to do with legal status obviously relevant at a time when asylum seekers were reported so prominently, and issues to do with identity formation and ability to act effectively.
- Many other countries had a form of education that addressed contemporary issues directly. Influences from within the European Union as well as initiatives in many countries around the world suggested that the education system in England had begun to look unbalanced. The action taken within England was in a sense not freestanding.

> **Summary box**
>
> A long period during which citizenship education remained a neglected curriculum area in the United Kingdom was followed in the 1970s, 1980s and 1990s by a determination to provide citizenship education with a curriculum place and status. Political, ideological and cultural motivations for this initiative were very different and consequently very different forms of citizenship education emerged.

What is citizenship? traditions and trajectories

The comments made above go some way towards describing developments in educational policy-making and explaining some of the causal factors. Implied in those comments is something about the meaning of citizenship. It is now important to try to flesh out a little more the different perspectives that have been used in discussions about citizenship. Heater (1999) provided an excellent analysis of the key trends and issues associated within citizenship debates. He argued that there were two distinct traditions associated with citizenship: the liberal (rights-based) and the civic republican (duties-based).

Of course, both positions can be represented negatively or positively. An individual who seeks his or her rights at the expense of others may be acting in an unacceptable manner; but, equally, a country that demands an unreasonable fulfilment of duties in the name of the common good is not acting democratically. For some the traditions may be in conflict. Wolfe (1999: 429), for example, suggested that it had not yet been convincingly argued how 'putting the common good *ahead* of one's private interests is compatible with liberal values such as autonomy'. This would seem to render the thoughts and activities of a person as a citizen to be either partial or contradictory. Perhaps, there are some more positive ways forward. The differences between rights and duties may break down fairly readily. For example, is it my right or my duty to look after my children? It is clearly both. We can argue that 'by being a virtuous, community-conscious participant in civic affairs (a republican requirement), a citizen benefits by enhancing his or her own individual development (a liberal objective). Citizenship does not involve an either/or choice' (Heater, 1999: 177).

Not all will be persuaded by such seemingly attractive compromises, and complete logical clarity cannot be expected. However, the dilemma of balancing rights with duties should not hinder good educational work, and the sort of balance offered by writers like Dagger (1997) and Heater is necessary and valid. There is, necessarily, continuing debate about the nature and meaning of citizenship but to work from a conceptual base that makes sense is possible. What, then, should a programme for citizenship education look like?

Summary box

Two key traditions associate with the development of citizenship education:

- a liberal, rights-based perspectives;
- a civic republican, duties-based perspective.

Citizenship education: a rich tapestry or a tangled mess

Rowe (1997) identified at least eight approaches to citizenship education competing for attention in England: the constitutional knowledge, the patriotic, the parental, the religious, the value conflict or pluralist, the empathetic, the school ethos and the community action. Other approaches may be possible from those, for example, who would wish to emphasize the importance of political matters. All these approaches, to some extent, relate to the very different conceptions of citizenship discussed above. Community action may, for example, be undertaken by those teachers who understand citizenship in terms of communitarianism. Perhaps they also relate to other considerations such as a teacher having to consider the extent to which different approaches lend themselves to exciting teaching activities which will lead to improvements in pupils' understanding and skills. The efforts of those in the 1970s to promote political literacy led to work that was issue-focused. They used a broader concept of politics than that which had been used in British Constitution courses. They valued procedural concepts (such as truth, respect for reasoning and respect for argument). They were concerned with skills as well as knowledge and attitudes so as to develop pupils' potential for action. The key publication was edited by Crick and Porter (1978).

Political literacy did seem by the end of the 1970s to have gained a strong position with key policy-makers. Legitimation had been achieved, however, without implementation and during the 1980s it was replaced by a raft of 'new educations'. These were, perhaps, not a coherent school of thought or action other than in their commitment to social justice. Some subjects, such as peace education and world studies had existed from the post World War One era (Heater, 1984); others, such as anti-sexist and anti-racist education were more recent. There were a number of key shifts made from the work of the 1970s. Whereas political literacy saw those from traditional academic subjects attempting to expand the nature of work on politics so that it had the potential for democratic understanding and action, the initiatives of the 1980s, while for the most part having similarly democratic credentials, had a harder edge and would not achieve the same level of support from key decision-makers. Instead of having a broad framework of politics which was applied to issues affecting everyday lives, the 'new educations' seemed to give more attention to specific issues. There were a number of key issues but four were always more important than others: the bomb; gender; development; and 'race' (the latter in inverted commas as the very existence of 'race' is, in my view, to be challenged). All four areas were concerned with social justice.

Work on education for citizenship emerging in the late 1980s was closely connected with the thinking of Marshall (1963) (although, of course, the earlier developments were all part of the citizenship agenda). Citizenship became one of the (impotent) five cross-curricular themes of the National Curriculum (National Curriculum Council, 1990) and the subject of a report by the Commission on Citizenship (1990) The council suggested eight essential components comprising community, pluralism, and rights and responsibilities of a citizen as well as specific explorations of the family, democracy in action, the citizen and the law, work employment and leisure and public services. The Speaker's Commission Report, although including many valuable suggestions, became associated narrowly and negatively with the recommendation for more voluntary action by young people. There is some uncertainty about the most recent versions of citizenship education (government thinking about the 14-19 curriculum seems confused) but the Crick Report (QCA, 1998) that led to the form of citizenship education within the National Curriculum seems to me to be (largely) an admirable way forward (Arthur *et al.*, 2001).

Citizenship education in practice

What does all this look like in real schools with real students? Three broad approaches will be briefly discussed with some examples given of work taking place in schools.

First, whole-school approaches are seen as significant. At times this can be rather intangible. Headteachers may talk expansively but rather imprecisely about the importance of an ethos that exemplifies mutual respect, open dialogue and collaborative action. This can be given more particular and precise expression (for example, Trafford, 1993). Organizations such as the Hansard Society, Schools Council UK, Citizenship Foundation, the Institute for Citizenship and Community Service Volunteers can help enormously with the organization of mock elections, school councils, special commemorative days (for example, United Nations Day), peer mediation programmes and community involvement. Schools occasionally provide one-off special events that highlight citizenship education. One particularly successful example of that (Davies *et al.*, 1998) included for the whole school on one day a mock election, activities on human rights, justice, parliamentary debates, Amnesty International and the ethics of scientific research.

A second general approach for the implementation of citizenship education is to target mainstream subjects. Some subjects are felt to have particularly strong links with citizenship. Geography for instance raises many issues about the politics of place: who lives where; who gets what? English requires a study and practice of effective communication in which the significance of support mobilization and audience manipulation can be explored. Although all subjects provide, potentially, opportunities for the citizenship educator perhaps history has been discussed most frequently. The meanings and purposes ascribed to the teaching and learning of citizenship and history are very similar. Dewey (1966: 93) in his key work believed that education utilized 'the past for a resource in a developing future'. Many related citizenship particularly to politics and there were some commentators who stressed the importance of seeing, consequently, a particular link with history. Oakshott (1956: 16) defined political education as 'knowledge as profound as we can make it of our tradition of political behaviour'. Seeley (quoted by Heater, 1974: 1) argued that 'politics are vulgar when they are not liberalised by history and history fades into mere literature when it loses sight of its relation to practical politics'. Heater himself even went so far as to say that history and politics are 'virtually identical subjects'. Crick (2001: xix) explained that had he not been successful in getting citizenship education as a full National Curriculum subject his 'fall back position to propose as a best possible second best: a Key Stage 4 statutory subject in modern history and citizenship'. The sort of work that can be undertaken in classrooms has been discussed by Arthur *et al.* (2001) with examples given for teachers and students.

The third approach to the implementation of citizenship education is to teach citizenship explicitly as separately organized lessons or activities. This is perhaps the most difficult approach to achieve. Arthur *et al.* (2001) expressed some concerns that it might become lost within a personal and social education programme. Innovation is always problematic. Schools always jealously guard the time given to existing subject departments and with the absence of a tradition of citizenship education (with no trained teachers or established career paths) it is very difficult to construct something that will have all the trappings of a *proper* subject. This will be especially noticeable when so many want that new area to be distinct from *normal* school work. That said, there are many fine examples of schemes of work that directly address citizenship education. To illustrate this it will be useful to refer to a very good project that is seeking to meet the challenges in what is arguably the most difficult of the citizenship topics: political literacy.

The project is being managed by the Citizenship Foundation and at the time of writing is still in a development phase. The project makes an argument (Huddleston and Rowe, 2001) for two of the normal approaches to political education to be put to one side. The teaching of the British Constitution is not advocated. This would be a boring and unrealistic way to teach politics. The Constitution is often not a good guide to what happens and why. Further, learning about the Constitution has in the past led to an unhelpful emphasis on factual recall and essay writing as opposed to the wider range of knowledge and skills needed by citizens. The project directors also reject what they have referred to as 'big issues'. A list of supposedly controversial issues often leaves students feeling disempowered in the face of a fragmented, crisis-ridden world. This approach can be particularly unhelpful if the choice of those issues is driven by media reports as it is then not possible to establish overarching perspectives on the nature of politics. Instead the project is focusing on what is referred to in unpublished project papers as 'public discourse'. The central aim of the project *should be* the development of the 'capacity to engage in political discourse' rather than, but not to the exclusion of, the acquisition of factual knowledge about political structures and procedures. A set of materials will be published during 2003 which will include opportunities for school students to debate a range of issues through which they will develop knowledge, but the emphasis will be on the ways in which they engage in increasingly sophisticated public discourse.

> **Summary box**
>
> Schools may decide to implement citizenship education in a variety of ways. Perhaps the three most common methods are:
>
> - whole-school approaches e.g. schools councils, mock elections etc;
> - the infusion of citizenship into other curriculum subjects e.g. history;
> - through explicit teaching through a tailor-made course e.g. political literacy.

The importance of coherence

Throughout this consideration of different approaches to citizenship education it is important to maintain a coherent approach. At times citizenship debates have been conducted philosophically and not pedagogically and with an absence of limits so that at best only a hazy undifferentiated altruism remained. It would not be helpful (in fact it would be contradictory) to insist on de-limiting debates and actions so that participatory democracy would not be relevant to the process of developing citizenship education. One way of working towards a more focused understanding of citizenship education would be to explore the underlying aspects of its nature and to establish more clearly what we mean when we say that students are doing well. A project in which there has been an attempt to do this was sponsored by the DfES (Davies and Thorpe, 2001). That project aimed to achieve coherence by focussing on procedural concepts. Procedural (or second order) concepts (such as evidence and interpretation) are distinct from substantive concepts that relate more narrowly to the study of particular issues (such as government or war). The project team wanted to help teachers to go beyond asking students to memorize details of specific cases, and also to go further than simply asking them to consider the nature of the contexts and substantive concepts which may relate to a number of cases. The ambitious position would be to assert that by identifying procedural concepts it would be possible to invite students not just to think *about* citizenship but to think *as* citizens. Teachers and others would be encouraged to move away from citizenship as merely a goal and allow for the possibility of a clearer identification of what students need to do and how they should think in order to demonstrate effective learning. Given that the preference is for active engagement, the expression of the procedural concepts is given in the form of active verbs. The three areas are: explaining; tolerating and participating. Expressed slightly more fully these areas would involve developing understanding dispositions and abilities associated with:

- rationality grounded in a critical appreciation of social and political realities;
- toleration within the context of a pluralistic democracy;
- participation arising from an acceptance of one's social and political responsibilities and appreciation of one's own rights and entitlements;

These concepts were selected following a careful consideration of the nature of the citizenship order, a review of the literature and discussion with experts (academics and teachers). It is a very provisional list and it is hoped that it will be modified as a result of further work in schools. It is, of course, necessary to relate the concepts to substantive concepts of citizenship, otherwise it would be possible for school students to explain and tolerate and participate in any lesson or activity in the school or community. Having asserted that there is something essential for citizenship education wrapped up in these procedural concepts we must be able to explain how they relate generally to an over-arching sense of citizenship and how they themselves can be seen as being made up of necessary features. As such our materials in history, English and PSE classrooms have been based around a key concept such as inequality or justice or identity. The materials and activities are designed to encourage students to:

- explain their views, their understandings and their arguments;
- tolerate, accommodate and reflect upon opinions and views that may be different from their own;
- participate in the consideration and debate of these ideas in the class-

room and (ideally) use this experience and understanding in their life outside school.

Some initial results show the sort of teaching materials that are being used and the sort of work that is expected from students (Davies *et al.*, 2002).

Conclusion

Citizenship education, in one sense, has always been a very clear part of what any school provides. At times, however, this is done in such a way that it is implicit rather than recognized and élitist rather than inclusive. The current context in England provides a great deal of hope and encouragement for those who wish to promote a professional form of citizenship education. Teachers are being trained, the National Curriculum recognizes the significance of the work, and resources for use in the classroom are flooding onto the market. Whether or not this opportunity can be seized remains to be seen but, in light of the very many issues raised above, if we are serious about the need to secure and promote democratic understandings and practice then a good deal of work lies ahead.

Task

(1) Read the quotations below (the authors are shown at the end of this chapter).

> Active citizenship is the free acceptance by individuals of voluntary obligations to the community of which they are members. It cannot be conjured up by legislation or by political speeches although both can help. It arises from traditions of civic obligations and voluntary service which are central to the thinking of this government and rooted in history.

> The practice of citizenship is about ensuring everybody the entitlements necessary to the exercise of their liberty. As a political question welfare is about rights, not caring, and the history of citizenship has been the struggle to make freedom real, not to tie us all in the leading strings of therapeutic good intentions.

(2) Think about the following:
-   Who do you think was the author of the quotations given here? Can you make an informed guess as to what sort of person they are? What sort of job do they do? What sort of views about citizenship do they hold? Why do you think they hold those particular views? What sort of traditions (as discussed) in this chapter relate most closely to the perspectives given in the quotations? What sort of work that could be undertaken within or outside school would emerge from the two different approaches represented in the quotations? Which of the two quotations (or what sort of blend between the two quotations) do you prefer and why?
(3) Teachers need to know what to look for in terms of students' work. Once they have made some initial judgements they will always explore matters further and it is possible that views will change over a period of time about what counts as good work. Consider the sorts of levels of understanding, skills and dispositions that might be demonstrated by students who are following a citizenship education programme. Thoughts about what good work looks like in relation to toleration are given in Davies *et al.* (2002). Come up with your own ideas about what sorts of student understandings are possible in relation to toleration. Check your views against those given in the article. Criticize the article and come up with a better overall position.

Indicative reading

Crick, B. (2001) *Essays on Citizenship*. London: Continuum. Bernard Crick chaired the advisory group on Education for Citizenship and the Teaching of Democracy in Schools. His report was highly influential and led to the introduction of citizenship as a National Curriculum subject. He is a respected academic who wrote the classic *In Defence of Politics* and was the principal figure in the political literacy movement of the 1970s. This book contains a range of his work written over a thirty year period.

Davies, I., Hatch, G., Martin, G. and Thorpe, T. (2002) "What is good citizenship education in history classrooms?", *Teaching History*, (106): 37-43.

Heater, D. (1999) *What is Citizenship?* Cambridge: Polity Press. Derek Heater provides a very good and fairly accessible account of the different strands and traditions associated with citizenship. He explores the work of Marshall (1963) who has been so influential in the setting of the contemporary agenda for citizenship education. Very good explanations are given for the rights-based liberal tradition and the duties-based civic republican tradition that relate to citizenship education.

Jowell, R. and Park, A. (1997) "Young people, politics and citizenship – a disengaged generation?" Paper delivered at the Citizenship Foundation Annual Colloquium. London: Citizenship Foundation. This paper was published by the Citizenship Foundation. It explores issues associated with young people's involvement in politics. If difficult to get hold of, it might be easier to see some of the issues in the following book: White, C., Bruce, S. and Ritchie, J. (2000) *Young People's Politics: political interest and engagement amongst 14 to 24 year olds.* York: Joseph Rowntree Foundation. Both these publications raise important issues about why young people are less interested in politics than we might hope. There is some concern that voting figures for young people are low and decreasing. However, some argue that we do not have enough evidence to know whether there is a real problem in terms of young people's alienation from the political process. It is possible that young people have always simply grown into the habit of voting as they age and that this will again occur for the current younger generation. Similarly, there is disagreement amongst teachers about whether young people should be encouraged to vote. Some forms of participation may take the form of an informed decision not to vote and it may not be professional for teachers to take a more limited view of what is meant by taking part in the political process.

Pike, G. and Selby, D. (1988) *Global Teacher, Global Learner.* London: Hodder and Stoughton. This book was written just before the National Curriculum was established and well before citizenship education in its present form was considered. In some ways the book is part of an earlier age of curriculum development work. There is something about the peace-loving, holistic, global approach that is, in the contemporary objectives driven commitment to literacy and numeracy, unusual. However, this book is also up-to-date. It is very popular with student teachers. It suits our determination to look beyond the borders of nation states. It contains very many thought-provoking ideas and it is full of practical suggestions for classroom action.

The websites of the following organizations provide useful insights into the key issues as well as providing examples of classroom-based and other activities. Often entering the site of one of the following (e.g. Citizenship Foundation) will give you an easy link to the other sites shown here and many others.

(Citizenship Foundation) http://www.citfou.org.uk/
(Institute for Citizenship) http://www.citizen.org.uk
(Association for Citizenship Teaching) http://www.teachingcitizenship.org.uk/test/
(Department for Education and Skills) http://www.dfes.gov.uk/
(Citizen 21) http://www.citizen21.org.uk
(Commission for Racial Equality) http://www.cre.gov.uk/

Information on the two quotations for task (1)

- The first quotation is from Hurd, D. (1988). Douglas Hurd was a key member of Margaret Thatcher's governments. At the time he made that statement he was at the Home Office responsible for law and order and immigration. His junior minister, John Patten, later became Secretary of State for Education and was involved with the attempt to implement a form of citizenship education in the early 1990s.
- The second quotation is from Ignatieff, M. (1989) Michael Ignatieff is a philosopher and occasional journalist. His most recent book is titled *Human Rights* (edited by Amy Gutman, 2001). He is currently Director of the Carr Center for Human Rights Policy at Harvard University.

Notes on Contributors

Ian Barron, a former primary school headteacher and schools advisor with wide experience in early years education, is principal lecturer and leader of educational studies programmes at Manchester Metropolitan University, where he specializes in co-ordinating and teaching courses on early childhood education.

Graham Boyes is headteacher at St. Bartholomew's County Primary School in Lancashire. He has worked in a variety of Lancashire schools, contributed to the delivery of continuing professional development programmes at Edge Hill College and worked as mentor in the professional development of head-teachers.

Dr Keith Crawford is a reader in education at Edge Hill College and educational research co-ordinator, and has published widely in the area of curriculum theory, the social construction of curriculum and curriculum history. Dr Crawford's research interests focus upon citizenship education and the politics and ideology of curriculum mediated through history and social studies textbooks. He is editor of *Citizenship, Social and Economics Education: an international journal* published by JP Publishing.

Professor Cedric Cullingford is head of educational research at the University of Huddersfield. His research interests include principles of learning and attitude formation; analysis and response to issues of bullying and truancy; the role of parents in the education system; effective teaching and ethnographic research methods. He is the author of fifteen books including *Children and Society*, Cassell; *Parents, Education and the State; the politics of primary education*, OUP; *Prejudice; from individual identity to nationalism in young people*, Kogan Page.

Dr Ian Davies is a lecturer in education studies at the University of York. He teaches undergraduates and graduates and supervises graduate research in history, humanities education and civic education. Dr Davies is a member of Children's Identity and Citizenship in Europe, a European Commission funded thematic network. Publications include *Citizenship through Secondary History*, published by RoutledgeFalmer in 2001, and *Good Citizenship and Educational Provision*, Falmer Press, 1999.

Dr Mike Davis is a senior lecturer in education at Edge Hill College where he is course leader for the BA honours degree in education and literacy. Dr Davis teaches undergraduates and graduates, and supervises graduate research in teaching and learning. His research interests include the development of curriculum for on-line learning.

Brenda Judge is a senior lecturer in education at Edge Hill College where she teaches on courses related to inclusive education; she has wide experience of the principles and practices of primary education including the headship of an inner city primary school. She is co-author of *Learning to Teach in the Primary School* published by Routledge in 1996.

Dr Dean Garratt is a research fellow in the Research and Graduate School of the Institute of Education at the Manchester Metropolitan University. Since completing his doctoral thesis, he has written extensively on issues concerning qualitative research methodology, curriculum and citizenship, with international publications in these areas. He has been involved in externally funded research and an evaluation of the Citizenship Values Award Pilot Scheme funded by the Institute of Global Ethics and the Citizenship Foundation.

Philip Prescott is a senior lecturer at Edge Hill College and course leader for the BA (hons) degrees in childhood and youth studies, and early childhood studies, and an Open University tutor. He spent nine years as a lecturer on the diploma in social work course responsible for childcare law, policy and practice. His research areas are child protection and sport. Before joining Edge Hill he had seventeen years professional experience as manager, guardian *ad litem* and as a practitioner in childcare social work.

Tony Shallcross is programme leader for international programmes and designated researcher at Manchester Metropolitan University. His research interests include children's participation in education for sustainable development, curricular applications of deep green ethical theory, and ethnographically focused self-evaluation strategies for schools. He has conducted funded evaluation projects for Scottish Natural Heritage, the World Wildlife Fund for Nature, the Institute for Global Ethics and the Citizenship Foundation. He is project director for the European Commission funded Sustainability Education in European Primary Schools Project (SEEPS) which supports the development of whole-school approaches to sustainability education. His responsibilities include PhD and masters' dissertation supervision, teaching on initial teacher education and continuing professional development (CPD) courses including course direction for European Commission funded COMENIUS CPD courses. He has had over twenty years experience teaching in schools involving senior academic and pastoral posts of responsibility.

Adrian Smith is a senior lecturer in education at Edge Hill College where he co-ordinates courses on educational studies for the MA degree and supervises post-graduate research. His research interests focus upon the principles and practices of effective schooling and school management where he has conducted funded research projects. He is joint editor with Catherine Sykes of *Leading School Improvement: what works and why?* published by Peter Francis in 2001.

Dominic Wyse is a former primary teacher and language co-ordinator in London, Bradford and Kirklees. He is principal lecturer in school-based research in the School of Education and Community Studies at John Moores University, Liverpool. Dominic Wyse lectures on childhood studies and education courses. His work has included papers on the teaching of reading, and the teaching of grammar which appeared in *The Journal of Educational Studies*. His book, *Teaching English, Language and Literacy*, has been described as the standard text for the 2000s. Books include *Becoming a Primary Teacher* published by RoutledgeFalmer, and *An Introduction to Childhood Studies*, published by Blackwell in 2003.

Bibliography

Abbott, L. and Pugh, G. (eds.) (1998) *Training to Work in the Early Years*. Buckingham: OUP.

Ainscow, M. (1995) "Education for all: making it happen", *Support for Learning* 10 (4).

Alderson, P. (2000) "Children's rights in schools: the implications for youth policy", *Youth and Policy*, 64: 56-73.

Alderson, P. (1999) "School students' views on school councils and daily life at school", *Children and Society*, 14: 121-34.

Alexander, R. (1984) *Primary Teaching*. London: Cassell.

Althusser, L. (1984) *Essays on Ideology*. London: Verso.

Althusser, L. (1981) "Marx's new science" in T. Bottomore (ed.) *Modern Interpretations of Marx*. Oxford: Blackwell.

Anning, A. and Edwards, A. (1999) *Promoting Children's Learning from Birth to Five: developing the new early years professional*. Buckingham: OUP.

Apple, M.W. (1993) *Official Knowledge: democratic education in a Conservative age*. London: Routledge.

Apple, M.W. (1990) *Ideology and Curriculum* (2nd edn). London: Routledge.

Aries, P. (1962) *Centuries of Childhood*. Harmondsworth: Penguin.

Arnot, M. (1997) "'Gendered citizenry': new feminist perspectives on education and citizenship", *British Educational Research Journal*, 23 (3): 275-95.

Arthur, J., Davies, I., Wrenn, A., Haydn, T. and Kerr, D. (2001) *Citizenship through Secondary History*. London: Routledge.

Ball, C. (ed.) (1994) *Startright: the importance of early learning*. London: Prentice Hall.

Ball, S.J. (1993b) "Education, markets, choice and social class: the market as a class strategy in the UK and the USA", *British Journal of Sociology of Education*, 14 (1): 3-19.

Ball, S.J. (1990) *Politics and Polict Making in Education: explorations in policy sociology*. London: Routledge.

Bandura, A. (1986) *Social Foundations of Thought and Action: a social cognitive theory*. Englewood Cliffs: Prentice Hall.

Bandura, A. (1973) *Aggression: a social learning analysis*. London: Prentice Hall.

Bartlett, S., Burton, D. and Peim, N. (2001) *Introduction to Education Studies*. London: Paul Chapman.

Batho, G. (1990) "The history of the teaching of civics and citizenship in English schools", *The Curriculum Journal*, 1 (1): 91-100.

Beane, J.A. and Apple, M.W. (1999) *Democratic Schools: lessons from the chalk face*. Buckingham: OUP.

Beckett, F. (2002) "Comprehensives: a minute to midnight", *New Statesman*, 14th October.

Behlemer, G.K. (1982) *Child Abuse and Moral Reform in England, 1870-1908*. Stanford: Stanford University Press.

Begg, A. (2000) *Empowering the Earth: strategies for social change*. Dartington: Green Books.

Belsky, J. (1993) "Etiology of child maltreatment: a developmental-ecological analysis", *Psychological Bulletin*, 114: 413-34.

Belsky, J. (1978) "Three theoretical models of child abuse: a critical review", *Child Abuse and Neglect*, (2): 37-49.

Benn, T. (1988) *Tony Benn: office without power – Diaries 1968-72*. London: Hutchinson.

Bennet, J., Gash, H. and O'Reilly, M. (1998) "Ireland: integration as appropriate, segregation where necessary" in T. Booth and M. Ainscow (eds.) *From Them to Us*. London: Routledge.

Berg, L. (1968) "Chained children", *Cambridge Review*, 8th November. Available from http:// www.aspects.net/~leilaberg/ChChildren.htm (accessed 12th June 2003).

Bernstein, B. (1970) "Education cannot compensate for society" in D. Rubinstein and C. Stoneman (eds.) *Education for Democracy*. Harmondsworth: Penguin.

Board of Education (1943) *Curriculum and Examinations in Secondary Schools* (Norwood Report). London: HMSO.

Board of Education (1928) *Report of the Consultative Committee on Secondary Education with Special Reference to Grammar Schools and Technical High Schools* (Spens Report). London: HMSO.

Bonnet, M. (1999) "Education for sustainable development: a coherent philosophy for environmental education", *Cambridge Journal of Education*, 29 (3): 313-24.

Bowers, C.A. (1997) *The Culture of Denial. Why the Environmental Movement Needs a Strategy for Reforming Universities and Public Schools*. Albany: State University of New York Press.

Bowlby, J. (1982) *Attachment and Loss* (vol. 1) (2nd edn). New York: Basic Books.

Bowles, S. and Gintis, H. (1976) *Schooling in Capitalist America*. London: Routledge and Kegan Paul.

Brennan, A. (1991) "Environmental awareness and liberal education", *British Journal of Educational Studies*, 39 (3): 279-95.

Brennan, T. (1981) *Political Education and Democracy*. Cambridge: Cambridge University Press.

Brodie, I. (2000) "Children's homes and school exclusion; redefining the problem", *Support for Learning*, 15 (1).

Bronfenbrenner, U. (1979) *The Ecology of Human Development: experiments by nature and design*. London: Harvard University Press.

Bruce, T. (1997) *Early Childhood Education* (2nd edn). London: Hodder and Stoughton.

Bruner, J. (1977) *The Process of Education*. London: Harvard University Press.

Bruner, J. (1966) *Towards a Theory of Instruction*. London: Harvard University Press.

Bruner, J. and Haste, H. (eds.) (1987) *Making Sense: the child's construction of the world*. London: Methuen.

Burman, E. (1994) *Deconstructing Developmental Psychology*. London: Routledge.

Burr, V. (1995) *An Introduction to Social Constructionism*. London: Routledge.

Callaghan, J. (1976) "Towards a national debate" (Ruskin College speech, 18th October). Reprinted in *The Guardian*, 15th October 2001. Available from http://education.guardian. co.uk/thegreatdebate/story/0,9860,574645,00.html (accessed 15th October 2001).

Cannella, G.S. (1997) *Deconstructing Early Childhood Education: social justice and revolution*. New York: Peter Lang.

Carr, M. and May, H. (2000) *"Te Whariki:* curriculum voices" in H. Penn (ed.) *Early Childhood Services: theory, policy and practice.* Buckingham: OUP.

Children and Young Person's Unit (2002) "Building a strategy for children and young people: a consultation from the CYPU", *Childright,* 183 (January/February): 3-5.

CRDU (1994) *UK Agenda for Children.* London: Children's Rights Development Unit.

Claxton, G. (1997) *Hare Brain, Tortoise Mind.* London: Fourth Estate.

Clayton, A.M.H. and Radcliffe, N.J. (1996) *Sustainability, a Systems Approach.* London: Earthscan, WWFNUK and The Institute for Policy Analysis.

Cole, M. (1992) "Culture in development" in M.H. Bornstein and M.E. Lamb (eds.) *Human Development, an advanced textbook.* Hillsdale, NJ: Lawrence Erlbaum.

Coles, R. (1997) *The Moral Intelligence of Children.* London: Bloomsbury.

Commission on Citizenship (1990) *Encouraging Citizenship.* London: HMSO.

Connell, S., Fien, J., Lee, J., Sykes, H. and Yencken, D. (1999) "'If it doesn't directly affect you, you don't think about it': a qualitative study of young people's environmental attitudes in two Australian cities", *Environmental Education Research,* 5 (1): 95-113.

Corby, B. (1993) *Child Abuse: towards a knowledge base.* Buckingham: OUP.

Cormack, M. (1992) *Ideology.* London: Batsford.

Cosin, B.R., Dale, I.R., Esland, G.M., Mackinnon, D. and Swift, D.F. (eds.) (1971) *School and Society.* London: Routledge and Kegan Paul.

Cox, C.B. and Boyson, R. (eds.) (1977) *Black Paper 1977.* London: Temple Smith.

Cox, C.B. and Boyson, R. (eds.) (1975) *Black Paper 1975.* London: JM Dent and Sons.

Cox, C.B. and Dyson, A. (eds.) (1970) *Black Paper Three.* London: Critical Quarterly Society.

Cox, C.B. and Dyson, A. (eds.) (1969a) *Fight for Education Black Paper.* London: Critical Quarterly Society.

Cox, C.B. and Dyson, A. (eds.) (1969b) *Black Paper Two.* London: Critical Quarterly Society.

Crain, W. (1992) *Theories of Development: concepts and applications.* Englewood Cliffs, NJ: Prentice Hall.

Crawford, K.A. (1998) "The social construction of the National Curriculum: a political and ideological analysis", *Research Papers in Educations,* 13 (3), 261-76.

Crick, B. and Heater, D. (1977) *Essays on Political Education.* Lewes: Falmer.

Crick, B. (2001) "Preface" in J. Arthur, I. Davies, A. Wrenn, T. Haydn, D. Kerr *Citizenship through Secondary History.* London: RoutledgeFalmer.

Crick, B. and Porter, A. (eds.) (1978) *Political Education and Political Literacy.* London: Longman.

Cullingford, C. (2000) *Prejudice: from individual identity to nationalism in young people.* London: Kogan Page.

Dagger, R. (1997) *Civic Virtues: rights, citizenship and republican liberalism.* Oxford: Oxford University Press.

Dahlberg, G. and Lenz Taguchi, H. (1994) *Forskola och skola – om tva skilda traditioner och om visionen om en motesplats (Preschool and school – two different traditions and a vision of an encounter).* Stockholm: HLS Forlag.

Dale, P. (1986) *Dangerous Families: assessment and treatment of child abuse.* London: Routledge.

Dalin, P. (1978) *Limits to Educational Change.* London. Macmillan.

David, T. (1990) *Five – Under Educated.* Buckingham: OUP.

David, T. (2001) "Curriculum in the early years" in G. Pugh (ed.) *Contemporary Issues in the Early Years: working collaboratively for children* (3rd edn). London: Paul Chapman.

David, T. (1999) "Valuing young children" in L. Abbott and H. Moylett (eds.) *Early Education Transformed.* London: Falmer Press.

Davies, I. (1999) "What happened to the teaching of politics in schools in England in the last three decades and why?", *Oxford Review of Education*, 25 (1&2): 125-40.

Davies, I. (1993) "Teaching political understanding in secondary schools", *Curriculum*, 14 (3): 163-77.

Davies, I. and Thorpe, T. (2001) "Exploring the procedural concepts of citizenship education". A paper for the conference on The Social and Moral Fabric of the School. University of Hull. September.

Davies, I., Hatch, G., Martin, G. and Thorpe, T. (2002) "What is good citizenship education in history classrooms?", *Teaching History*, (106): 37-43.

Davies, I., Gray, G., and Stephens, P. (1998) "Education for citizenship: a case study of 'Democracy Day' at a comprehensive school", *Educational Review*, 50 (1): 15-27.

Delair, H.A. and Erwin, E. (2000) "Working perspectives within feminism and early childhood education", *Contemporary Issues in Early Childhood*. (1): 2.

Derrida, J. (1991) "Of grammatology" in P. Kamuf (ed.) *The Blinds*. New York: Harvester Wheatsheaf.

DES (1990) *Starting with Quality* (Rumbold Report). London: HMSO.

DES (1987) *The National Curriculum 5-16: a consultation document*. London: HMSO.

DES (1985) *Education for All* (Swann Report). London: HMSO.

DES (1981) *The School Curriculum*. London: HMSO.

DES (1980) *A Framework for the Curriculum*. London: HMSO.

DES (1978) *Special Educational Needs* (Warnock Report). London: HMSO.

DES (1977) *Education for Schools: a consultative document*. London: HMSO

DES (1976) *Schools and Education in England: problems and initiative*. London: HMSO.

DES (1967a) *Children and their Primary Schools* (Plowden Report). London: HMSO.

DES (1967b) *Towards World History*. Pamphlet No. 52. London: HMSO.

Dewey, J. (1966) *Democracy and Education*. London: Free Press/Macmillan.

DfEE (2000) *Raising Ethnic Minority Pupil Achievement*. London: DfEE Publications.

DfEE (1997) *Excellence for All: meeting special educational needs*. London: DfEE Publications.

DfEE (1994) *The Education of Children being Looked after by Local Authorities* (Circular 13/94). London: HMSO.

DfEE and QCA (1999) *Citizenship*. London: QCA.

DHSS (1974) *Report of the Committee of Inquiry into the Care and Supervision Provided in Relation to Maria Colwell*. London: HMSO.

Dimbleby, J. (2001) "Change is in the air", *Resurgence*, (207): 16-17.

Donoughue, B. (1987) *Prime Minister: the conduct of policy under Harold Wilson and James Callaghan*. London: Jonathan Cape.

Douglas, J.W.B. (1964) *The Home and the School*. London: McGibbon and Kee.

Driver, E. and Droisen, A. (eds.) (1989) *Child Sexual Abuse: feminist perspectives*. London: Macmillan.

Early Childhood Education Research Forum (1998) *Quality in Diversity in Early Learning*. London: National Children's Bureau.

Edwards, A. and Whitty, G. (1992) "Parental choice and educational reform in Britain and the United States", *British Journal of Educational Studies*, 40 (2): 101-17.

Entwistle, H. (1973) "Towards an educational theory of political socialisation". Paper read at the Philosophy of Education Society conference, New Orleans, USA, 15th April.

Farrer, F. (2000) *A Quiet Revolution: encouraging positive values in our children*. London: Rider.

Flekkøy, M.G. (1995) "The Scandinavian experience of children's rights" in B. Franklin (ed.) *The Handbook of Children's Rights*. London: Routledge.

Fogelman, K. (ed.) (1991) *Citizenship in Schools*. London: David Fulton.

Foster, S.L., Matinez, C.R., and Kulberg, A.M. (1996) "Race, ethnicity and children's peer relations" in T.H. Ollendick and R.J. Prinz (eds.) *Advances in Clinical Child Psychology No. 18*. New York: Plenum Press.

Foucault, M. (1980) "Truth and power" in C. Gordon (ed.) *Power/Knowledge: selected interviews and other writings 1972-1977*. Brighton: Harvester.

Franklin, B. and Horwath, J. (1996) "The media abuse of children: Jake's progress from demonic icon to restored childhood innocent", *Child Abuse Review*, (5): 310-18.

Franklin, B. and Petley, J. (1996) "Killing the age of innocence: newspaper reporting of the death of James Bulger" in J. Pilcher and S. Wagg (eds.) *Thatcher's Children? politics, childhood and society in the 1980s and 1990s*. London: Falmer Press.

Freeman, C. (1999) "Children's participation in environmental decision-making" in S. Buckingham-Hatfield and S. Percy (1999) *Constructing Local Environmental Agendas: people places and participation*. London: Routledge.

Fullan, M. and Hargreaves, A. (1992) *What's Worth Fighting for in Your School?* Buckingham: OUP.

Gardner, H. (1993) *Frames of Mind. The Theory of Multiple Intelligences*. London: Heinmann.

Gelles, R. (1979) "Psychopathology as cause: a critique and reformulation" in D. Gil (ed.) *Violence Against Children*. Cambridge, Mass: Harvard University Press.

Giddens, A. (1998) *The Third Way: the renewal of social democracy*. London: Polity Press.

Gil, D. (1975) "Unravelling child abuse", *American Journal of Orthopsychiatry*, (45): 3.

Gillard, D. (2001) "A brief history of education in England". Available from http://www.kbr30.dial.pipex.com/educ19.shtml (accessed 20th June 2003).

Gillborn, D. (1997) "Ethnicity and educational performance in the United Kingdom: racism, ethnicity and variability in achievement", *Anthropology and Education Quarterly*, 28 (3).

Gillborn, D. and Gipps, C. (1996) *Recent Research on the Achievements of Ethnic Minority Pupils*. London: HMSO.

Gillborn, D. and Mirza, H. (2000) *Educational Inequality: mapping race, class and gender; a synthesis of research evidence*. London: OFSTED.

Gilmour, I. (1992) *Dancing with Dogma*. London: Pocket Books.

Giroux, H.A. (1996) "Towards a postmodern pedagogy" in L.E. Cahoone (ed.) *From Modernism to Postmodernism: an anthology*. Oxford: Blackwell.

Gittins, D. (1998) *The Child in Question*. London: Macmillan.

Goldson, B. (1997) "'Childhood': an introduction to historical and theoretical analyses" in P. Scraton (ed.) *Childhood in Crisis?* London: UCL Press.

Goldstein, L.S. (1997) *Teaching with Love: a feminist approach to early childhood education*. New York: Peter Lang.

Goleman, D. (1996) *Emotional Intelligence*. London: Bloomsbury.

Goodman, P. (1971) *Compulsory Miseducation*. Harmondsworth: Penguin.

Goodson, I. (1989) "Curriculum reform and curriculum theory: a case study of historical amnesia", *Cambridge Journal of Education*, 19 (2): 131-43.

Goodson, I. (1988) *The Making of Curriculum: collected essays*. Lewis: Falmer.

Gramsci, A. (1971) *Selections from the Prison Notebooks*. Translated by Q. Hoare and G. Nowell-Smith. London and New York: Lawrence & Wishart.

Greenstein, F. (1965) *Children and Politics*. London: Yale University Press.

Greig, A. and Taylor, J. (1999) *Doing Research with Children*. London: Sage.

Greig, S., Pike, G. and Selby, D. (1989) *Greenprints for Changing Schools*. London: WWF and Kogan Page.

Grundy, S. (1987) *Curriculum: product or praxis*. Lewes: Falmer.

Habermas, J. (1972) *Knowledge and Human Interests* (2nd edn). London: Heinemann.

Hague, T. (1998) "Promoting children's interests and rights in education: the contribution of the ombudsman for children to the compulsory school reform", *International Journal of Early Childhood*, 30 (1): 52-5.

Hall, C. (1998) "A family for nation and empire" in G. Lewis (ed.) *Forming Nation, Framing Welfare*. London: Routledge.

Hardman, B. (2002) *Birthright*, unpublished poem.

Harrington, R.F. (1996) "Bringing education down to earth", *Trumpeter*, 13 (3). Available from http://www.icaap.org/iuicode?6.13.3.5 (accessed 20th June 2003).

Hart, R. (1997) *Children's Participation; the theory and practice of involving young citizens in community development and environmental care*. London: UNICEF/Earthscan.

Hatcher, R. and Troyna, B. (1994) "The policy cycle: a ball by ball account", *Journal of Education Policy*, 9 (2): 155-70.

Haviland, J. (1988) *Take Care Mr Baker*. London: Fourth Estate.

Hayden, C. (1997) *Exclusions from Primary Schools*. Buckingham: OUP.

Hazareesingh, S., Simms, K. and Anderson, P. (1989) *Educating the Whole Child*. London: Building Blocks Educational.

Heater, D. (1984) *Peace Through Education. The Contribution of the Council for Education in World Citizenship*. Lewes: Falmer.

Heater, D. (1983) "The origins of CEWC. (Council for Education in World Citizenship)". Paper presented at a seminar in the Department of Educational Studies, University of York.

Heater, D. (1974) *History Teaching and Political Education* (Occasional Pamphlet, number 1). Manchester: Politics Association.

Hendrick, H. (1990) *Child Welfare England 1872-1989*. London: Routledge.

Hillgate Group (1987) *The Reform of British Education*. London: Hillgate Group.

Hillgate Group (1986) *Whose Schools? a radical manifesto*. London: Hillgate Group.

Holden, C and Clough, N. (1998) "The child carried on the back does not know the length of the road: the teacher's role in assisting participation" in C. Holden and N. Clough (eds.) *Children as Citizens: education for participation*. London: Jessica Kingsley.

Holland, P. (1992) *What is a Child? Popular Images of Childhood*. London: Virago Press.

Holt, J. (1964) *Why Children Fail*. Harmondsworth: Penguin.

Houghton Report (1974) *Pay of University Teachers*. London: HMSO.

Huddleston, T. and Rowe, D. (2001) "Political literacy in secondary schools: process or product?" Paper presented to Diverse Citizenships conference, University of North London, March.

Hurd, D. (1988) "Freedom will flourish where citizens accept responsibility", *The Independent*, 13th February.

Ignatieff, M. (1989) "Citizenship and moral narcissism", *Political Quarterly*, (60): 1.

Illich, I. (1973) *Deschooling Society*. Harmondsworth: Penguin.

Irvine, R. (1988) "Child abuse and poverty" in S. Becker and S. MacPherson (eds.) *Public Issues: private pain*. London: Insight.

Jack, G. (2001) "An ecological perspective on child abuse" in P. Foley, J. Roche and S. Tucker (eds.) *Children in Society: contemporary theory, policy and practice*. Hampshire: Palgrave.

Jack, G. and Jordan, B. (1999) "Social capital and child welfare", *Children and Society*, (13): 242-56.

Jackson, B. and Marsden, D. (1962) *Education and the Working Class*. Harmondsworth: Penguin.

Jenks, C. (1996) *Childhood.* London: Routledge.

Jensen, B.B. (ed.) (1995) *Concepts and Models in a Democratic Health Education: research in environmental and health education.* Copenhagen: Royal Danish School of Educational Studies.

Johnson, R. (1991) "A new road to serfdom? A critical history of the 1988 Act" in R. Johnston *Education Limited.* London: Unwin Hyman.

Johnston, E. and Rahilly, S. (2001) *Opportunity for Childcare? The impact of government initiatives upon childcare provision.* Liverpool: Save the Children (UK) and Liverpool John Moores University.

Kagan, J. (1984) *The Nature of the Child.* New York: Basic Books.

Katz, L.G. (1999) "Curriculum disputes in early childhood education", *ERIC,* December. Available from http://www.ericeece.org (accessed 11th June 2001).

Katz, L.G. (1996) "Balancing Constructivism and Instructivism in the Early Childhood Curriculum". The Annual Maya Zuck Lecture in Early Childhood Education Series, Washington University, St. Louis, MO.

Kempe, C.H., Silverman, F., Steele, B., Droegmueller, W. and Silver, H.K. (1962) "The battered baby syndrome", *Journal of the American Medical Association,* (181): 17-24.

King, R. (1978) *All Things Bright and Beautiful? A Sociological Study of Infant Classrooms.* Wiley: Chichester.

Kingston, P. and Penhale, B. (eds.) (1995) *Family Violence and the Caring Professions.* London: Macmillan.

Knight, C. (1990) *The Making of Tory Education Policy in Post-War Britain.* Lewis: Falmer Press.

Krech, D., Crutchfield, R.S. and Egerton, L. (1962) *Individual in Society.* Tokyo: McGraw-Hill.

Kress, G. (1999) "A creative spell", *Guardian Education,* 16th November.

Langan, M. (ed.) (1998) *Welfare: needs, rights and risks.* London: Routledge.

Laura, R.S. and Cotton, M.C. (1999) *Empathetic Education: an ecological perspective on educational knowledge.* London: Falmer.

Leather, N., Hawtin, A., Napier, N. and Wyse, D. (2000) *Children: a multi-professional perspective.* London: Arnold.

Lester Smith W.O. (1957) *Education.* Harmondsworth: Penguin.

Lind, U. (1998) "Positions in Swedish child pedagogical research" in T. David (ed.) *Researching Early Childhood Education: European perspectives.* London: Sage.

Lipsky, D.K. and Gartner, A. (1996) "Inclusion, school restructuring, and the remaking of American society", *Harvard Educational Review,* 66 (4).

Livingstone, D.W. (1997) "The limits of human capital theory: expanding knowledge, informal learning and underemployment", *Policy Options.* Available from http://www.irpp.org/po/archive/jul97/livingst.pdf (accessed 20th June 2003).

Mackenzie, R.F. (1970) *State School.* Harmondsworth: Penguin.

Marshall, T.H. (1963) *Sociology at the Crossroads.* London: Heinemann.

Marwick, A. (1990) *British Society Since 1945.* London: Penguin.

Matheson, C. and Limond, D. (1999) "Ideology in education in the UK" in D. Matheson and I. Grosvenor (eds.) *An Introduction to the Study of Education.* London: Fulton.

May, M. (1978) "Violence in the family: an historical perspective" in J.P. Martin (ed.) *Violence in the Family.* Chichester: Wiley.

McClure, H.M. and Fischer, G. (1969) *Ideology and Opinion Making: general problems of analysis.* New York: Columbia University Bureau of Applied Social Research.

McLellan, D. (1986) *Ideology.* Milton Keynes: OUP.

Medforth, N., Fenwick, G. and Wyse, D. (2000) "Images of childhood" in D. Wyse and A. Hawtin (eds.) *Children: a multi-professional perspective.* London: Arnold.

Meredith, P. (2001) "Editorial comment: the child's right to education", *Education and the Law,* 13 (1): 5-8.

Ministry of Education (1963) *Half Our Future: a report of the Central Advisory Council for Education, England* (Newsom Report). London: HMSO.

Ministry of Education (1959) *15-17: a report of the Central Advisory Council for Education, England Volume 1* (Crowther Report). London: HMSO.

Ministry of Education (1949) *Citizens Growing Up. Pamphlet No. 16.* London: HMSO.

Ministry of Education (1947) *The New Secondary Education. Pamphlet No. 9.* London: HMSO.

Mooney, G. (1998) "'Remoralizing the poor?': gender, class and philanthropy in Victorian Britain" in G. Lewis (ed.) *Forming Nation, Framing Welfare.* London: Routledge.

Moore, R. (1984) "Schooling and the world of work" in I. Bates, J. Clark, P. Cohen, D. Finn, R. Moore and P. Willis (eds.) *Schooling for the Dole.* London: Macmillan.

Morris, M. and Schagen, I. (1996) *Green Attitudes or Learned Responses?* Slough: National Foundation for Educational Research.

Morris, M. and Griggs, C. (eds.) (1988) *Education – thirteen wasted years.* Lewis: Falmer.

Morrison A. and McIntyre, D. (1971) *Schools and Socialisation.* Harmondsworth: Penguin.

Morss, J.R. (1996) *Growing Critical. Alternatives to Developmental Psychology.* London: Routledge.

Moscovici, S. (1976) *La Psychanalyse, son image et son public.* Paris: Presses Universitaires de France.

Moyles, J. (2001) "Passion, paradox and professionalism in early years education", *Early Years,* 21 (2): 81-95.

Naess, A. (1993) "Beautiful action: its function in the ecological crisis", *Environmental Values,* 2 (1): 67-71.

Nasman, E. (1994) "Individualization and institutionalization of childhood in today's Europe" in J. Qvortrup, M. Bardy, G. Sgritta and H. Wintersberger (eds.) *Childhood Matters: social theory, practice and politics.* Vienna and Aldershot: European Centre and Avebury.

National Curriculum Council (1990) *Education for Citizenship. Curriculum Guidance 8.* York: NCC.

Neill, J.W. (1969) *Neill and Summerhill: a man and his work. A Pictorial Study.* Harmondsworth: Penguin.

Nelson, B. (1984) *Making an Issue of Child Abuse.* Chicago: Chicago University Press.

Oakshott, M. (1956) "Political education" in P. Laslett *Philosophy, Politics and Society.* Oxford: Basil Blackwell.

Oates, J. (ed.) (1994) *The Foundations of Child Development.* Milton Keynes: OUP.

Oliver, D.W. and Shaver, J.P. (1966) *Teaching Public Issues in the High School.* Boston: Houghton Mifflin Co.

Orr, D.W. (1992) *Ecological Literacy: education and the transition to a postmodern world.* Albany: State University of New York Press.

Orr, D.W. (1994) *Earth in Mind on Education, Environment, and the Human Prospect.* Washington, DC: Island Press.

Ortiz, A. (1984) "Texas: a State policy for Hispanic children with special needs" in P. Williams (ed.) *Special Education in Minority Communities.* Milton Keynes: OUP.

Orwell, G. (1937) *The Road to Wigan Pier.* Harmondsworth: Penguin.

Osler, A. (1997) "Black teachers and citizenship: researching differing identities", *Teachers and Teaching: theory and practice,* 3 (1): 47-60.

Parton, N. (1985) *The Politics of Child Abuse.* London: Macmillan.

Pascal, C. and Bertram, T. (1997) *Effective Early Learning.* London: Hodder & Stoughton.

Patten, J. (1993) *Letter of Response to David Pascal, NCC in English for Ages 5 to 16* (1993 Proposals to the Secretary of State). London: DfEE.

Pavlov, I.P. (1927) *Conditioned Reflexes*. Oxford: Oxford University Press.

Pence, A. and Ball, J. (2000) "Two sides of an eagle's feather: University of Victoria partnerships with Canadian First Nations communities" in H. Penn (ed.) *Early Childhood Services: theory, policy and practice*. Buckingham: OUP.

Penn, H. (1998) "Comparative research: a way forward?" in T. David (ed.) *Researching Early Childhood Education*. London: Sage.

Peters, R.S. (1966) *Ethics and Education*. London: Allen and Unwin.

Peters, R.S. (ed.) (1973) *The Philosophy of Education*. London: Oxford University Press.

Piaget, J. (1950) *The Psychology of Intelligence*. London: Routledge and Keegan Paul.

Posch, P. (1999) "The ecologisation of schools and its implications for educational policy", *Cambridge Journal of Education*, 29 (3): 341-48.

Posch, P. (1993) *Approaches to Values in Environmental Education in OECD/ENSI Values in Environmental Education*. Dundee: SCCC.

Postman, N. and Weingartner, C. (1971) *Teaching as a Subversive Activity*. Harmondsworth: Penguin.

Price, C. (1998) "Crosland aloft", *London Review of Books*, 20: 19.

Prout, A. and James, A. (1990) "A new paradigm for the sociology of childhood?" in A. James and A. Prout (eds.) *Constructing and Deconstructing Childhood: contemporary issues in the sociological study of childhood*. Brighton: Falmer.

QCA/DfEE (2000) *Curriculum Guidance for the Foundation Stage*. Sudbury: QCA.

QCA (1999) *Early Learning Goals*. Sudbury: QCA.

QCA (1998) *Education for Citizenship: the teaching of democracy in schools* (Crick Report). London: QCA.

Quicke, J. (1988) "The New Right and education", *British Journal of Educational Studies*, 26 (1): 5-21.

Rauch, F. (2000) "Schools: a place of ecological learning", *Environmental Education Research*, 6 (3): 245-56.

Reynolds, M.C. (1989) "An historical perspective: the delivery of special education to mildly disabled and at-risk students", *Remedial and Special Education*, 10 (6).

Reynolds, P. (2000) "Childhood and sexuality: some conceptual considerations" in K. Crawford and K. Straker (eds.) *Citizenship, Young People and Participation*. Stoke: John Price.

Rickinson, M. (2001) "Learners and learning in environmental education: a critical review of the research", *Environmental Education Research*, 7 (3): 207-320.

Robb, M. (2001) "The changing experiences of childhood" in P. Foley, J. Roche and S. Tucker (eds.) *Children in Society: contemporary theory, policy and practice*. Hampshire: Palgrave.

Robbins (1963) *Report of the Committee on Higher Education* (Robbins Report). London: HMSO.

Rogoff, B., Mistry, J., Goncu, A. and Mosier, C. (1993) "Guided participation in cultural activity by toddlers and caregivers", *Monograph of the Society for Research in Child Development*, 58 (8).

Ross, A. (2000) *Curriculum Construction and Critique*. London: Falmer.

Roszak, T. (1995) "Where Psyche meets Gaia" in T. Roszak, M.E. Gomes and A.D. Kanner (1995) *Ecopsychology Restoring the Earth Healing the Mind*. San Francisco: Sierra Club Books.

Rousseau, J.J. (1762) *Emile*. Reprinted (1993) London: Dent/Everyman Publications.

Rowe, D. (1997) "Value pluralism, democracy and education for citizenship" in M. Leicester, C. Modgil and F. Modgil (eds.) *Values, Culture and Education: political and citizenship education*. London: Cassell.

Rutter, M. (1981) *Maternal Deprivation Reassessed* (2nd edn). Harmondsworth: Penguin.

Rutter, M. and Mortimer, P. (1990) *Fifteen Thousand Hours*. Harvard: Harvard University Press.

Sameroff, A.J. (1991) "The social context of development" in M. Woodhead, R. Carr and P. Light (eds.) *Becoming a Person*. London: Routledge.

Sanders, R. (1999) *The Management of Child Protection Services: context and change*. Aldershot: Arena.

Saraga, E. (1998) "Children's needs: who decides?" in M. Langan (ed.) *Welfare: needs, rights and risks*. London: Routledge.

SCAA (1996) *Desirable Outcomes for Children's Learning on Entering Compulsory Education*. London: SCAA/DfEE.

Scarce, R. (1990) *Eco-Warriors Understanding the Radical Environmental Movement*. Chicago: The Noble Press.

School Councils UK (2002) "School Councils in Primary Schools". Available from http://www.schoolcouncils.org/NewFiles/Primary%20Schools.html (accessed 9th July 2002).

Schools Council (1967) *Society and the Young School Leaver: a humanities programme in preparation for the raising of the school leaving age. Working paper No. 11*. London: HMSO.

Schweinhart, L.J. and Weikart, D.P. (1997) *Lasting Differences: the High/Scope pre-school curriculum comparison through age 2-3*. Ypsilanti: High/Scope Press.

Scraton, P. (ed.) (1997) *Childhood in Crisis*. London: UCL Press.

Shahar, S. (1990) *Childhood in the Middle Ages*. London: Routledge.

Shallcross, T. and Wilkinson, G. (1998) "The primacy of action: the basis of initial teacher education for sustainability", *International Journal of Environmental Education*, 17 (3): 243-56.

Sharp, R. and Green, A. (1975) *Education and Social Control*. Routledge and Kegan Paul.

Shore, R. (1997) *Rethinking the Brain*. New York: Families and Work Institute.

Sinclair Taylor (1995) "Less better than the rest: perceptions of integration in a multi-ethnic special needs unit", *Educational Review*, 47 (3).

Skilbeck, M. (1976) *Three Educational Ideologies*. Milton Keynes: OUP.

Skinner, B.F. (1974) *About Behaviourism*. New York: Vintage.

Smith, J.K. (1993) *After the Demise of Empiricism: the problem of judging social and educational inquiry*. New Jersey: Ablex.

Stainton Rogers, W. (2001a) "Constructing childhood, constructing child concern" in P. Foley, J. Roche and S. Tucker (eds.) *Children in Society: contemporary theory, policy and practice*. Hampshire: Palgrave.

Stainton Rogers, W. (2001b) "Theories of Child Development" in P. Foley J. Roche and S. Tucker (eds.) *Children in Society: contemporary theory, policy and practice*. Hampshire: Palgrave.

Stenhouse, L. (1983) *Authority, Emancipation and Education*. London: Heinemann.

Stenhouse, L. (1975) *An Introduction to Curriculum Research and Development*. London: Heinemann.

Sterling, S. (2001) *Sustainable Education Revisioning Learning and Change*. Dartington: Green Books.

Stradling, R. (1977) *The Political Awareness of the School Leaver*. London: Hansard Society.

Stradling, R. and Noctor, M. (1981) *The Provision of Political Education*. London: Curriculum Review Unit.

Sweet, J. and Resick, P. (1979) "The maltreatment of children: a review of theories and research", *Journal of Social Issues*, 35 (2): 40-59.

Sylva, K. (1999) "The role of research in explaining the past and shaping the future" in L. Abbott and H. Moylett (eds.) *Early Education Transformed*. London: Falmer.

Sylva, K., Siraj-Blatchford, I., Melhuish, E., Sammons, P. and Taggart, B. (1999) *An Introduction to the EPPE*. London: Institute of Education.

Thane, P. (1981) "Childhood in history" in M. King (ed.) *Childhood, Welfare and Justice*. London: Batsford.

The Children's Secretariat (1999) "Early years study – reversing the real brain drain", Toronto, Ontario. Available from http://www.childsec.gov.on.ca (accessed 13th October 2001).

The Mental Health Foundation (1999) *The Big Picture. Promoting Children and Young People's Mental Health.* London: The Mental Health Foundation.

Torney-Purta, J., Schwille, J. and Amadeo, J-A. (1999) *Civic Education across Countries: twenty-four national case studies from the IEA civic education project.* Amsterdam: The International Association for the Evaluation of Educational Achievement.

Trafford, B. (1993) *Sharing Power in Schools: raising standards.* Ticknall: Education Now.

Trevarthen, C. (1998) "The child's need to learn a culture" in M. Woodhead, D. Faulkner and K. Littleton (eds.) *Cultural Worlds of Early Childhood.* London: Routledge.

UNESCO (1997) *Educating for a Sustainable Future: a transdisciplinary vision for concerted action.* Paris: UNESCO.

United Nations (1989) *The United Nations Convention on the Rights of the Child.* New York: UN.

Uzzell, D. (1999) "Education for environmental action in the community: new roles and relationships", *Cambridge Journal of Education*, 29 (33): 397-414.

Uzzell, D., Davallon, J., Fontes, P.J., Gottesdiener, H., Jensen, B.B., Kofoed, J., Uhrenholdt, G. and Vognsen, C. (1994) *Children as Catalysts of Environmental Change.* Brussels: European Commission Directorate General for Science Research and Development.

Vygotsky, L.S. (1978) *Mind and society: the development of higher psychological processes.* Cambridge, MA: Harvard University Press.

Wagg, S. (1996) "'Don't try to understand them': politics, childhood and the new education market" in J. Pilcher and S, Wagg (eds.) *Thatcher's Children? politics, childhood and society in the 1980s and 1990s.* London: Falmer.

Webb, L. (1974) *Purpose and Practice in Nursery Education.* Oxford: Blackwell.

Whitbread, N. (1995) "Celebrating 10/65 thirty years on", *Forum*, (37): 2. Available from http://www. triangle.co.uk/for/for_372-.htm (accessed 20th June 2003).

White, J. (1990) *Education and the Goodlife: beyond the national curriculum.* London: Kogan Page.

White, J. (1982) *The Aims of Educational Reform.* London: Routledge and Kegan Paul.

Whitmarsh, G. (1974) "The politics of political education: an episode", *Journal of Curriculum Studies*, 6 (2): 133-42.

Williams, K. (2002) "Children's views in school – reality or paper exercise" (unpublished dissertation), Liverpool, John Moores University.

Willis, P. (1993) *Learning to Labour: how working class kids get working class jobs.* Aldershot: Ashgate.

Wolfe, D. (1999) "Visions of citizenship education", *Oxford Review of Education*, 25 (3): 425-30.

Wolff, S. and McCall Smith, A. (2001) "Children who kill: they can and should be reclaimed", *The British Medical Journal*, (322): 61-2.

Woodhead, M. (1999) "Reconstructing developmental psychology: some first steps", *Children and Society*, 13 (1): 1-17.

Woodhead, M. (2000) "Towards a global paradigm for research into early childhood" in H. Penn (ed.) *Early Childhood Services: theory, policy and practice.* Buckingham: OUP.

World Commission on Environment and Development (1987) *Our Common Future* (Brundtland Report). Oxford: OCED.

Wyse, D. (2001) "Felt-tip pens and student councils: children's participation rights in four English schools", *Children and Society*, (15): 209-18.

Young, M.F.D. (1971) *Knowledge and Control.* London: Collier Macmillan.

Zohar, D. and Marshall, I. (2000) *Spiritual Intelligence. The Ultimate Intelligence.* London: Bloomsbury.

Index

A

accountability 5, 23, 62, 122, 127, 137, 141, 148
Althusser 28-30
Apple 26, 31, 32, 45, 128
assessment 140, 141
attitudes 19, 24, 39-41, 44, 47, 49, 61, 79, 91-3, 95, 125, 129, 158, 159, 161, 163, 177

B

Baker, Kenneth 22, 125
Ball 34, 70, 74, 121, 125, 128
Bernstein 37
better schools 124
Black Papers 18, 21, 120
Blunkett 129, 130, 162, 163
Bowles and Gintis 91
Bulger, James 101, 102
bullying 95, 98, 100, 185
Butler Act, The *see* The 1944 Education Act

C

Callaghan, James 17, 19, 20, 120, 122
child abuse 53, 59, 64-9, 71
childhood 3, 4, 37, 45, 52-7, 59-61, 63, 69, 70, 73, 74, 77, 81-5, 91-3, 95, 101-3, 106, 114, 117, 119, 185, 187

children 1, 3, 4, 8-12, 14-16, 21, 23, 34, 35, 40-8, 50, 52-97, 99-119, 121, 126, 127, 130, 132, 155-60, 163, 164, 167, 168, 172, 176, 185, 186
Circular 10/65 7, 13-15, 17
citizenship 5, 22, 43, 55, 90, 91, 96, 113, 131, 132, 166, 171-86
citizenship education 6, 22, 90, 91, 131, 132, 171-6, 178-85
community 6, 39, 44, 45, 49, 50, 63, 66, 68, 77, 87, 98, 100, 129, 132, 147, 150, 156-60, 175-8, 181, 182
comprehensive re-organisation 14
schools 14, 15
Crick Report, the 43, 178
Crowther Report, the 172
cultural socialization 25
culture 30, 44, 46, 47, 53, 54, 59, 61, 77, 79, 94, 98, 99, 123, 124, 126, 127, 131, 150, 163
curriculum 2, 4, 5, 9, 10, 15, 17-19, 21-3, 25, 26, 30-6, 39, 40, 42, 43, 49, 53, 56, 60-4, 69, 70, 72, 73, 75-80, 85-92, 94, 96, 99, 100, 107, 117, 120, 122-34, 139, 150, 161, 163-6, 169, 171-5, 177-9, 182-6

D

democracy 5, 45, 131, 175, 178, 180, 181
Department for Education and Employment 168
Department for Education and Skills 180

desirable learning outcomes 75, 76, 80, 86
DfEE *see* Department for Education and
    Employment
DfES *see* Department for Education and
    Skills
disability 3, 57, 59, 72, 155, 157-9, 165,
    167
Disability Discrimination Act 157, 166
duties 115, 138, 151, 166, 167, 176, 183

E

early childhood studies. 3, 52
early years education 73
economics 63, 70, 127
education for sustainable development 25,
    36, 37, 39, 186
Education Reform Act, The 21
educational change 23
effective schools 5
eleven-plus, the 8-10, 14
employers 14, 19, 20, 23, 122, 123, 125,
    127
empowerment 17, 30, 70, 77
Engels 27, 28, 30, 31
environmental education 45
equality of opportunity 11, 13, 87, 169
evaluation 140-3, 146, 147
examinations 14, 17, 144

F

fairness 13, 95, 141
family 98

G

gender 5, 34, 48, 59, 62, 66, 158, 159, 163,
    165, 177
Goodson 126-8
government 4, 10, 13, 15, 17, 18, 22, 74-6,
    78, 79, 81-3, 97, 108-10, 120, 122-5,
    128, 130, 131, 155, 157, 161, 163-5,
    167-9, 175, 178, 181, 182

governors 88, 143, 146, 147, 151, 152,
    161, 166
grammar schools 9, 11, 13, 14
Gramsci 29, 30, 90
grant maintained schools 23
Great Debate, The 19
Grundy 33-6, 39

H

Habermas 33, 34, 36
headteachers 113, 135, 138, 139, 143, 145
High Scope 77
Hillgate Group, the 126, 127
human capital 7, 16

I

identity 185, 186
ideology 3, 23, 25-32, 34, 35, 37-40, 42,
    43, 45, 46, 49-51, 74, 127, 133, 185
inclusion 157-60, 162, 165, 169, 170
inclusive education 159, 160, 185
industry 19, 20
inspection 5, 10, 75, 81, 88, 90, 92, 107,
    127, 129, 135, 136, 138, 151, 152

K

knowledge 2-4, 6, 16, 25, 27, 29, 31-7, 40,
    50, 52-4, 56-8, 61, 63, 64, 69-71, 76, 79,
    80, 84, 90-3, 99, 111, 118, 120, 126,
    127, 132, 141, 149, 151, 153, 163, 169,
    176, 179, 180

L

language 19, 30, 39, 50, 62, 67, 77, 94, 98,
    99, 103, 123, 124, 157, 158, 165, 187
LEAs *see* local education authorities

learning 2, 3, 5, 6, 16, 20, 21, 33-6, 40, 43, 46, 48, 49, 55, 57, 58, 61, 62, 67, 69, 73, 75-7, 79, 80, 82, 84, 86-9, 91-4, 96, 99, 100, 122, 125, 130, 132, 140, 141, 149, 150, 154, 157, 159, 160, 163-5, 167, 172, 173, 179, 181, 185, 186
literacy and numeracy strategies 79
local education authorities 14, 73, 161
local management of schools 22

M

Macpherson Report, the 161
managing change 137
Mannheim 31, 32
Marx 27, 28, 30, 31
Matheson and Limond 26, 27

N

National Curriculum 22, 79, 120, 123, 126, 128, 134, 164, 178
national literacy strategy 130
Neo-Conservative 126, 128
New Labour 23, 120, 129, 131, 132, 162-5, 168, 169
Newsom Report, the 172
Nursery Voucher Scheme, the 75

O

Office for Standards in Education *see* OFSTED
OFSTED 5, 75, 76, 79, 81, 88, 89, 114, 141, 147, 148, 151, 168

P

parents 1, 3, 4, 14, 19, 22, 23, 42, 47, 65, 72-5, 78, 81, 82, 86, 91, 95, 104-9, 121-3, 125, 127, 147, 149, 150, 161, 167, 185

participation 4, 16, 30, 35, 36, 43, 45, 48, 49, 55, 101, 107, 111, 113, 118, 145, 160, 162, 184, 186
pedagogy 31, 35, 40, 43, 48, 61, 67
Plowden Report, the 35, 79, 88
politicians 3, 11, 17, 19, 56, 72, 145, 174
politics 4, 17, 23, 55, 63, 70, 91, 93, 96, 97, 127, 133, 173, 177-79, 184, 185
postmodern 126
post-war educational consensus 7, 11
poverty 3, 7, 8, 57, 65, 72, 78, 81, 86, 90, 97, 104, 109, 168
power 3, 10, 18, 22, 28-32, 37, 45, 56, 62, 63, 66-70, 74, 88, 90, 94, 97-9, 115, 116, 121, 122, 127, 129, 131, 133, 154, 169
prejudice 94-7, 99, 100, 105, 126, 158-61, 169
propaganda 126, 174

Q

QCA 5, 43, 78, 80, 85, 86, 131, 165
Qualifications and Curriculum Authority *see* QCA

R

Race Relations Act 157, 166
racism 99, 126, 161, 162
racist 92, 161, 175, 177
responsibilities 5, 48, 113, 114, 122, 131, 138, 143, 178, 181, 187
restorationist discourse 127
rights 4, 45, 56, 62, 63, 66, 67, 74, 86, 87, 99, 101, 105-11, 113, 115, 117, 118, 159, 163, 166, 176, 178, 181-3
Rousseau 35, 57, 79, 101, 103
Ruskin College 18, 19, 122

S

school councils 111, 117
school improvement 136, 138, 140, 141, 144-6, 151-4
school leadership 140

schools 4, 10, 12, 18, 19, 23, 51, 76, 84, 89, 91-3, 95, 96, 98, 124, 127, 128, 130, 135, 137, 144, 147, 150, 172, 173, 178, 179, 183, 187
schools and industry 19
secondary education 8, 122
secondary modern schools 9, 10, 20
'Secret garden', the 7, 17
SEN *see* special educational needs
Sex Discrimination Act 165
skills 20, 48, 57, 61, 72, 77, 79, 80, 83, 84, 90, 92, 121, 122, 125, 127, 128, 132, 163, 164, 168, 175, 177, 179, 183
social class 12
society 1, 3, 4, 6, 16, 17, 20, 23, 24, 26, 27, 31, 33, 36, 41, 47, 53-7, 60, 61, 63, 66, 68, 73, 75, 78, 90-6, 98, 100-3, 105, 108-10, 117, 123, 124, 127, 131, 132, 137, 140, 142, 144, 145, 156, 158, 161-3, 167-9, 172
special education 155, 167
special educational needs 157, 158, 167
Special Educational Needs and Disability Act 157, 167
standards 4, 5, 19, 20, 22, 62, 67, 78, 79, 84, 89, 91, 106, 108, 120-2, 124, 126-30, 136, 154, 162
sustainability 37-9, 41, 51, 187

T

target-setting 149
Teacher Training Agency 84
teachers 1, 6, 9, 10, 12, 14, 15, 17-23, 33, 35, 36, 40, 42, 44, 45, 47-51, 81, 84, 88, 89, 91, 94, 95, 98, 100, 110-13, 115, 116, 120-3, 125, 127, 129, 130, 138, 158, 168, 169, 171-4, 177, 179, 181-5
teaching 1, 2, 5, 15, 19-21, 33, 35, 36, 45, 47, 48, 50, 61, 79, 80, 84, 90, 91, 121-3, 125, 130, 131, 138, 141, 147, 150, 154, 157-60, 164, 177, 179, 182, 185-7
technical schools 9
Thatcher, Margaret 17
The 1944 Education Act 7, 8, 88
theory 16, 57
transactional model 34

transformatory model 35
transmissional model 3
TTA *see* Teacher Training Agency

U

UN Convention on the Rights of the Child 101, 107, 111

V

vocational education 20, 128

W

Warnock Report, the 156
wealth 20, 163
Wilson, Harold 13, 15, 16

Y

Young 32, 34, 60, 73, 93, 94, 96, 111, 117, 129